'This book provides an excellent overview of the types of digital technologies that are being introduced into the clinic and the way that they are changing clinical practice. Using carefully selected case studies, the book analyses the complex ethical, legal and regulatory issues that are raised by implementing digital innovation. Carolyn Johnston is a lawyer who is well equipped to do this, having had many years working with clinicians and scientists who are navigating these issues. The threads that go through this book will provide readers with a rich understanding of these complex issues and generate insights into the way that clinical practice is changing.'
—**Jane Kaye**, *Professor of Health, Law and Policy and Director of the Centre for Health, Law and Emerging Technologies (HeLEX) at University of Oxford*

'Carolyn Johnston's book offers plain language insights into the complex and rapidly expanding world of digital health technologies. Consumers want the best, most convenient technologies to manage their health, yet clinicians may be wary of the traditional relationship power shifts and treatment efficacy concerns that result from the digital health care revolution.

Johnston explores eight new technologies and takes us back to the fundamentals of ethics, respect, humanity and evidence that should guide consumers, clinicians, regulators and society more broadly as this revolution unfolds. A timely scholarly contribution.'
—**Mark Cormack**, *Honorary Professor at the College of Health and Medicine, Australian National University (ANU)*

DIGITAL HEALTH TECHNOLOGIES

Increasingly digital technologies are used in healthcare. This book explores eight digital health technologies, situated the context of a life span, from high-throughput genomic sequencing technologies and do-it-yourself (DIY) insulin delivery for diabetes management in paediatrics, to the use of robotic care assistants for older adults and digital advance care decisions.

A scene-setting case scenario at the start of each chapter describes the digital technology and identifies the sometimes competing interests of the key stakeholders. Broad themes of resource allocation, access to technologies, informed consent, privacy of health data and ethical concerns are considered in context, alongside analysis of legal duties owed by healthcare professionals to act in their patients' best interests.

This book addresses legal and ethical issues arising from the use of emerging digital health technologies and is of interest to academics, clinicians and regulators and anyone interested in the development of health technologies and the challenges they may present. It focusses on the Australian legal framework, with some comparison to other jurisdictions.

Carolyn Johnston is a legal scholar and currently research fellow at the University of Tasmania, exploring legal and ethical obligations to provide raw genomic information to research participants. She was previously a member of the Centre for Health, Law and Emerging Technologies research team at the University of Melbourne and taught at Melbourne Law School. Carolyn is an experienced clinical ethicist and is chair of the Clinical Ethics Response Group at Monash Children's Hospital, Melbourne, providing clinical ethics consultation.

Law and Change: Law in Times of Crisis
Series Editor
Professor Mark Findlay
Singapore Management University, Singapore

Artificial Intelligence (AI) is touted as the remedy for many of the economic, social, political and cultural contentions in an epoch where social demographics are unbalance, economic growth is slowing, labour markets are fragile, and global trade is wracked with protectionism. The arrival of the pandemic has heightened calls for AI and big data to help innovate economies out of the worst. This transition presents significant challenges for the ecosystems of law firms, and the requirements of due process in the exercise of litigation. Against the realisation of seismic shifts brought about by current and impending global watersheds, this series reflects how first the pandemic and then inevitable future crises will change the law, and how law can be understood as a change agent, talking to today in upheaval, and to new tomorrows.

The series provides a space for scholars, educators, practitioners and leaders to share their contributions on the present and future relevance of the law and reflect on law and change and change through law in times of global crises. The contributions will be critical, focusing on contemporary challenges to social ordering and global sustainability where law in context has much to say. In addition, the series will question law's regulatory relevance across a wide range of substantive and procedural fields currently facing transition.

Titles in this series include:

Digital Health Technologies
Law, Ethics and the Doctor-Patient Relationship
Carolyn Johnston

DIGITAL HEALTH TECHNOLOGIES

Law, Ethics and the Doctor-Patient Relationship

Carolyn Johnston

LONDON AND NEW YORK

Cover image: © Getty Images

First published 2023
by Routledge
4 Park Square, Milton Park, Abingdon, Oxon OX14 4RN

and by Routledge
605 Third Avenue, New York, NY 10158

Routledge is an imprint of the Taylor & Francis Group, an informa business

© 2023 Carolyn Johnston

The right of Carolyn Johnston to be identified as author of this work has been asserted in accordance with sections 77 and 78 of the Copyright, Designs and Patents Act 1988.

All rights reserved. No part of this book may be reprinted or reproduced or utilised in any form or by any electronic, mechanical, or other means, now known or hereafter invented, including photocopying and recording, or in any information storage or retrieval system, without permission in writing from the publishers.

Trademark notice: Product or corporate names may be trademarks or registered trademarks, and are used only for identification and explanation without intent to infringe.

British Library Cataloguing-in-Publication Data
A catalogue record for this book is available from the British Library

Library of Congress Cataloging-in-Publication Data
Names: Johnston, Carolyn, author.
Title: Digital health technologies : law, ethics, and the doctor-patient relationship / Carolyn Johnston.
Description: Abingdon, Oxon ; New York, NY : Routledge, 2023. | Series: Law and change | Includes bibliographical references and index.
Identifiers: LCCN 2022035708 | ISBN 9781032115061 (hardback) | ISBN 9781032115054 (paperback) | ISBN 9781003220190 (ebook)
Subjects: LCSH: Medical technology—Law and legislation—Australia.
Classification: LCC KU1525 .J64 2023 | DDC 344.9404/1—dc23/ eng/20221101
LC record available at https://lccn.loc.gov/2022035708

ISBN: 978-1-032-11506-1 (hbk)
ISBN: 978-1-032-11505-4 (pbk)
ISBN: 978-1-003-22019-0 (ebk)

DOI: 10.4324/9781003220190

Typeset in Bembo
by Apex CoVantage, LLC

To Anthony, Amy, Patrick and Grace.

CONTENTS

Acknowledgements   *x*

1   Introduction   1

2   Digital genomic sequencing: who should have access to genomic information?   10

3   Internet of Things and personalised medicine: DIY-ing diabetes management   28

4   Smartphone apps for mental health   47

5   AI in the diagnosis of health conditions   63

6   Symptom checker chatbots and informed consent   81

7   Telehealth: what has been learned through the COVID-19 pandemic?   98

8   Robotic care assistants and older adults   116

9   A new use for existing technology: digital advance care decisions   135

Index   *152*

ACKNOWLEDGEMENTS

Thank you to the following people who have offered their comments and thoughts on book chapters, and in particular to Max Slattery, a former law student (Juris Doctor) at Melbourne Law School, University of Melbourne, who has read through and commented on all the chapters and with whom I have had interesting conversations on these digital health technologies.

Max Slattery, Lawyer, Ashurst Australia

Dr James Breen, Telethon Kids Institute & Australian National University

Ms Jasmine Schipp, PhD Candidate, Deakin University, Melbourne and the Australian Centre for Behavioural Research in Diabetes

Dr Jo Emmanuel, Central and NorthWest London NHS Foundation Trust, London

Sam Wilson, Lawyer, Australian Securities and Investments Commission

Dr Selena Stellman, General Practitioner, London, and Member of the Nuffield Council on Bioethics

Dr Megan Prictor, Senior Lecturer, Melbourne Law School and the Centre for Digital Transformation of Health, University of Melbourne

Associate Professor Ralph Hampton, Department of Social Work, University of Melbourne

1
INTRODUCTION

Introduction to the book

The range of digital health technologies, their potential to transform delivery of healthcare and how much they impact on the traditional provision of treatment and care are the subjects of this book. Digital technologies are increasingly part of everyday life – how often do we use mobile phone apps to measure our daily step rate, or meditation time, or connect to our healthcare practitioner through a screen rather than face to face? Digital health technologies have a very broad scope. As the Australian Institute of Health and Welfare noted in its report in 2022, they include mobile health and wellness applications, SMS reminders via mobile messaging, electronic health records, telehealth and telemedicine, wearable devices, robotics and artificial intelligence.[1]

We can immediately see how such technologies enable individuals to take more control over their health and wellbeing. A woman using a smartphone app to track her menstrual cycles, identifying when she is most fertile, can empower her contraceptive or fertility choices without the need for interaction with a healthcare professional. In comparison individuals with a susceptibility to mental illness can use an app which utilizes voice analysis and pairs it with behavioural data to flag decline in mood, and this information can be shared with clinicians to trigger interventions. These examples demonstrate more personalised management of health issues.

Other digital technologies can improve access to healthcare. As we have seen during the COVID-19 pandemic, telehealth became the norm for healthcare interactions between clinician and patient, and the success of this improved accessibility underscores the role of telehealth as an everyday mode of delivery of healthcare. Chatbots provide a way of triaging care, using artificial intelligence (AI) to recommend courses of action based on input of data by the user. Such technology

DOI: 10.4324/9781003220190-1

can also enable a more efficient use of resources, identifying the most appropriate management for a health condition.

We may also consider the role of digital health technologies in improving the management of health conditions. Software algorithms which enable individuals to do-it-yourself (DIY) their insulin dosage based on real-time glucose levels is an example of citizen science and how digital technologies have been developed by users themselves. The estimated 10,000 people worldwide who use these open-source algorithms may testify to the improvement in managing their type 1 diabetes over commercial systems[2]; yet there is a lack of regulation and guidance for healthcare professionals faced with patients who opt to use these DIY systems. Providers of digital technologies transcend national boundaries and the jurisdiction of the regulator in the country where it is used.

At their best digital technologies enable more personalised, targeted and accessible healthcare. But what of the downsides? The enormous amounts of data collected by these technologies raise concerns about data privacy and with whom it is appropriate to share this information. Transborder flows of information require adequate protections both in countries where data is collected and where it is going. London's Royal Free hospital failed to comply with the UK Data Protection Act when personal data of 1.6 million patients was given to DeepMind, a Google subsidiary, and the scandal of Cambridge Analytica which collected information of Facebook users and their friends and used it for predictive profiling services (without their consent) underscores the importance of the adequacy of privacy laws. In Australia a review of the Commonwealth Privacy Act 1988 is being undertaken by the attorney general's office,[3] addressing its adequacy in the digital era. The attorney general recently commented that he hoped to bring in sweeping reforms to the Privacy Act, noting that the greatest dangers to privacy are people losing control of their own information and personal information being used in ways that is invasive and that they have not consented to. Reforms should give people greater control over their own information and allow them to make informed choices about the use of their data.[4] Another concern is health data poverty, defined as "the inability for individuals, groups or populations to benefit from a discovery or innovation due to a scarcity of data that are adequately representative,"[5] which is an emerging problem in digital health. Although AI may be more diagnostically accurate than a human expert, algorithms underlying AI depend on the datasets that direct them. If these datasets are drawn from mostly white, male individuals, their applicability and utility are of limited value – AI which reads the likelihood of skin cancers will not be as accurate for dark-skinned individuals if it is enabled by datasets from Caucasian individuals, and might promote racial, gendered bias.[6]

There is also a tension between public and private interests. Whole genome sequencing produces large datasets that are shared with other research enterprises to further knowledge and medical science. But are participants in research fully apprised of the way their biomedical samples, and data derived from them, are shared with other researchers? It is in the public interest for data to be shared for research purposes to develop generalisable knowledge for the benefit of society, and consent to data sharing and de-identification of data are important in this realm.

We also have an interest in controlling who has access to our private information. The Nuffield Council on Bioethics recognises that as individuals are embedded in communities, "each has a private interest in protecting their privacy but also in contributing to the public good because, as a member of the public, they and those they care about benefit from the good that they bring about through cooperation with others in society."[7] Understanding how data is and should be shared, and the type of consent required to do so, is foundational to the trust placed in digital technologies.

In this book I refer to trust, consent, autonomy and dignity, and these concepts readily apply to interactions between individuals. But digital technologies which harness AI to perform tasks and take on decision-making capabilities do not currently have emotional capacities and may lack the nuance to identify and balance these interests. A trite example outside the health sphere is the automated car which must choose whether to run over passengers and perhaps kill them to avoid harm to the 'driver'/passengers in the car. Where an older person uses a robotic care assistant, how far they should be afforded the dignity of risk-taking and decision-making autonomy where this might place them at risk of harm is a decision to be made by a programmed machine. As Michael Sandel has questioned,

> Can smart machines outthink us, or are certain elements of human judgment indispensable in deciding some of the most important things in life?[8]

It may not just be human judgement that is missing when digital technologies are used but also human interaction, which is so fundamental in the provision of healthcare. Digital technologies have the potential to disrupt the patient-doctor paradigm and the way society seeks to care for and protect the most vulnerable. We go to a health practitioner not just to receive a diagnosis and treatment but to have our narratives of illness heard and recognised. William Ostler, described as the father of modern medicine, who wrote *The Principles and Practices of Medicine* over 100 years ago, noted that "medicine is learned by the bedside."[9] Narrative medicine underscores the need for clinicians to listen to and seek to understand the stories of their patients with the aim of providing more compassionate, humane and appropriate care. Digital technologies learn from data inputs rather than human stories, and so the traditional doctor/patient relationship is changed. Increasingly health provision is compartmentalised and distributed by specialists, rather than by one health practitioner who has knowledge of the social and cultural contexts of their patient's illness, and the importance of an ongoing relationship with a healthcare provider, taking into account the inherent access and resource costs, remains to be seen.

Different stakeholders — healthcare practitioners, patients, their family members and carers and health services — may have different perspectives on the use and value of these digital health technologies. I like the concept of 'epistemic humility' proposed by Anita Ho, the "recognition of the boundary of one's expert domain as well as the appreciation of the limitation of one's knowledge in making appropriate decisions,"[10] which acknowledges the importance of considering diverse perspectives. These all have a place in the future development and use of digital technologies in healthcare.

This book addresses the adequacy of regulation and how the law provides a framework for the protection of rights and interests. There may be a time lag between the development of these health technologies and regulation and a lack of case law to articulate legal standards of care. I have therefore analysed the issues from first principles and am mindful of the suggestion by Brazier and Glover that by 2050 medical law as it has been known and practised "is unlikely to exist,"[11] with more emphasis developing in areas of consumer and public law.

There is a broad spread of subjects at play here, including law, ethics, science, biotechnology, computer science and social science. I am a scholar in law and ethics and have explored many of the issues covered in this book in previous academic legal research, particularly around mental capacity, best interests' decision making, advance decisions and through discussion with clinical colleagues in my role as clinical ethicist, currently at Monash Children's Hospital, Clayton, Melbourne. The impetus for this book arose from my appointment with the Health Law and Emerging Technologies (HeLEX) research group at the University of Melbourne and through teaching a legal research subject called Emerging Technologies in Healthcare at Melbourne Law School. I have enjoyed discovering more about a range of digital health technologies as I have written this book, and I am grateful to my friends and colleagues around the world who have provided comments and insights.

My aim is to provide interest in and an understanding of some digital technologies from a lay person's perspective and to address relevant legal and ethical issues from a broad standpoint, with a focus on Australian and English jurisprudence and academic literature. As the range of health technologies develops with increasing pace, this book provides a timely consideration of the challenges that they raise.

Digital technologies explored in the book

This book explores eight digital health technologies, situated the context of a life span, from genomic sequencing used to personalise treatment for children with cancer and DIY diabetes management in paediatrics, to the use of robotic care assistants for the elderly and digital advance care decisions. Broad themes of resource allocation, access to digital technologies, privacy and ownership of health data and informed consent are considered throughout the book, and I cross reference themes across the chapters. A scene-setting case scenario at the start of each chapter describes the digital technology and identifies the sometimes-competing interests of key stakeholders, and the legal and ethical issues are addressed in the context of the case scenario.

Chapter 2

Digital genomic sequencing: who should have access to genomic information?

Next-generation genomic sequencing technologies produce large amounts of useful data that are shared with other research enterprises to further knowledge and medical science. But do participants in research and their genetic relatives have a right to receive data that may be of value to them? In this chapter I consider three different case scenarios to address this question. I consider whether legal principles and ethical frameworks underpin a right to access 'raw' genomic data, and I compare this with return of secondary findings in research. There are clearly resource implications for healthcare providers, genetic services and healthcare systems if a right to return is recognised. Knowledge about risk of a genetic condition enables choices to be made, about treatment, lifestyle and reproduction, but it can also give rise to "anxious introspection."[12] I consider a right to know and not to know and how the common law, privacy legislation and ethical guidance frame a defensible approach.

Chapter 3

Internet of Things and personalised medicine: DIY-ing diabetes management

In management of type 1 diabetes the #WeAreNotWaiting movement has pushed forward new ways to personalise care, rather than wait for commercial companies to develop hardware and software systems. In this chapter I consider the use of DIY 'looping' technologies to manage type 1 diabetes in children. I explore the reported benefits and relative risks of this new technology, whether the choice of parents to use such a system for their child is legally and ethically supportable and 'sharenting' – parents willingly sharing information on social media for peer support. Open-source software to manage type 1 diabetes created by a programmer in the United States can be downloaded and used anywhere in the world. In Australia regulation operates to check safety and efficacy of medical devices (including software as a medical device) before they are accessed on the market, but open-source software presents a challenge to the paradigm; it can be used free of charge and therefore not 'marketed.' A health practitioner may have concerns about supporting the use of a DIY system for their paediatric patient and whether they could be legally liable in doing so, and the potential for a claim in negligence is explored.

Chapter 4

Smartphone apps for mental health

William Lowrance, writing in 1997, talks about a "future envisaged by seers" in which "many aspects of public health surveillance (such as scanning for infectious disease outbreaks), compilation of statistics, (use of hospital outpatient services), development of registries (vaccination) . . . will simply be derived, whenever and in whatever form needed, from the networked lifetime dossiers."[13] During the coronavirus pandemic we saw the use of smartphones to track and trace people in the interests of public health. The ubiquitous use of wearable devices and smartphone apps enable people to manage their wellbeing and health. Health data such as a person's weight, menstrual cycle, fertility, alcohol consumption and pregnancy status captured on the apps is a resource that can also be used by commercial companies, but health data privacy laws may not apply to health data collection outside a hospital system or traditional healthcare provider. In this chapter I focus on the use of apps in supporting patients to manage their mental health, and increasingly as a way for healthcare professionals to monitor their patients diagnosed with schizophrenia to alert them for a relapse. I consider evidence of utility and harms of digital phenotyping and how this may be used in the future to support clinical care. The enormous amounts of data collected by apps highlight data privacy and with whom it is appropriate to share this information, and I consider the adaptability of regulation to address these concerns.

Chapter 5

AI in the diagnosis of health conditions

Evidence is emerging that AI may be more accurate in diagnosing skin conditions such as melanoma than a human expert, and if that is the case, is there an argument that dermatologists should be using AI as a standard provision of care? In this chapter I consider ultimate responsibility for decisions using AI and whether the tort of negligence would provide legal redress for harm that arises through use of AI. I consider the relevance of bias in datasets and how this may exacerbate healthcare disparities. In dermatology if the data from which the machine learns does not reflect the diversity of skin types in society, this will have an impact on its utility in identifying skin cancers in dark-skinned individuals. The Nuffield Council on Bioethics[14] recognised data bias and public acceptance as key aspects in use of AI in healthcare. AI may impact on the doctor-patient relationship, and trust in the AI system, and in the healthcare professionals' use of it, is fundamental to ensure that health outcomes are improved for all.

Chapter 6

Symptom checker chatbots and informed consent

Digital heath technologies have the potential to dramatically improve the efficiency of healthcare delivery and the quality of patient care, but they do give rise to legal and ethical challenges, and in this chapter, I focus on informed consent and the complexity of privacy laws. In 2004 Roger Magnusson wrote that "privacy legislation has tended to be added, layer upon layer, in a less than coordinated way, atop a disparate mix of confidentiality provisions and common law,"[15] which he calls a "lasagne effect." Symptom checker chatbots require consent for their use, but are 'notify and consent' provisions adequate to ensure properly informed consent? Privacy policies are notoriously long and difficult to understand, and research[16] has identified that they became longer after the European General Data Protection Regulation came into effect in 2018, which ironically was intended to secure privacy of personal data. The reasons why people seek health services are not dependent solely on symptoms of disease but are multi-faceted and culturally determined. 'Connecting' with a symptom checker chatbot for health information is no substitute for empathetic connection from a human health professional.

Chapter 7

Telehealth: what has been learned through the COVID-19 pandemic?

During the COVID-19 outbreak, with lockdown policies to minimise transmission, telemedicine came into its own, enabling ongoing provision of healthcare. Although geographical distance in Australia promoted the initial development of telehealth there, during the pandemic most uptake was in metropolitan areas. For many the convenience of 'seeing' a doctor from their own homes can be an advantage – it saves time and cost of travel and may be of benefit to those who find it a challenge to speak with a healthcare professional face to face. Telehealth enables more than a one-to-one interaction, and the expertise of specialist and allied health can provide input when needed, collaborating in caring for a patient and sharing data to do so. Satisfaction with ongoing use of telehealth, for patients and doctors, remains to be seen. It will never be an appropriate format to deliver diagnosis of a challenging condition or outcome, but post lockdown, future use of this digital technology should augment rather than replace face-to-face healthcare.

Chapter 8

Robotic care assistants and older adults

As Neil Postman noted when he spoke about 'Five things we need to know about Technological Change' in 1998, "all technological change is a trade-off . . . technology giveth and technology taketh away. This means that for every advantage a new technology offers, there is always a corresponding disadvantage."[17] The lack of regulation of robots who monitor and provide care for the elderly in their own homes raises concerns about the safety and the propriety of such technology. Can a robot improve the wellbeing of an older person, or does it exacerbate loneliness and isolation, and how do we frame ethical concepts of dignity and respect for autonomy when the monitoring of an elderly person is performed by AI rather than by healthcare professionals and family? Consent should be acquired through clear and understandable provision of information, but issues of declining decision-making capacity and the complexity of AI decision making may lead to questions about the adequacy of consent to use of a robot care assistant by an older person in their own home.

Chapter 9

A new use for existing technology: digital advance care decisions

There are many good reasons for a person to decide about their medical treatment and care for a future time when they may lose decision-making capacity – it can support family to know they have 'done right' by their loved one, and it enables healthcare professionals to provide patient-centred care. Making an advance decision promotes a person's current autonomous choice which impacts future decisions. As John Harris notes,

> Autonomy, the values expressed as the ability to choose and have the freedom to choose between competing conceptions of how to live and indeed of why we do so, is connected to individuality in that it is only by the exercise of autonomy that our lives become in any sense our own. By shaping our lives for ourselves we assert our own values and our individuality.[18]

But people do not readily put pen to paper and write an advance care decision or complete a template form. This may be because people do not like to contemplate illness and loss of capacity, or they may not know in advance what they would want. Enabling advance decision making to be as accessible as possible could be achieved through recording, rather than writing, our wishes, and the concept of a 'values video' recorded on our ubiquitous smartphones could be a way forward.

Notes

1. Australian Institute of Health and Welfare, 'Digital Health' 07 July 2022. www.aihw.gov.au/reports/australias-health/digital-health.
2. K. Braune et al. 'Open-source Automated Insulin Delivery: International Consensus Statement and Practical Guidance for Health-care Professionals' (2022) 10(1) *The Lancet. Diabetes & Endocrinology* 58–74.
3. Australian Government, Attorney-General's Department, Privacy Act Review, Discussion Paper, October 2021.
4. Attorney General speaking on Radio National Australia, The Law Report 5.30 pm Tuesday 28th June 2022.
5. D. Wen et al. 'Characteristics of Publicly Available Skin Cancer Image Datasets: A Systematic Review' (2020) 4(1) *The Lancet Digital Health* e64, at e71.
6. M. Makhortykh, A. Urman, R. Ulloa, 'Detecting Race and Gender Bias in Visual Representation of AI on Web Search Engines,' In: Boratto, L., Faralli, S., Marras, M., Stilo, G. (eds) Advances in Bias and Fairness in Information Retrieval. BIAS 2021. Communications in Computer and Information Science, vol 1418 (Springer, Cham, 2021).
7. R. Anderson, *The Collection, Linking and Use of Data in Biomedical Research and Health Care: Ethical Issues*, para 3.27 (Nuffield Council on Bioethics, London, 2015).
8. C. Pazzanese, 'Great Promise but Potential for Peril,' *The Harvard Gazette*, October 26, 2020.
9. W. Ostler, *The Principles and Practice of Medicine* (Lea & Febridge, Philadelphia, 1907–1910).
10. A. Ho, '"They Just Don't Get It!" When Family Disagrees with Expert Opinion' (2009) 35(8) *Journal of Medical Ethics* 497–501, page 500.

11 M. Brazier, J. Glover, 'Does Medical Law Have a Future?' In: Hayton (ed) *Law's Future(s): British Legal Developments in the 21st Century* (Hart, Oxford, 2000) 371–388 at page 388.
12 R. Magnusson, 'The Changing Legal and Conceptual Shape of Health Care Privacy' (2004) 32(4) *The Journal of Law, Medicine & Ethics* 680–691, page 688.
13 W. Lowrance, *Privacy and Health Research, A Report to the U.S. Secretary of Health and Human Services* (U.S. Dept. of Health and Human Services, Office of the Assistant Secretary for Planning and Evaluation, Washington, DC, 1997).
14 R. Anderson, *The Collection, Linking and Use of Data in Biomedical Research and Health Care: Ethical Issues*, (Nuffield Council on Bioethics, London, 2015), para 1.36.
15 R. Magnusson, 'The Changing Legal and Conceptual Shape of Health Care Privacy' (2004) 32(4) *The Journal of Law, Medicine & Ethics* 680–691, page 686.
16 I. Wagner, 'Privacy Policies Across the Ages: Content and Readability of Privacy Policies 1996–2021'. arXiv:2201.08739.
17 Neil Postman, 'Five Things We Need to Know about Technological Change,' Talk Delivered in Denver Colorado, March 28, 1998 https://web.cs.ucdavis.edu/~rogaway/classes/188/materials/postman.pdf.
18 J. Harris, 'Consent and End of Life Decisions' (2003) 29(1) *Journal of Medical Ethics* 10–15, page 10.

2
DIGITAL GENOMIC SEQUENCING

Who should have access to genomic information?

Introduction

The development of new cures for disease requires the collection of data, ongoing research and innovation. High-throughput sequencing technologies offer rapid and cost-effective sequencing of nucleic acids, deoxyribonucleic acid (DNA) and ribonucleic acid (RNA), providing large datasets for researchers and information to clinicians about an individual's predisposition to genetic disease,[1] leading to the potential for targeted therapies. But what information should be shared with those whose biosamples have undergone genetic sequencing and their family members who are at risk of the same genetic disease? Does their genome sequence data 'belong' to them? Should they only be provided with genome sequence data that has some clinical utility, leading to preventative measures or treatments? In this chapter I address the legal and ethical obligations of researchers, healthcare professionals and individuals to share genomic information, and I explore these issues in three different settings. I start with genomic sequencing in research and the ethical and legal duties of biobanks to return secondary findings to research participants. I then consider high-throughput sequencing technologies in translational medicine, where information from research can be used for targeted treatments, hence the blurring of boundaries between research and clinical care. I focus on an issue that is anticipated to have increasing impact – the return of raw genomic data to patients and research participants. In the final section I turn to the use of high-throughput sequencing technologies in clinical care where whole genome sequencing (WGS), whole exome sequencing (WES) and RNA sequencing (which is far cheaper than both WES and WGS) is used to identify a genetic component of disease. I explore the legal duty of healthcare professionals and the moral[2] duty of individuals to share relevant information with genetic relatives who are at risk of the same genetic condition.

DOI: 10.4324/9781003220190-2

Data from high-throughput sequencing technologies has a big impact on our understanding of disease, leading to treatment and lifestyle and reproductive choices that can be exercised with such knowledge. There are undoubtedly benefits of having and sharing genome sequencing information, and individuals may feel a strong sense of entitlement to 'their' genomic data. In this chapter I explore ownership of and access to genetic data, how such data is protected and rights 'to know and not to know'.

It is helpful to clarify some terminology at the outset:

DNA – Deoxyribonucleic acid. DNA is a unique personal identifier. It contains the genetic information that directs the body's growth, maintenance and reproduction and is found in all human cells.
RNA – Ribonucleic acid. A nucleic acid present in all living cells, which converts the information stored in DNA into proteins.
NGS – Next-generation sequencing involves fragmenting DNA into multiple pieces and reassembling it into a genomic sequence.
Exome – The coding parts of genes which provide a functional role.
Genome – The entire set of DNA, 3 billion nucleotides, or 'letters,' of DNA.
Secondary findings (also known as 'incidental findings') – Health-related findings discovered during research which are not looked for within the aims of the study. Individual research results are called 'primary findings' when they relate to the outcome measure of the research. In contrast, secondary findings are unsought but not uncommon, as current technologies mean that researchers now have a greater chance of encountering secondary findings.[3]

DNA sequencing technologies

The Human Genome Project, which commenced in 1990, aimed to sequence all 3.2 billion base pairs of the human genome. At the time the enormous potential of genome mapping may not have been fully appreciated, but the success of the project and the recent completion of the human reference genome has had a massive impact on clinical interpretation from 2000 and led to a new era of genomic medicine which utilises an individual's genomic information for diagnosis and targeted therapies.

There have been significant advances in the technologies used to sequence DNA. NGS techniques use semiconductors and nanotechnology that increase the speed with which genomes are sequenced,[4] enabling an entire human genome to be sequenced in a day and at reduced cost compared to the conventional 'Sanger' sequencing technology. High-throughput sequencing technologies also provide a depth of information, enabling variants in just a few percent of cells to be identified. WGS looks at all portions of the genome, and WES sequences only the protein coding parts of genes and is used by researchers to search for rare mutations. Sequencing 'panels' of genes related to a suspected disorder provides a more targeted approach and increases the likelihood of identifying an underlying genetic cause.

Huge amounts of data are produced from high-throughput sequencing technologies, and this raises questions about who has a right to that data and who it should be shared with. I address three situations arising in genomic sequencing that give rise to ethical and legal challenges:

- Sharing information from research – legal duties and ethical obligations of biobanks to return secondary findings to research participants.
- Providing access to raw genomic data, which comprises genomic sequence data before annotation and interpretation, to research participants/patients.
- Genomic sequencing in the clinical context – legal duties and ethical obligations of healthcare professionals to share information with the genetic relatives of the person undergoing testing.

Case scenario 1: sharing information from research biobanks

Ally is 57 years old and has been diagnosed with type 1 diabetes. Her general practitioner has discussed with Ally whether she would be interested in contributing to research on this condition. Ally participates in the national biobank, providing a tissue sample (biosample) and information about her current health and lifestyle, and she agrees to be followed up over the next five years. Ally's sample undergoes genomic sequencing using high-throughput sequencing technology, and genetic markers for BRCA1 and BRCA2 are discovered, which predisposes to breast and ovarian cancer.[5] The researchers ponder their obligations to return this information to Ally, as it was discovered beyond the specific aims of the study (a secondary finding).

Return of secondary findings: obligations of researchers

A biobank describes the storage of tissue samples and health data with an aim of understanding how genes influence the health of a population. There are biobanks in many countries around the world, including Iceland, Sweden, Denmark, Estonia, Canada, South Korea, Japan, Singapore and the United States. The UK Biobank has, since 2006, collected biological and health data from half a million people, aged between 40 and 69 years old, as part of a large-scale prospective study looking at the relationship between disease, lifestyle and genes and identifying factors that affect individual response to specific treatments.

> Participants in a biobank voluntarily undergo a battery of tests as part of an observational study and allow the resultant data to be stored by the biobank for use in future research.[6]

The aim of research is to provide generalisable knowledge which has impact for society, and future generations. Researchers are not looking for information at the level of an individual participant, and participants do not receive 'treatment' as they would in a clinical situation (a 'disease-agnostic' biobank). But do researchers have an obligation to inform participants in research about secondary findings which may be clinically significant and which may then be used by the individual to make treatment, reproductive and lifestyle choices? If Ally was informed of her genetic predisposition to cancer, she could seek medical advice and perhaps undergo treatment. The UK Biobank Ethics and Governance Council identifies the tension between respecting the interests of individual participants in biobanks and the effective use of public resources, such as funding and research time, for the benefit of society.[7]

Participants in biobanks provide samples and personal information, which enables the research to be carried out, and for a biobank to continue to function, it requires the ongoing cooperation of participants. Participants will, like other members of society, receive the public health benefits created by the biobank, but is that sufficient to recognise their contribution? The principle of reciprocity gives rise to an expectation of some response/reward in recognition of their input. Participants in a biobank may justifiably expect some feedback, and this may include the return of relevant information to them. General research findings from a research project will often be provided through public formats. The UK 10K Project (100,000 Genomes Project) provides an update of the project, media releases and publications in peer-reviewed scientific journals and on its website (www.uk10k.org). Increasingly there is an expectation that findings which have relevance for the individual participant will be provided to them.

A biobank's protocol will state the position on feedback of health-related findings – which should be returned and which should not. The initial governance framework for UK Biobank stated that "UK Biobank will not provide participants with information, genetic or otherwise, derived from examination of the database or samples by research undertaken after enrolment."[8] This 'no feedback' approach was justified on the basis that the time, cost and complexity of the procedures necessary to provide feedback findings to individual participants would prevent or impair the research purposes of the biobank.[9] However, where research undertaken in the biobank study shows that a participant carries a genetic mutation for a serious disease that is treatable, then arguably this position is not legally or ethically defensible.[10]

The legal obligation to return secondary findings rests on the existence of a duty of care owed by the biobank to the participants. A duty of care is established where harm is foreseeable, there is sufficient nexus between the biobank and its participants and it is fair and reasonable to impose such a duty. I have previously argued that UK Biobank does owe a duty of care to provide feedback of a gene mutation for a serious genetic disorder which is treatable or the symptoms of which could be ameliorated.[11] Harm is foreseeable, and proximity can be established, as UK Biobank will maintain a continuous relationship with participants over many years, and it is fair to impose a duty – based on a notion of reciprocity – because participants supply confidential information over a period of up to 20 years, undergo a health screen and continue to update the project with relevant information.

A policy not to provide feedback contravenes a fundamental principle in medical research (and clinical practice) of respect for self-determination. Autonomous choices depend on the person having sufficient information to make an informed choice, "to be forewarned presents individuals with choices, most importantly, with the possibility of forearming oneself against disease."[12]

Data and samples provided to biobanks have personal identifiers removed, but given the amount of data generated during genomic sequencing, it is now a reality that an individual could be identified from the genotyping process, and findings can be linked to an individual (a 'linkage key' may be used by to re-identify the individual) and provided to them. Nevertheless, the practical and resource issues necessary to implement a meaningful return process would place a burden on the biobank.[13] The genotyping results arising from the research would have to be redone and validated before being used to confirm the existence of a gene mutation for clinical purposes. But there is growing consensus that findings which are analytically valid should be returned if they are 'clinically significant.' There may be some controversy about the meaning and scope of 'clinically significant' findings. The governance framework of the UK10K project, for example, defines clinically significant findings as "variants that contribute to the current disease status or alter assessment of the future disease risk of the research participant."[14] There are different views about what might be an appropriate 'floor' for return of secondary findings, ranging from those secondary findings which are medically actionable, higher penetrance and for serious conditions[15] to those which inform reproductive decisions. A process for return should avoid swamping a person with information which is not of use in making treatment, management and reproductive choices.[16] For Ally, knowledge that she carries *BRAC1* and *BRCA2* gene mutation would enable her to make informed choices about regular screening and/or treatment.

Although biobanks do not have an obligation to search for such findings, they should establish robust management processes for handling potential clinically significant secondary findings where they do arise to meet their ethical obligations. The World Medical Association Declaration of Taipei (2016) recommends that the return of secondary findings (referred to as 'incidental findings') is "gradually integrated into global ethical norms."[17]

Right not to know

The right 'not to know' is recognised in international biomedical instruments, including the European Convention on Human Rights and Biomedicine, which states that "everyone is entitled to know any information collected about his or her health. However, the wishes of individuals not to be so informed shall be observed" (Article 10.2).

It is broadly accepted that health-related findings should only be returned when participants have consented to being given this feedback. Respecting individual autonomy means respecting their decision not to receive such information too – they may waive any benefit of their right to know and exercise their right not to know about secondary findings. This can be ethically challenging for researchers and those involved in establishing governance frameworks for biobanks. If genome sequencing reveals the possibility of a genetic condition that could lead to serious harm and where that harm could be easily avoided, should there not be a requirement that the person is told? But individuals may worry *more* knowing of a potential health risk, and the Danish Council of Ethics used the term 'morbidification' to describe the notion of living in fear of onset of symptoms and the inescapable fate through knowledge about risk of a genetic disease.[18] Certainly, if discrimination in employment and limited availability of insurance becomes a reality, there would be strong arguments for not wanting to receive secondary findings which could have an impact on the individual beyond their healthcare. Where researchers do identify the possibility of a serious genetic condition for which treatment is available and the participant has not agreed to receive secondary findings at the outset, this presents an ethical dilemma.[19] A paternalistic approach points towards overriding the patient's choice in the interests of providing an opportunity to protect the patient's health or quality of life (and as genetic information is inherently familial, information of risk is also of importance to family members). If a right not to know should be 'activated' by the individual's explicit choice, rather than being presumed then, this requires the individual to have enough information to weigh up risks and benefits of such a choice, "but this is precisely what the individual wanted to avoid."[20]

The tension between public and private interests in biobank research could be considered through a utilitarian perspective, identifying the consequences of (non) provision of individual feedback, whether feedback would do more harm than good. I have already considered the relative harms and benefits for the *individual* of receiving such information. It is worth considering the reputational damage to the research enterprise where individual feedback which may save the life of the individual is not provided,

> Not to feedback in such a situation could result in damage to the public trust in medical researchers, as well as having severe repercussions for medical research in general and the UK Biobank project in particular.[21]

In this section I have sought to demonstrate the tension between a societal interest in research and the interests of individual participants to receive feedback of findings which may have relevance to them. Ethical principles of autonomy, trust and reciprocity should be foremost when determining strategies and policies of biobanks to provide information that is of value to research participants.

Genomic research can lead to discoveries about the genetic basis for disease. Although many of the sequence variants identified in whole genome/whole exome sequencing are not clearly pathogenic, high-throughput sequencing technologies can identify significant biological markers associated with the development of disease and its response to treatment, resulting in targeted therapies. Hospital-based genomics research, especially in paediatric contexts, often has a translational component, where genomic sequencing can be used to identify tumour-specific 'markers' –

gene alterations unique to an individual patient.[22] Patients whose clinical symptoms do not suggest a recognisable syndrome, or who are not responding to treatment, may undergo genomic sequencing, and a great deal of genomic data that is being used directly for patient management options is being generated in the research environment through trials. I will address an issue that is starting to gain consideration – the return of raw genomic data to patients/research participants.

Case scenario 2: right to access genomic data

Berta has seen her oncologist over the past two years and has not responded to treatment. Her clinician discusses with her the possibility of enrolment in a research study which focusses on rare cancers. She does enrol, hoping that the research may identify a genetic component of her condition leading to personalised treatment. She provides a tissue sample, and genomic sequencing is carried out. Her clinician is provided with a summary report of the interpreted data and discusses it with Berta. Unfortunately, genomic sequencing has not revealed data which leads to treatment. Berta's partner is a bioinformatician and thinks it would be a good idea to get the raw uninterpreted data so they can seek further analysis of it. Berta requests a copy of the raw genomic data. Her clinician is unsure whether he should provide her with a copy and whether she has a right to access it.

Raw genomic data is genomic sequence data before any annotation and interpretation have been undertaken, it is 'non-curated,' and it has been considered a 'meaningless code' without clinical value until further analysed.[23] Raw datasets include the data generated by a next-generation sequencer such as FASTQ files, Binary Alignment/Map format (BAM files) or Variant Call Format files (VCF files). There is no information in raw genomic data that in itself communicates risk of genetic disorders, and so such data is not viewed as 'results' of genomic sequencing.[24] The justification for return of raw genomic data is thus not based on its clinical utility, but rather is framed by ethical arguments of respect for the autonomy of research participants/patients and the personal meaning and value that genomic information has for them. In principle it should be more straightforward to return raw data, compared to returning secondary 'findings,' where decisions need to be made about the relevance of findings and whether or not they are actionable.[25]

In Australia the *National Statement on Ethical Conduct in Human Research* updated 2018 (paragraph 3.3.28) states that researchers are not expected to return raw genomic data to research participants (doubtless to avoid creating onerous obligations on researchers and to manage expectations of participants). Berta in the case study is a participant in research, but she is also a patient. The long-established division between clinical care and research is becoming increasingly distorted as clinicians may have a role in recruiting patients to research studies and then translating genomic results into clinical care. Patients can be provided with results of investigations such as imaging and x-rays to take home, and the doctor may discuss them with the patient during the consultation. Arguably raw genomic data is different because of the potential for further clinical interpretation, which could provide health information for themselves and their genetic relatives outside the current clinical relationship. There is no consensus on return of raw genomic data to clinical patients who are enrolled in a research study.

If interpretive hurdles can be overcome, raw genomic data provides huge amounts of information of potential importance to an individual's current and future health. They may seek further analysis by their clinician or by using a third-party interpretative service. In a survey of attitudes of <7000 "members of the public, genomic researchers, genetic health professionals and non-genetic health professionals," when asked to suggest what they would do with a raw sequence, if offered it, 62% (n = 4320) were interested in using raw genomic data to seek out their own interpretation of it, and this could be using a clinical genetics service, general practitioner or genomics researcher.[26] Of course, individuals may want their raw data for other reasons, such as supporting data sharing initiatives, to "'create some art work' or simply to have as 'an amazing memento.'"[27] The increasing genetic literacy of the public, commoditisation of sequencing and resulting rapid emergence of third-party interpretative services which may be used to interpret raw genomic data have hastened patient trends to request raw genomic data. There is growing support for patients and research participants to have access to their raw genomic data in both clinical and research contexts.

But there is no standard approach to return of raw genomic data. Some research protocols provide that they will not return raw data; other studies may return it on a case-by-case basis to those who request it. Despite current practice, do legal and ethical principles point to a right of individuals to access their raw genomic data? People feel strong ownership over their genomic data, giving rise to a sense of entitlement to it, and they may request possession of the data because it is something they believe they 'own.'

Ownership

Could the concept of ownership provide the basis for a legal right to return of raw genomic data once a sample has been donated for research? Empirical studies show that many people believe that their genomic data 'belongs' to them, thereby giving them a right to access it.[28] The applicability and utility of property law to resolve issues of ownership and control depends on whether the subject of debate is a biological sample or data derived from it. At what point in the continuum from tissue sample to data does a person have, or cease to have, property rights?

Property and biosamples

A rationale for ownership of tissue samples and genetic information derived from them is the protection of privacy and autonomy of the donor. Ownership may also enable the individual to share in the tangible benefits of genetic research.[29] Historically application of the 'labour theory' gave rise to property rights through the application of work and skill. In 1908 the High Court of Australia in *Doodeward v Spence*[30] decided that a human body part can become the subject of property and that rights can be acquired through the lawful exercise of work or skill. Nearly a century later the English Court of Appeal in *R v Kelly*[31] confirmed a right to retain possession of a body part through the labour of a person in lawful possession of it. Applying this legal principle to a tissue sample provided for genomic analysis, we can conclude that ownership rights are much more plausible for health services and researchers than for the individual donor.[32]

Property and data

Raw genomic data is the consequence of genomic sequencing of a biological sample, requiring the expertise of researchers and funding of their institutions.[33] Just by 'investing' bodily samples to be tested, an individual does not become the owner of data that is produced through the expertise of researchers. Ballantyne notes that a person can have relevant interests in data without the need to conclude that data 'belongs' to them, and indeed, data 'ownership' presents a barrier to the use of data in research.[34] She proposes that since genomic data is co-produced between participants/patients and other health professionals, the narrative of collective ownership is "more compelling than private property claims."[35] This might lead to a conclusion that in publicly funded research, the output of professionals' labour should be co-owned by the individual and the state and should be used for public benefit and/or kept in the public domain.

Nevertheless, the metaphor of 'ownership' and of data 'belonging' to someone is certainly used in the debate around management of health data in an amorphous non-legal way, exemplified by the 'Your DNA, Your Say' online survey gathering global attitudes towards genomic data sharing.[36] In a discussion paper on the *Ethical and Legal Aspects of Whole Sequencing of the Human Genome*, the EURAT project group states that raw data "continues to belong to the study participants in an irrevocable and unchangeable sense"[37] because of the continuing relationship between these individuals and the research enterprise. Ownership is better conceived of as a moral rather than legal claim of research participants so that biomedical research is not unduly hampered. It is worth noting the High Court of Australia decision in *D'Arcy v. Myriad Genetics Inc*.[38] that no patent or other intellectual property rights can be granted in *BRCA1* and *BRCA2* nucleotide sequences because, although the isolation of the nucleotide sequence comprising the *BRCA1* gene is a man-made process, it does not involve any element of inventiveness.[39]

Privacy: access to personal data

We give information to governments and their institutions and other bodies anticipating that they can be trusted not to share it with others inappropriately. The dominant articulation of privacy laws, such the Health Insurance Portability and Accountability Act 1996 (United States), Data Protection Act 2018 (UK), General Data Protection Regulation (GDPR, Europe) and Privacy Act 1988 (Commonwealth legalisation, Australia) is the prevention of unauthorised disclosure, although such legal frameworks also provide a right of access to personal data by the individual to whom it relates.

In Europe the GDPR provides protections for an individual's personal information, and Article 15 gives a right to access personal data unless this would lead to serious impairment of the research project. Genomic data is a form of personal data and so, arguably, study participants and patients have a right to have their raw genomic data released to them. The EURAT project group notes that the moral and legal rights of participants/patients to access their raw genomic data are established.[40]

In Australia the equivalent Privacy Act 1988 (Cth) (as amended) and state and territory provisions provide less clear guidance with respect to access to raw genomic data. At the federal level, the Privacy Act 1988 regulates how personal information is handled by Commonwealth public-sector bodies and some private-sector health service providers. 'Personal information' is data which identifies an individual or from which that individual's identity can be reasonably ascertained (section 6(1) 'information or an opinion about an identified individual, or an individual who is reasonably identifiable'). There is some debate about whether genomic information meets the criteria of personal information.[41] Information *about* an individual has a low bar and is easily established for genetic information.[42]

Genomic information used in research often has personal identifiers removed, as scientific researchers "are seeking trends and correlations across broader populations, rather than conclusions about known individuals."[43] Whether an individual is reasonably identifiable from their genomic information, and in particular raw genomic data, is the key issue. Eckstein et al. note the lack of clarity as to whether sequence data constitutes 'personal information,' given ambiguity around the possibility of reidentification from WGS data.[44] As technology improves, however, individuals "may be reidentified on the basis of genetic raw data even when traditional identifiers such as the name or date of birth are removed."[45] Where genomic sequencing is carried out within a research study to inform clinical care, the clinician and/or researcher will have a linkage key with IDs and names so the genomic sequencing data can be linked to an individual. That raw genomic data is, in practice, being returned to individuals who request it demonstrates that a person is identifiable from the data held.

Implications for return of raw genomic data

What are the likely implications for researchers and clinicians of projected increases in requests for raw genomic data? Research seeks to enhance understanding at a societal rather than individual level, and research findings may not meet clinical standards for quality. Therefore, the recipient of that information will need to seek further analysis in order to produce information which meets a level of interpretation to be clinically reliable. It takes time and resources to set up processes to check that raw data is accurate and being returned to the right person. Sample swaps and mis-annotations, where a sample is incorrectly attributed to the wrong donor, are common yet "are a high stakes issue for large consortium projects and clinical science."[46] Logistical questions are associated with appropriate storage and transfer mechanisms for large data files. Genetic counsellors are likely to be gatekeepers in the sense that they will be called upon to play a greater role in managing expectations around what can be gleaned from raw genomic data.[47]

Aside from an increased burden of the process for return, however, are the liability ramifications. Where raw data is subsequently subjected by patients to third-party analysis, there may be a potential need to provide clinical advice on that interpretation. There is evidence that many third-party interpretative services (TPIs) websites recommend that customers discuss results with their healthcare provider. One issue that requires consideration is whether researchers/clinicians should inform recipients of raw genomic data about the foreseeable impact of use of TPIs. The health reports and risk estimates produced by these interpretation tools can be difficult for both consumers and healthcare professionals to interpret.[48] Harms that could be associated with using raw genomic data should be discussed prior to handing it over so that the person is making an informed choice.

Myriad legal, ethical and practical challenges arise when a patient requests their raw genomic data. Irrespective of the legal framework, there are strong ethical grounds to compel the release of data. However, associated burdens and challenges must be addressed, and it is essential that researchers and clinicians address these challenges before data requests become routine.

Case scenario 3: sharing information with genetic relatives

Charlie, aged 50 and has been experiencing abnormal facial movements and muscle spasms. He is referred by his general practitioner to the local clinical genetics service. WGS reveals that he has the gene mutation for Huntington disease. Charlie has three adult children, and the genetic counsellor informs Charlie that each of his children have a 50% chance of having the gene mutation. The genetic counsellor offers to support Charlie to share the difficult news with them, but he is adamant that he does not want his children to know, as there is no treatment, and he feels the information would be a burden to them. The genetic counsellor is unsure whether she should let Charlie's children know of the genetic risk so they have the opportunity to have genetic testing, but she is aware of the importance of her duty of confidentiality.

The clinical application of high-throughput sequencing technologies is becoming more commonplace in providing a diagnosis for an individual. A referral may be made to a genetics service (public or private) by a primary care doctor, and the results of the genome sequencing will be discussed with the individual tested (the proband) by a genetic counsellor. Genetic data is not only highly personal but also inherently familial, and high-throughput technologies produce health data that is relevant for the proband and his or her genetic relatives. Knowledge of the genetic component of disease can enable prevention, surveillance and treatment and can inform reproductive choices. Most patients diagnosed with a hereditary condition are keen to notify their at-risk family members so that they can take steps to be tested, and a genetic counselling service will support the patient in the process of disclosure to relatives.[49] Rarely the proband may be unwilling to share this information with his or her relatives, and they may not feel it is their responsibility to do so for distantly related family members or for those with whom they are no longer in touch.[50] Genetic counsellors then will consider how to manage their legal duty of confidentiality and maintain privacy of health information in respect of their patient and the ethical obligation to prevent harm to at-risk relatives. Although this dilemma may happen rarely in practice, non-disclosure will be of increasing concern as NGS becomes more commonplace. Of recent significance is the legal duty to warn genetic relatives of the risk of disease.

Confidentiality and duties to share genetic information

Patient autonomy in healthcare decision making is not limited to treatment decisions but also extends to how their health information is shared. Autonomy is not absolute, however, and a person's right to control how their information is shared with others is constrained by an obligation not to harm them. John Stuart Mill in 1859 observed that the exercise of personal freedom may be legitimately limited if it places others at risk of harm.[51] Arguably there is a moral obligation on the proband to share information with at-risk relatives in order to avoid potentially preventable harm and to enhance *their* autonomous decision making, but do healthcare professionals owe a legal duty to do so? The tension between privacy and avoiding harm to others presents a challenge for those involved in clinical genetics services, who owe a duty of care to the individual who has undergone genomic sequencing. How should maintaining trust with the proband (a 'patient' in the context of a clinical genetics service) be balanced with avoiding harm to relatives who, if they knew about the genetic risk, may choose to pursue testing, allowing early treatment/diagnostic options?

A duty of care exists between a patient and the health professional because of the established relationship between them. Healthcare information, such as the results of genetic testing, is confidential information, and health professionals owe their patients a duty to respect patient confidentiality, disclosing the information to others only with the patient's express up-to-date consent or as required or authorised by law.

The common law duty of confidentiality is owed in respect of confidential information received in the context of the professional relationship,

> a duty of confidence arises when confidential information comes to the knowledge of a person (the confidant) in circumstances where he has notice, or is held to have agreed, that the information is confidential, with the effect that it would be just in all the circumstances that he should be precluded from disclosing the information to others.[52]

The expectation that healthcare information will remain confidential encourages patients to be open and truthful with their clinician. If genetic test results are disclosed without the agreement of the proband, this may lead to the patient disengaging with health services, including monitoring or treatment programmes. Additionally, there is a public interest in maintaining medical confidentiality, as public trust in a clinical genetics service would be undermined if information is disclosed without justification.

Parker and Lucassen have argued that the traditional approach to confidentiality, what they term the 'personal account' model, does not adequately account for the familial nature of genetic information.[53] The personal account model, which has been the default position, states that information divulged by patients to their healthcare professionals should generally be treated as confidential – patients have a right to decide what happens to information given by them to their clinician. Parker and Lucassen prefer a 'joint account' model, in which all those who share the genetic information have an equal right to that information, and this approach is gaining ground from other academic commentators.[54] The joint account model also addresses the inequity that would arise when patients who are aware of a familial genetic factor have the knowledge to then seek treatment but those who do not have such information cannot.

Privacy

Legislation in many countries sets out the thresholds for lawful disclosure of certain kinds of information. The threshold for lawful sharing of genetic information is compliance with privacy law principles, irrespective of the ethical acceptability of disclosure. In the UK professional guidelines from the General Medical Council provide that even if a patient has explicitly refused consent, healthcare professionals can disclose personal information when "the benefits to an individual or to society of the disclosure outweigh the public and the patient's interest in keeping the information confidential."[55] In Australia, numerous statutory provisions govern the handling of personal information, including health information, and the Commonwealth Privacy Act 1988 promotes the privacy of individuals while recognising the need to balance this with the interests of others. Health and other sensitive information (including genetic information) are provided higher levels of protection than other personal information. The legislation applies to information collected, used and disclosed by private-sector entities such as private hospitals and health practitioners. It does not apply to public health services, where most of the genetic testing in Australia currently takes place. Disclosure of genetic information within the public sector is covered by relevant state or territory legislation.

In response to the Australian Law Reform Commission Report *Essentially Yours – The Protection of Human Genetic Information in Australia* (ALRC Report 96), the Privacy Act 1988 (Cth) was amended,[56] and it now provides that health information can be disclosed without consent if the doctor with care of the patient reasonably believes that disclosure is necessary to lessen or prevent a serious threat to the life, health or safety of a genetic relative. Disclosure must be carried out in accordance with guidelines, developed by the National Health and Medical Research Council (Use and Disclosure of Genetic Information to a Patient's Genetic Relatives under Section 95AA of the Privacy Act 1988 Cth).

There are considerable challenges for healthcare professionals working in a genetic service in applying these principles. The serious *threat* to the life, health or safety of genetic relatives need not be imminent, but should present a *significant* danger to the relative. This could include a potentially life-threatening situation or one that might reasonably result in an illness or psychological harm unless a timely decision is taken. A scenario for disclosure described in the NHMRC guidelines is the genetic mutation for Huntington disease (HD). The manifestation of this disease involves substantial psychological and emotional elements, and the mode of inheritance and penetrance of HD are clear-cut, although currently there is no treatment and the physical effects are unable to be prevented or lessened. A relative at risk might claim they are at serious risk of psychological harm through ignorance of his or her genetic risk and so they should be informed of their at-risk status, even if the proband does not agree. However, it cannot be known whether disclosure might in fact have entirely the opposite effect and introduce or increase a threat to their psychological or emotional wellbeing.[57] It is known that very few (5–15%) of those at 50% risk of developing HD actually choose to learn their genetic status through predictive testing,[58] and "the vast majority prefer to remain ignorant, possibly to preserve hope that they may not carry the gene mutation."[59]

The Australian NHMRC guidelines do not oblige health practitioners to make disclosure but legally permits them to do so if they see fit, balancing the harms and benefits. Respecting the proband's views about disclosure as far as possible engages the ethical principle of autonomy, on the other hand, disclosure enables at-risk relatives to seek testing themselves and then take appropriate action, so the principle of beneficence is relevant for them. The ethical obligation to avoid harm (non-maleficence) requires both a consideration of the harm arising to the proband from disclosure without consent and the harm to the genetic relatives of not knowing their genetic risk and therefore not seeking testing and perhaps treatment. The ethical principle of justice requires that all genetic relatives should be aware of their at-risk status, rather than just some, and this is a premise of Parker and Lucassen's joint account model. Disclosure to a genetic relative should in any event be limited to information that is necessary for communicating the increased risk.

I and colleagues have argued elsewhere that "while the harms of disclosure without consent may be justified to avoid or reduce physical harms emanating from the genetic condition for the at-risk relative, this balance is unlikely to be achieved for psychological or emotional harms because of the difficulty in establishing that notification would lessen, and not of itself cause, psychological harm."[60]

So far, I have considered the duty of confidentiality and privacy obligations owed to patients and the ethical considerations which inform a discretion to disclose to at-risk relatives. Recently a legal challenge in England focussed on the extent of a legal duty owed to genetic relatives to inform them of their risk status.

Balancing harms and benefits of disclosure

The case of *ABC v St George's Healthcare NHS Trust*[61] explored the legal duty of healthcare professionals in England and Wales in balancing their duty of confidentiality to a patient with the duty to avoid harm to others. In brief, the facts of the case are as follows: A man shot and killed his wife and, following conviction for manslaughter, was detained under hospital order. His doctors suspected that he might be suffering from HD, and genetic testing confirmed this. He refused to inform his daughters of the diagnosis, despite knowing that one was pregnant. That daughter, ABC, brought a legal claim, arguing that the doctors treating her father had been negligent in failing to alert her to the risk that she may have the HD gene mutation. She said that clinicians with care of her father should have informed her of her father's diagnosis when they knew that she was pregnant, so she would have the opportunity to undergo testing.

The Court of Appeal, hearing the case by judicial review, found that although ABC was not a patient, on the particular facts of the case, there was a relationship of proximity between her and her father's clinicians. It was reasonably foreseeable that she might suffer psychological harm and the loss of opportunity to terminate her pregnancy, and so the court considered that it was "fair, just and reasonable" that a legal duty is owed in these circumstances. A key concern of the father's clinicians was that to impose a duty here would be to effectively impose a duty of care to non-patients and would conflict with the duty of confidentiality owed to existing patients. But genetics is different from other fields of medicine because clinicians acquire definite, reliable and critical medical information about a third party (ABC in this case). Justice Yip found that in the circumstances a duty was owed to ABC, but that it did not amount to a duty to disclose confidential information when a patient has refused consent for that disclosure. Rather, it is a duty for the healthcare team to conduct a balancing exercise, taking into account the public interest in protecting individual privacy and the public interest in using that information for the benefit of others.[62] Nevertheless "in the context of genomic medicine, this has important consequences for clinical practice."[63]

Conclusion

Genomic data produced by high-throughput sequencing technologies, such as WGS, WES and RNA sequencing, is of value in both research and clinical contexts. Whether an individual has a right to access this information depends on the nature of the relationship in which it arises and the value of that information. In the research context there is an ethical obligation to return secondary findings that have clinical utility (and, arguably, a legal duty). There is a need for greater clarity to members of the public about ways that their biomedical data is used and may be used in the future. Providing access to raw genomic data is an emerging issue for NGS in translational medicine. Here, raw data has value, where further interpretation can lead to understanding of the genetic component of disease. But it may have value to an individual just because it is 'their data' – something that belongs to them and therefore they should have access to. Where genome sequencing is used in a clinical setting, it has value to the person tested and also to genetic relatives at risk. The duties owed by healthcare professionals to the proband may need to be tempered to avoid harm to at risk genetic relatives.

Notes

1 K. Snell, 'Health as the Moral Principle of Post-Genomic Society: Data-Driven Arguments Against Privacy and Autonomy' (2019) 28(2) *Cambridge Quarterly of Healthcare Ethics* 201–214.
2 Although the terms 'ethics' and 'morals' tend to be used interchangeably, the term 'morals'/'morality' refers to the values of an individual and their sense of right and wrong, whereas 'ethics' refers to rules from an external source, such as codes of conduct or frameworks.
3 J-C Lin, et al. 'Managing "Incidental Findings" in Biobank Research: Recommendations of the Taiwan Biobank.' (2019) 17 *Computational and Structural Biotechnology Journal* 1135–1142.
4 B. Berkman, Z. Shapiro, L. Eckstein and E. Pike, 'The Ethics of Large-Scale Genomic Research.' In: Colman, J., and Matei, S. A. (eds) *Ethical Reasoning in Big Data: An Exploratory Analysis* (Springer, New York, 2016).
5 N. Petrucelli, et al. 'BRCA1- and BRCA2-Associated Hereditary Breast and Ovarian Cancer.' In Adam, M. P. (ed.) *GeneReviews* (University of Washington, Seattle, 1998).
6 M. Graham et al. 'Taking it to the Bank: The Ethical Management of Individual Findings Arising in Secondary Research' (2021) 47 *Journal of Medical Ethics* 689–696, page 689.
7 Ethics and Governance Council of UK Biobank, *Feedback of Health-Related Findings: Foreground Principles and Background Perspectives* (Ethics and Governance Council of UK Biobank, London, 2015).
8 Wellcome Trust, Medical Research Council, *UK Biobank Ethics and Governance Framework* (V 1.0 Department of Health, London, 2004).
9 It is worth noting that for medical imaging UK Biobank will inform participants of secondary (incidental) findings that could have a major impact on the participant's quality of life and where abnormalities are potentially life-threatening. Lorna Gibson et al. 'Factors Associated with Potentially Serious Incidental Findings and with Serious Final Diagnoses on Multi-modal Imaging in the UK Biobank Imaging Study: A Prospective Cohort Study' (2019) 14(6) *PLoS One* e0218267
10 C. Johnston, J. Kaye, 'Does the UK Biobank have a Legal Obligation to Feedback Individual Findings to Participants?' (2004) 12(3) *Medical Law Review* 239–267.
11 C. Johnston, J. Kaye, 'Does the UK Biobank Have a Legal Obligation to Feedback Individual Findings to Participants?' (2004) 12(3) *Medical Law Review* 239–267.
12 N. Halliwell et al. 'Balancing Autonomy and Responsibility: The Ethics of Generating and Disclosing Genetic Information' (2003) 29(2) *Journal of Medical Ethics* 74–79, page 76.
13 I. Budin-Ljøsne 'Feedback of Individual Genetic Results to Research Participants: Is It Feasible in Europe?' (2016) 14(3) *Biopreservation and Biobanking* 241–248.
14 *UK 10K Rare Genetic Variants in Health and Disease, Ethical Governance Framework, Version 21* (London, 2010) page 8. http://www.uk10k.org/assets/ef_uk10k_v21.pdf
15 G. Jarvik, et al. 'Return of Genomic Results to Research Participants: The Floor, the Ceiling, and the Choices in Between' (2014) 94(6) *American Journal of Human Genetics* 818–826.
16 E. Ormondroyd et al. 'Not Pathogenic Until Proven Otherwise": Perspectives of UK Clinical Genomics Professionals Toward Secondary Findings in Context of a Genomic Medicine Multidisciplinary Team and the 100,000 Genomes Project' (2018) 20(3) *Genetics in Medicine* 320–328.
17 J.-C. Lin et al. 'Managing "Incidental Findings" in Biobank Research: Recommendations of the Taiwan Biobank' (2019) 17 *Computational and Structural Biotechnology Journal* 1135–1142, page 1141.
18 Danish Council of Ethics, *Ethics and Mapping of the Human Genome* (Danish Council of Ethics, Copenhagen, 1993).
19 R. Brownsword, J. Wale. 'The Right to Know and the Right Not to Know Revisited: Part One' (2017) 9(1) *Asian Bioethics Review* 3–18.

20 R. Andorno 'The Right Not to Know: An Autonomy-based Approach' (2004) 30(5) *Journal of Medical Ethics* 435–439, page 436.
21 C. Johnston, J. Kaye, 'Does the UK Biobank Have a Legal Obligation to Feedback Individual Findings to Participants?' (2004) 12(3) *Medical Law Review* 239–267, page 243.
22 Germline mutations are mutations in the DNA in cells that are carried onto the next generation and are far more likely to be implicated in early onset genetic diseases such as Cerebral Palsy, Epilepsy, Developmental delay. Somatic mutations occur in other cell types and cannot be inherited by offspring but are a key component of the majority of diseases and cancer. Gene alterations may be not only unique to an individual, but one "tissue" might have a gene alteration that is unique compared to other "tissues" in the body.
23 A. Middleton, et al. 'Potential Research Participants Support the Return of Raw Sequence Data. (2015) 52(8) *Journal of Medical Genetics* 571–574, page 571.
24 C. Schickhardt, et al. 'Do Patients and Research Subjects Have a Right to Receive their Genomic Raw Data? An Ethical and Legal Analysis' (2020) 21(1) *BMC Medical Ethics* 7.
25 J. Lunshof, et al. 'Information Access. Raw Personal Data: Providing Access' (2014) 343, 6169 *Science (New York, N.Y.)* 373–374.
26 A. Middleton et al. 'Potential Research Participants Support the Return of Raw Sequence Data' (2015) 52(8) *Journal of Medical Genetics* 571–574, page 571.
27 A. Middleton et al. 'Potential Research Participants Support the Return of Raw Sequence Data' (2015) 52(8) *Journal of Medical Genetics* 571–574, page 572.
28 A. Thorogood et al. 'APPLaUD: Access for Patients and Participants to Individual Level Uninterpreted Genomic Data' (2018) 12(1) *Human Genomics* 7.
29 R. Spinello, 'Property Rights in Genetic Information' (2004) 6(1) *Ethics and Information Technology* 29–42.
30 *Doodeward v Spence* [1908] HCA 45.
31 *R v Kelly* [1999] QB 621.
32 J. Montgomery, 'Data Sharing and the Idea of Ownership' (2017) 23(1) *New Bioethics* 81–86.
33 A. Middleton, 'Your DNA, Your Say' (2017) 23(1) *The New Bioethics* 74–80.
34 A. Ballantyne, 'How Should We Think about Clinical Data Ownership?' (2020) 46(5) *Journal of Medical Ethics* 289–294, page 292.
35 A. Ballantyne, 'How Should We Think about Clinical Data Ownership?' (2020) 46(5) *Journal of Medical Ethics* 289–294, page 292.
36 A. Middleton, 'Your DNA, Your Say' (2017) 23(1) *The New Bioethics*, 74–80.
37 E. Winkler et al. 'Ethical and Legal Aspects of Whole Genomic Sequencing,' In: *On the Release of Raw Genomic Data to Patients and Study Participants* (Position paper, EURAT Project Group, Heidelberg, 2019), page 39.
38 *D'Arcy v Myriad Genetics Inc.* [2015] HCA 35.
39 D. Nicol, J. Nielsen, V. Dawkins, 'D'Arcy v Myriad Genetics: The Impact of the High Court's Decision on the Cost of Genetic Testing in Australia' (2018) *Occasional Paper No 9, Centre for Law and Genetics*.
40 E. Winkler et al. 'Ethical and Legal Aspects of Whole Genomic Sequencing,' In: *On the Release of Raw Genomic Data to Patients and Study Participants* (Position paper, EURAT Project Group, Heidelberg, 2019).
41 S. Jowett, E. Dallaston, B. Bennett, 'Genomic Research and Data-Sharing: Time to Revisit Australian Laws?' (2020) 39(2) *The University of Queensland Law Journal* 341–369.
42 M. Paterson, N. Witzleb, 'The Privacy-related Challenges Facing Medical Research in an Era of Big Data Analytics: A Critical Analysis of Australian Legal and Regulatory Frameworks' (2015) 26(1) *Journal of Law and Medicine* 188–203.
43 Australian Government, Australian Law Reform Commission, Essentially Yours: The Protection of Human Genetic Information in Australia (Report 96), para 3.12.
44 L. Eckstein et al. 'Australia: Regulating Genomic Data Sharing to Promote Public Trust' (2018) 137 *Human Genetics* 583–591, page 587.
45 A. Schwab et al. 'Genomic Privacy' (2018) 64(12) *Clinical Chemistry*, 1696–1703, page 1696.

46 N. Javed et al. 'Detecting Sample Swaps in Diverse NGS Data Types Using Linkage Disequilibrium.' (2020) 11(1) *Nature Communications* 3697.
47 J. Nielsen, C. Johnston, T. O'Brien, V. Tyrell, 'Returning Raw Genomic Data: Rights of Research Participants and Obligations of Health Care Professionals.' (2022) 216 (11) *Medical Journal of Australia* 550–552.
48 S. Nelson et al. 'Third-party Genetic Interpretation Tools: A Mixed-methods Study of Consumer Motivation and Behavior.' (2019) 105(1) *American Journal of Human Genetics* 122–131.
49 R. McWhirter, C. Johnston, J. Burke, 'Disclosure of Genetic Results to At-risk Relatives without Consent: Issues for Health Care Professionals in Australia' (2019) 27(1) *The Journal of Law, Medicine & Ethics* 108–121.
50 N. Meggiolaro et al, 'Disclosure to Genetic Relatives without Consent – Australian Genetic Professionals' Awareness of the Health Privacy Law.' (2020) 21(1) *BMC Medical Ethics* 13.
51 John Stuart Mill, *'On Liberty'* (Harper Collins, London, 1962)
52 *Attorney-General v Guardian Newspapers Ltd (No 2)* ('Spycatcher') 1988 3 *W.L.R.* 766, Lord Goff at page 805.
53 M. Parker, A. Lucassen, 'Genetic Information: A Joint Account?' (2004) 1329(7458) *BMJ* 165–167.
54 M. Parker, A. Lucassen, 'Genetic Information: A Joint Account?' (2004) 1329(7458) *BMJ* 165–167.
55 General Medical Council, *'Confidentiality'* para 22 (General Medical Council, London, 2017).
56 *Privacy Legislation Amendment Act 2006* (Cth); *Privacy Act 1988* (Cth) s95AA)
57 R. McWhirter, C. Johnston, J. Burke, 'Disclosure of Genetic Results to At-risk Relatives without Consent: Issues for Health Care Professionals in Australia' (2019) 27(1) *The Journal of Law, Medicine & Ethics* 108–21.
58 R. Tassicker et al. 'Problems Assessing Uptake of Huntington Disease Predictive Testing and a Proposed Solution' (2009) 17(1) *European Journal of Human Genetics* 66–70.
59 R. McWhirter, C. Johnston, J. Burke, 'Disclosure of Genetic Results to At-risk Relatives Without Consent: Issues for Health Care Professionals in Australia' (2019) 27(1) *The Journal of Law, Medicine & Ethics* 108–121, page 117.
60 R. McWhirter, C. Johnston, J. Burke, 'Disclosure of Genetic Results to At-risk Relatives Without Consent: Issues for Health Care Professionals in Australia' (2019) 27(1) *The Journal of Law, Medicine & Ethics* 108–121, page 120.
61 *ABC v St George's Healthcare NHS Trust* [2020] EWHC 455 (QB).
62 W. Nixson 'Has the Right to Breach Patient Confidentiality Created a Common Law Duty to Warn Genetic Relatives?' (2017) 17(1) *QUT Law Review* 147–159.
63 A. Middleton et al. 'Professional Duties are Now Considered Legal Duties of Care within Genomic Medicine.' (2020) 28 *European Journal of Human Genetics* 1301–1304, page 1301.

3
INTERNET OF THINGS AND PERSONALISED MEDICINE

DIY-ing diabetes management

Case scenario

Zoe is five years old. Last year she was diagnosed with type 1 diabetes (T1D), and after a steep learning curve, her diabetes has been well managed by her parents. They are very involved in her care and pay close attention to Zoe's glucose level and collaborate well with Zoe's paediatric endocrinologist, who works in the local public hospital. Zoe's mother, Sue, is a nurse, and her father, Bob, is an IT programmer, and they have done some research on management of T1D using an open-source insulin delivery system called a hybrid 'closed loop' system. Bob is confident that he can build this do-it-yourself (DIY) system by following instructions from the website OpenAPS, and they join the closed Facebook group Aussie, Aussie, Aussie, Loop, Loop LOOP! which helps and supports the implementation and running of a 'loop' for Australians and New Zealanders. They are motivated to build the system to optimize Zoe's diabetes management. At Zoe's next scheduled outpatient appointment Bob and Sue tell the endocrinologist about their plans to set up a DIY insulin delivery system for Zoe and ask for support, including monitoring Zoe's glucose readings and ongoing provision of prescriptions for insulin. The endocrinologist knows that Zoe's parents are committed and caring, but she is worried about her involvement, as the system they propose is not standard treatment and she is concerned that it is not registered as a medical device with the regulating body in Australia, the Therapeutic Goods Administration.

Introduction

The UK case of Charlie Gard[1] highlights the desire of parents to seek innovative or experimental treatments for their children where current therapies are ineffective.

> The parents in this case have done what any parent would do for their child. They have searched far and wide for the possibility of a cure or, if

DOI: 10.4324/9781003220190-3

a cure is not available, treatment that would prolong life or even slightly improve the condition.[2]

Families of patients for whom evidence-based therapies have proved ineffective may seek out innovative treatments, or modifications of existing treatments, and the Internet provides a wealth of information to explore options. People with T1D and their families are increasingly using the Internet of Things to build 'looping' systems that monitor glucose levels and automate insulin delivery in a way they consider an improvement on standard management.

The Internet of Things (IoT) is described as "a new technological paradigm that allows any object or thing to be connected to other things, services or people through the Internet."[3] By 2030, it is estimated that there will be more than 21 billion IoT devices connected to the Internet globally, with the highest estimations predicting over 64 billion devices.[4] A broad range of medical devices can be linked through a networked system so that they can function in real time, pushing data across the Internet, and healthcare devices represent one of the fastest-growing areas of IoT.[5] Wearable devices, such as fitness trackers on smartphones, are driving the trend for self-monitoring, and some smartphone applications may gather data and communicate with the patient's medical team, providing information about changes in wellbeing that could give rise to concern. I explore the use of smartphone apps in Chapter 4. In this chapter I focus on IoT technologies which enable a DIY approach to automated insulin delivery for people with T1D.

Do-it-yourself 'artificial pancreas system'

A developing technology for managing T1D is known as a DIY 'artificial pancreas system' (APS) or 'automated insulin delivery' (AID) system. The *International Consensus Statement and practical guidance for health-care professionals* refers to 'open-source automated insulin delivery system,' which is the most exact term.[6] But people in the community are more likely to refer to 'DIY looping' and those who use such systems as 'loopers,'[7] and I use these terms in this chapter. Such a system consists of a continuous glucose monitor (CGM) which measures glucose levels every few minutes, an insulin pump, a sensor with a transmitter attached and an algorithm within the pump that automatically works out how much insulin is needed.[8] The DIY part is the algorithm which decides how much insulin is required based on glucose levels, which are monitored by the CGM.[9] Currently, there is no fully automated system, and human intervention is required to manage spikes in blood glucose levels arising from exercise and food intake, so more appropriately the system is known as a *hybrid* closed loop system.

Although traditionally the pathway for digital innovations in healthcare has been top-down, increasingly patient groups are developing the technology to augment or improve standard healthcare delivery using IoT technologies.[10] Under the banner #WeAreNotWaiting, those tired of waiting for progress to be made in commercial systems to manage T1D share information and develop their own resources. The Open Artificial Pancreas System (OpenAPS) was created in February 2015 by Dana Lewis and her partner, Scott Leibrand, who produced and then shared a free predictive algorithm which links a CGM and insulin pump to automate insulin delivery based on real-time readings from the CGM.

> OpenAPS is a simplified Artificial Pancreas System (APS) designed to automatically adjust an insulin pump's basal insulin delivery to keep blood glucose (BG) in a safe range overnight and between meals. It does this by communicating with an insulin pump to obtain details of all recent insulin dosing (basal and boluses), by communicating with a Continuous Glucose Monitor (CGM) to obtain current and recent BG estimates, and by issuing commands to the insulin pump to adjust temporary basal rates as needed. It follows the same basic diabetes math that a person would do to calculate a needed adjustment to their BG – but it's automated and precise in its measurements.[11]

Other DIY looping systems are AndroidAPS (based on the platform of the OpenAPS algorithm and adjusted for smartphones with the Android system) and Loop (adjusted for smartphones with the iOS system).[12] In 2018 it was estimated that over 725 people worldwide used a DIY system, whereas in 2021 that increased to 10,000 individuals.[13] A 2018 survey found that 20 individuals were actively looping in Australia, one under 10 years of age and two between 10 and 19 years.[14] People are turning to this DIY management because of the high cost and lack of availability of commercial systems such as the Medtronic 670G, although in April 2022 both the Coalition and the Australian Labor Party in Australia gave a bipartisan commitment to provide subsidised access to continuous glucose monitoring for all people living with T1D.[15] DIY systems are flexible and customisable, enabling a more personalised titration of insulin and a way to ease the burden of living with T1D,[16] and that seems to be the reason why Zoe's parents want to use this way of managing their daughter's T1D. As the smartphone can monitor the system remotely, this is particularly helpful where the child cannot manage their own T1D, and parents can read their child's blood glucose levels and manage insulin delivery when the child is away from home.

> While these systems are cocreated by the DIYAPS community, each user has to build his/her own system and use it at his/her own risk. This includes children and adolescents whose caregivers build and maintain these systems on their behalf.[17]

The hardware, CGM and insulin pump, are both 'medical devices,' although they are often modified for use in the DIY system. Medical devices and software which is used as a medical device (SaMD) are subject to regulation by national bodies such as the Therapeutic Goods Administration (TGA) in Australia and the Food and Drug Administration (FDA) in the United States. But DIY hybrid closed loop systems use open-source software,[18] and that means that the program can be inspected, modified and enhanced by programmers who have access to it. As DIY hybrid closed loop systems have not undergone the usual testing and analysis required by therapeutic approval processes, healthcare practitioners may have justifiable concerns about their safety and are not prescribing such a system.[19] Rather, it is the users (and their families) who are the 'experts' in this new technology, often turning to support from other loopers through online communities, thus changing the traditional paradigm of care.

In this chapter I consider whether it is ethically and legally permissible for healthcare professionals to support this DIY approach for their paediatric patients. The open-source aspect of these medical devices is continuously developing, and many of these technologies are codesigned across jurisdictional boundaries, so what is the role of regulation and what does it seek to achieve? Parents using the DIY looping system are creating data and may share this with a closed social media community to gain support and information, and I consider the concept of 'sharenting' and the appropriate limits on sharing of a child's health data.

Benefits of looping

The management of T1D in a child has significant impact on the emotional wellbeing, financial situation, leisure activities and physical health of parents and other members of the family.[20] Benefits of open-source looping systems include availability and access, device and platform interoperability, and customisability.[21] DIY looping systems enable users to personalise their diabetes management, and a recent research study of use of these open-source DIY systems in adults showed improved glycaemic outcomes with no clinical safety concerns compared with a commercially available system.[22] Use of DIY looping systems is associated with reduced episodes of hypoglycaemia and improved overnight control, leading to a higher quality of life among adults with T1D.[23] A pilot study of 22 children 6–15 years of age exposed to prolonged physical activity over the study period showed the feasibility of the AndroidAPS as a tool for the optimization of T1D management during and after prolonged physical activity,[24] and an online survey of caregiver self-reported clinical outcomes of a paediatric population using a DIY system showed improved glycaemic outcomes in all paediatric age groups, including adolescents and very young children.[25]

DIY looping is reported to reduce the mental burden of managing T1D. There is some emerging evidence that shows the beneficial impact of DIY systems on quality of life and psychological wellbeing of children and adolescents,[26] and a small interview study of parents who were using looping technology noted an improved independence for their child and quality of life for their families.[27]

> Imagine going from you being the sole person keeping your child alive, because that is really what it's like to be a type 1 parent, and if your involvement isn't there every hour of every day for the next 15 years, the child will die. Simple as that. And, the looping is a lot like having a nurse 24/7 checking and correcting every five minutes.[28]

So user-led evidence certainly recognises the benefits of DIY looping systems. Clinical trials are taking place on commercial hybrid closed loop systems,[29] and the first randomised control trial on open-source automated insulin delivery, the

CREATE (Community deRivEd AutomaTEd insulin delivery) clinical trial run from New Zealand, is evaluating the safety and efficiency of an automated insulin delivery system.[30]

Challenges of looping

Although there may be benefits of using a DIY looping system, there are also challenges. Parents need to be tech savvy to set up a DIY system, the software and hardware that are used require updating and the insulin dosage needs to be understood and managed. Peer support groups on social media can help users navigate these challenges and provide 24/7 online support. It is apparent that the first tranche of DIY hybrid closed loop system users are highly motivated and competent consumers who engage with their diabetes care on a frequent basis.[31] Where parents are fully engaged and carefully monitor blood glucose levels using a DIY system, the risk to their child may be lower than the risks to a child who is not monitored as often even using approved devices.[32]

As with any insulin pump system, there is an inherent risk of device failure.[33] Concerns about malfunction of the device and potential safety issues arising from the high rates of use of out-of-warranty devices (the insulin pump and CGM), which are linked by the software, is exacerbated by the lack of regulation of DIY looping systems. However, clinically validated real-world data based on self-report, physician report and device data show no safety concerns compared with a commercially approved system[34] and suggest that open-source automated insulin delivery systems are safe and effective treatment options for people with diabetes.[35] In a news release, the lead investigator of the CREATE study said that the findings demonstrate that open-source automated insulin delivery is a 'safe and effective technology.'[36] A DIY system has alerts to notify users prior to hyper/hypoglycaemia if their DIY system is failing, and users can always resort to finger pricks and insulin injections as a back-up. If the child is away from home, the smartphone provides parents with real-time information, and arrangements can be made with their child's school or camp organiser about action to be taken in the event of a malfunction/failure of the system.

Dana Lewis notes the "almost constant risk of insulin management for people living with diabetes,"[37] and it is against that backdrop that safety of open-source automated insulin delivery systems should be considered. She argues that "the discussion of safety by some healthcare providers and also by regulators may include an overestimation of risks and may be anchored on a comparison to the risk to a person without diabetes, overlooking the daily and ongoing danger of living with insulin-requiring diabetes."[38]

Parental choice to use DIY looping

In this section I consider whether use of a DIY looping system in a child, a non-standard therapy for T1D, could be said to be in the *best* interests of the child, and even if it is not the best option for the child, then whether the parental decision to use a DIY system should in any event be supported by the child's clinician.[39]

The use of a DIY looping system in children engages different legal and ethical considerations from its use by an adult. The adult is making an informed choice, thereby exercising their autonomy, and taking on risks, and benefits, according to their values. As Beauchamp and Childress note, "competent patients who can make informed and voluntary choices should have more latitude than other parties in balancing benefits and burdens and in accepting and refusing treatment."[40]

Consent provides legal authority for treatment. For a person to provide valid consent to treatment, the person must be informed about the nature of the treatment,[41] have capacity to make the choice about whether to go ahead with the treatment and make that decision free from coercion (Chapter 6). In respect of minor children (children who have not yet attained the age of 18 years) who lack the capacity to make their own health decisions, parents have the responsibility and authority to make decisions for their children, known as 'parental responsibility.' In England and Wales section 3(1) Children Act 1989 provides that parents have "all the rights, duties, powers, responsibilities and authority which by law a parent of a child has in relation to the child and his property," and section 61B of the Family Law Act 1975 (Cth) in Australia has the same definition. This includes the duty of parents to make decisions on medical and health matters. As autonomy emerges, the views of the minor assume greater weight. Children under 16 may be considered 'Gillick competent' to make their own treatment decisions.[42]

Competence is an essential legal requirement for valid consent to medical treatment, and for adult patients, and arguably Gillick-competent minors, the principle of autonomy outweighs issues of maleficence.[43] In the paediatric context parental autonomy is constrained, as 'best interests' is the over-arching principle in decision making for children. The United Nations Convention on the Rights of the Child Article 3 provides that in all actions concerning children "the best interests of the child shall be a primary consideration." 'Best interests' is the standard for decision making on behalf of children as both a guidance principle, informing parents on how they should make healthcare decisions for their child, and as a rationale for intervention when the child's interests may be harmed by the parent's decision making.[44]

A parental request for novel or non-standard treatment represents a challenge to the treatment offered by the healthcare provider and what is conventionally 'best' for the child. Whether looping could be in the best interests of a child requires consideration of the benefits of such a DIY system for the child and whether the benefits outweigh the risks and burdens of this method of management compared to the standard treatment. The short- and longer-term consequences of a medical treatment are relevant in determining best interests, especially for lifelong chronic conditions such as T1D, and a broad range of medical and non-medical factors are relevant in the determination.

The weighting that parents of the child (and, of course, the child themselves if able to express a view) attach to relative benefits and challenges of DIY looping may legitimately differ from those of the clinical team, heavily influenced by their experiences. The customisability of insulin dosage and increased independence of the child may be prioritised by parents. Some authors argue that it is appropriate to include the interests of parents and family members as well in determining the overall welfare of the child[45] because of the interdependence of members of a family. So, the reduced cognitive burden on parents and positive impact on family life are also relevant in determining the best interests of the child. In contrast, healthcare professionals may be more concerned about the risks in the use of DIY systems – risks of 'hacking,' malfunction and errors made by parents – "there's great risk that people will go on these devices and get it wrong."[46]

How to resolve the conundrum where there are different perspectives on whether DIY looping is the *best* form of management for the child? Indeed, as Auckland and Goold state "where there is room for reasonable disagreement, there is essentially no right or 'best' answer, and so the question of 'best interests' cannot be properly answered."[47] The law recognises the importance of the parents' view, as expressed by Baker J in *Re Ashya King*,

> In most cases, the parents are the best people to make decisions about a child and the State – whether it be the court, or any other public authority – has no business interfering with the exercise of parental responsibility unless the child is suffering or is likely to suffer significant harm as a result of the care given to the child not being what it would be reasonable to expect a parent to give.[48]

As Gillam notes, courts' judgments seem sometimes more consistent with a harm threshold than a best interests standard.[49] Diekema[50] and more recently Auckland and Goold[51] reject the best interest standard as the threshold for intervention and propose that only where the child is at significant risk of serious harm is intervention in parental decision making justified. In their legal battle for experimental treatment for their baby son Charlie Gard, his parents argued in the England and Wales Court of Appeal that the law should "not interfere with a decision by parents in the exercise of their parental rights and responsibilities with regard to their child's medical treatment, save where there is a risk the parents' proposed course of action may cause significant harm."[52] This approach was not accepted by the Supreme Court or by the European Court of Human Rights, and the legal standard for intervention remains the best interests of the child. In any event, the harm principle was proposed for parental *refusals* of treatment. Parents like that of Zoe, from our case scenario are not refusing treatment for their child, but rather wish to modify a standard treatment and continue to engage productively with healthcare professionals, and the law recognises the value of the parents' perspective and the need for doctors to accommodate parental wishes "as far as professional judgment and conscience" allow.[53]

Zone of parental discretion

The Zone of Parental Discretion, described by Gillam, is the *ethically* protected space where parents may legitimately make decisions for their children if those decisions are 'good enough' even if not the 'best' for the child and focusses on whether the child will be harmed by the parents' decision, rather than what is optimal. The first stage of the inquiry is to decide whether carrying out the decision of the parents is so bad as to constitute probable significant harm to the child. Where parents are informed and supported in setting up a DIY system, have alternative ways to provide insulin if the automated system malfunctions and maintain an ongoing relationship with their child's clinical team, then DIY looping is not likely to cause significant harm to the child, and I consider that it falls within the Zone of Parental Discretion.

> If the effects on the child of the course of action wanted by the parents do not constitute probable significant harm, the parents' decision falls within the Zone of Parental Discretion: it should be acceded to, even if it is sub-optimal for the child.[54]

But even if use of a DIY system were to constitute probable significant harm, we then look to the second stage of the Zone of Parental Discretion inquiry, which considers the effect of overriding the parents' decision and whether that would cause greater harm to the child than the harm expected from the parents' original decision. Maintaining a therapeutic long-term relationship is an essential part of medical care, and the role of parents in managing their child's T1D is crucial. If parents are not supported by their child's paediatric endocrinologist in the use of a DIY system, there is a risk that parents may end the relationship with that healthcare practitioner or disengage with mainstream care, and, if so, then the negative effects on the child would likely constitute greater harm to the child than the harm expected from the parents' responsible use of a DIY system.

In the case scenario Zoe's parents are knowledgeable and confident in setting up and running the system, they have alternative ways to provide insulin if the automated system malfunctions, they carefully monitor Zoe, they engage with the paediatric endocrinologist and they attend outpatient appointments. I consider that this responsible use of a DIY system can be legally and ethically justified and within the scope of parental responsibility as a mode of management of their child's T1D.

Duties of parents: 'sharenting'

Usually, a child's health data such as blood pressure, x-rays and written notes of medical examinations are produced in a clinical setting, and healthcare practitioners owe legal and professional obligations not to disclose such information without express up-to-date consent or other legally recognised authorisation.[55] If a CGM has been provided to parents by the child's healthcare practitioner to monitor the child's blood glucose, there is an expectation that parents will share that information with the healthcare practitioner, who must keep it confidential.

However, it is less clear what obligations parents owe in respect of sharing their children's health information with others, such as relatives or on social media. Naturally, parents share information about their children with family and friends and increasingly on social media networks. The company *Nominet* found that parents share an average of 100 photos and videos of their children on social media every year, and more than half (51%) never ask, or do not feel the need to ask, their children if they mind their image is posted online.[56] The term 'sharenting' is used to describe the ways parents share details about their children's lives online.[57] There are potential harms of sharing photos of holidays and birthdays which can be pieced together to create a personal profile of the child.

> Personal data are now used to construct profiles of people that can have major implications for their life opportunities, such as their access to employment, travel, health and life insurance and credit.[58]

Inappropriate disclosure of health information by parents will have even greater implications for the future interests of the child, and a "digital biography created in childhood may have the effect of limiting that person's future life choices about employment and insurance options,"[59] which may be currently unforeseen.

So, what legal and moral obligations curtail the choice of parents to share their child's health data? Although "the individuals responsible for sharing the children's information are the same people tasked with protecting the children's privacy – the parents,"[60] as the Australian Law Reform Commission noted, there have not been many cases in which a person has brought an action for invasion of privacy against his or her spouse, partner or other family member.[61] It would generally not be reasonable to expect the same level of privacy from partners, family members and parents.[62]

Fiduciary obligations arise where one person is under an obligation to act in the interests of another.[63] The actions of parents may be constrained if they are characterised as owing fiduciary obligations in respect of their child. Canada deems the relationship of parent/child as fiduciary,[64] although in Australia the parent/child relationship is considered to have "fiduciary aspects."[65] McHugh J noted in *Marion's Case* in 1992 that "the role of the parent, when acting for the benefit of his or her child, and the role of a fiduciary are sufficiently similar to make at least some of the principles concerning fiduciaries applicable to the parent-child relationship"[66] and noted that a parent has no authority to act on behalf of their child where a conflict arises between their interests. As Joyce comments, "doubtless the imposition of fiduciary duties upon parents will require difficult line-drawing."[67] Whilst parents posting their children's health data on social media sites may not be considered to provide a gain for the parent, it could be considered an action which violates the trust of the children and betrays their future interests.

Steinberg considers that "sharenting includes a moral obligation to act with appropriate discretion and with full regard for the child's safety and well-being."[68] Parental autonomy may justifiably be restricted to preserve the autonomy rights-in-trust of the child. Feinberg's concept of a child's right to an open future[69] describes the interests of the child against having important life choices determined by others before they have the ability to make them. Posting information about a child's chronic health condition on a social media site could credibly impact future employment and insurance options, thus limiting their future options. But where parents share their child's health data from the DIY looping system with healthcare professionals and peer support groups on a closed social media site for the purpose of supporting the management of the child's health condition, I consider that this is a proper exercise of parental responsibility because it promotes the child's best interests overall.

Duties of healthcare professionals: the therapeutic relationship

T1D is a chronic condition which requires daily self-management, and so patients, or initially their parents if minors, become experts, with skills and confidence to manage their own care.[70] Health professionals can choose to acknowledge as a valuable resource a person's expertise with their own T1D,[71] and adults with T1D attribute value to health professionals showing support and understanding for their choice to use an open-source APS.[72] Although a DIY looping system is a patient-driven innovation, it nevertheless requires the 'support' of clinicians through the provision of insulin, which is a prescription-only drug, and ongoing monitoring of glucose readings from the CGM. In 2018, Diabetes Australia issued a position statement which included the view that "if a person with type 1 diabetes (or a parent or family member) chooses to build a DIY system, they must continue to receive support and care from their diabetes healthcare professional and the health system."[73] Diabetes UK recommended that "people who wish to use DIY closed-loop systems should continue to receive support and care from their diabetes team. Diabetes healthcare professionals should respect an individual's right to make informed choices about their own care, or that of their child."[74]

The Australian Medical Association in its document Good Medical Practice states that doctors have a duty to make the care of patients their first concern and to practise medicine safely and effectively.[75] Healthcare professionals in paediatric endocrinology may lack understanding of this non-standard management of T1D and have concerns about their legal liability and impact on indemnity insurance if they support parents through ongoing monitoring and prescribing insulin. Despite the myriad of legal and ethical difficulties which the use of DIY systems gives rise to, as Roberts et al. note, both in the United Kingdom and internationally, "there is an almost complete lack of specific guidance – legal, regulatory, or ethical – for clinicians caring for DIY APS users,"[76] although clinicians "are increasingly encountering patients who are using (or are considering using) these systems."[77] In the UK general guidance issued by the General Medical Council (including Good Medical Practice, consent guidance and prescribing guidance) has been interpreted as *not* precluding clinicians from initiating discussions about DIY systems or prescribing such unapproved medical devices.[78] The International Consensus statement on open-source AID states that "health-care professionals should support people with diabetes or their caregivers who might choose to manage their diabetes with an open-source AID system"[79] and makes recommendations for safe practice for healthcare professionals in discussing, supporting, documenting and reporting on use of DIY looping.

Potential legal liability of healthcare professionals who support use of DIY systems

The International Consensus statement notes the substantial variation in potential legal consequences for healthcare professionals supporting the use of unregulated systems in different countries and the ensuing "uncertainties in respect to accountability if adverse events occur."[80] The child's paediatric endocrinologist, diabetes educator and members of the healthcare team owe duties of care to the child, including the duty to treat competently and to provide adequate ongoing management of the condition. Although it is unlikely that a child would suffer harm from a DIY system set up and managed by informed and engaged parents and where there is adequate back-up if the system fails, *if* something goes wrong causing harm, parents on behalf of their child may bring a claim in negligence.

A healthcare practitioner is negligent if they have breached their duty of care which results in foreseeable harm. The duty of care is breached if the healthcare professional fails to meet the standard of care, which is led by peer professional opinion.[81] A doctor/diabetes educator is not negligent if they act in accordance with a practice accepted at the time as proper by a responsible body of medical opinion even though other doctors/diabetes educators adopt a different practice.

Guidelines and policy statements from professional bodies are likely to be influential in establishing what reasonable professionals would do. In Australia a working group of Australian specialist diabetes groups issued a consensus statement in which they rather cursorily address the issue of 'do it yourself technology',

> The Working group does not endorse the use of any technology unless approved by the TGA and used according to manufacturer instructions. However, clinicians should be aware of these devices/systems and be able to discuss the functionality and potential risks of using them.[82]

This can be taken as a view of a responsible body of medical opinion. However, peer professional opinion may not be determinative of an appropriate standard of care. As stated in *Bolitho v City and Hackney Health Authority*,[83] before accepting a body of opinion as being responsible, reasonable or respectable, a judge would "need to be satisfied that, in forming their views, the experts have directed their minds to the question of comparative risks and benefits and have reached a defensible conclusion on the matter."[84] As more evidence as to the comparative risks and benefits, safety and effectiveness of DIY systems emerges, healthcare professionals may be seen to be acting reasonably in supporting the use of a DIY system, even for their paediatric patients. I have argued elsewhere that "a healthcare professional working in paediatric endocrinology would fulfil their duty of care if they have discussed with parents the calibration of the device, safety issues, including when to take the child to hospital, and have authenticated the blood glucose readings from the device."[85] Academics from the United Kingdom also consider that applying established principles of negligence, clinicians are unlikely to be negligent if they discuss DIY systems with patients, provide information or even recommend their use.[86]

Role of regulation

The Australian government has issued a Code of Practice, *Securing the Internet of Things for Consumers*, 2020. Key principles include privacy of data collected and the security of software on IoT devices, including open-source software. These comprise a voluntary set of principles, where compliance is encouraged but optional. DIY systems also fall under the regulation of therapeutic goods, which include medical devices and software as a medical device.[87] In the United States the FDA is the regulatory body, and in Australia regulation of therapeutic goods is overseen by the TGA, part of the Commonwealth government's Department of Health.

To be lawfully supplied in Australia, a medical device must undergo conformity assessment procedures and be registered on the Australian Register of Therapeutic Goods (ARTG). In August 2018, the first commercial hybrid closed loop system for managing T1D, the Medtronic 670G, received approval from the TGA.[88] The CGM and insulin pump used in a DIY system are medical devices and so should be listed on the ARTG, although, until recently, devices that are used in a DIY system may have been modified to accommodate the software. The algorithm which calculates insulin dosage based on a patient's blood glucose is also a medical device because it is used for therapeutic purposes (the monitoring and treatment of T1D). In contrast health software apps as sources of information or tools to manage a healthy lifestyle are not medical devices and are not regulated (Chapter 4). An Australian entity could take on accountability and sponsor the product; however, to date no application has been made by an Australian sponsor for such open-source software to be listed on the ARTG. Therefore open-source systems are unregulated, and this operates as a barrier to accessing those items on the open market. But open-source software for a DIY system can be used free of charge (people have to code it themselves), and it is not advertised or marketed for profit, so listing on the ARTG is not actually required for it to be available for use. AndroidAPS, OPENAPS and Loop have openly shared algorithms and instructions online although AndroidAPS states that "it is legal to build the app for your own use, but you must not give a copy to others."[89] The Therapeutic Goods Act does not address the *use* of medical devices and software, and it is not illegal for parents to use a DIY system to manage their child's T1D.

So, what might be some barriers to regulation of DIY systems? The dominant voice in regulation is established by medical professional bodies and international scientific evidence of efficacy, quality and safety. The TGA has identified potential risks and harms of software, and it notes, in respect of diabetes management software, that there are few randomised control trials, case-control studies and cohort studies due to the "constant feature evolution and improvement, the inability to devise placebo effect, and the financial cost and resources required to conduct studies relative to commercial value of products during its short life cycle."[90] Gleeson has argued, in respect to regulation of medicinal cannabis in Australia, that there should be ongoing dialogue with and between all parties to the regulatory relationship to ensure political legitimacy.[91] Patients are experts in their own diabetes management, and now it is being recognised how important their voice is in the regulatory system.

> The patient voice is of course one that is important, but it is also under recognised in most of our systems and structures in Australia today. It is not the same as a professional voice or a manufacturer voice, but that is its benefit. . . . A patient's assessment of risk is not the same as that of a regulator.[92]

Although the inclusion of patient-reported outcomes may be more difficult to measure than traditional clinical trial outcomes, the TGA has said that there is more to do in including the role of the patient voice to enable it to assess the impact a medicine or device has on patients' quality of life.[93]

In the United States the FDA has warned patients and healthcare professionals of risks associated with the use of unapproved or unauthorized devices for diabetes management, including automated insulin dosing systems.[94] Nevertheless the FDA is working proactively with Tidepool (a non-profit organisation founded by people with diabetes, caregivers and leading healthcare providers) to develop *Tidepool Loop*,[95] a mobile app designed for AID devices, and as this would be an off-the-shelf, downloadable, commercial product, it would no longer be considered DIY.

Some in the DIY movement do not see regulation as a necessity for adoption, and in fact regulation is perceived as an unnecessary brake to the ongoing development of the open-source code. Some participants in a study of adults using open-source APS in Australia believed that "commercial companies could not catch up to the fast pace at which open-source APS were able to change and evolve."[96] Until commercial regulated systems are developed that allow individualisation and interoperability to the same level as a DIY system, some people will choose the latter.

Conclusion

DIY looping systems provide an example of patient-led IoT solutions to improve management of T1D and a "case study in how increasingly informed and connected patients are shaping the direction of technological innovation in diabetes care and, potentially, for other areas of health care."[97] There are many motivations for setting up a DIY system, including interoperability, customisation and reduced cognitive burden, and also they are cheaper to set up and run than commercial hybrid automated systems. Worldwide the number of users of DIY systems is currently low, but numbers are increasing.

Management of a chronic condition such as T1D has always required self-care, and patients and their families are seen as 'experts' in their own diabetes. Users of DIY systems are highly motivated, and their knowledge of this technology often exceeds that of the healthcare professional. This illustrates a paradigm shift in the traditional healthcare provider/patient relationship, with users turning to those in the looping community for information and assistance with technology. Nevertheless, the support of a healthcare professional is required for provision of insulin and checking of data and looking for development of complications. Despite real-world data providing information that DIY systems are safe and effective, they are not regulated, and this may result in healthcare professionals' uncertainty in deciding whether to support patients who use them.

The principle of respect for patient autonomy suggests that adults should be supported to make an informed choice about the use of a DIY system and take on relative benefits and risks in accordance with their values, but parental autonomy in use of a DIY looping system for their minor child is curtailed by the welfare of the child. A DIY system is not standard and, from a medical perspective, may not provide the *best* management of T1D. However, I argue that the decision falls within the Zone of Parental Discretion because, in circumstances where they are informed, engaged and have adequate back-up in the event of a malfunction, use of a DIY system does not pose a probable significant harm to child.

Whilst I have used the case scenario of DIY systems for minor children, this emerging digital technology has the potential to reduce inequalities in outcomes that are linked to individual disparities in the capacity to cope with the burdens of T1D across various age groups, genders and socioeconomic communities.[98] DIY and IoT technologies can widen access, lessen health inequalities and promote patient engagement, and the #WeAreNot Waiting movement has achieved that for T1D.

Notes

1 The High Court heard expert evidence and considered representations of counsel for the parents and the hospital (*Great Ormond Street Hospital v Yates, Gard and Gard* [2017] EWHC 972). The Court of Appeal unanimously dismissed the appeal by Charlie's parents (*Yates and Gard v Great Ormond Street Hospital for Children NHS Foundation Trust and Gard* [2017] EWCA Civ 410). The European Court of Human Rights gave a final judgment (*Gard and Others v. UK Application no. 39793/17*)
2 *Great Ormond Street Hospital v Yates and Gard* [2017] EWHC 972 (Fam) Francis J at para 70.
3 D. Castro et al., 'Survey on IoT solutions Applied to Healthcare.' (2017) 84 (203) *DYNA* 192–200, 192.
4 Australian Government. *Code of Practice: Securing the Internet of Things for Consumers*, 2020, page 1.
5 10 internet of things (IoT) healthcare examples, https://ordr.net/article/iot-healthcare-examples
6 K. Braune et al. 'Open-source Automated Insulin Delivery: International Consensus Statement and Practical Guidance for Health-care Professionals' (2022) 10(1) *The Lancet. Diabetes & Endocrinology* 58–74.

7. TM Hng and D Burren, 'Do-It-Yourself Closed-loop Systems to Manage Type 1 Diabetes.' (2018) 48(11) *Journal of Internal Medicine* 1400–1404.
8. J. Chiang et al. 'Type 1 Diabetes in Children and Adolescents: A Position Statement by the American Diabetes Association' (2018) 41(9) *Diabetes Care* 2026–2044.
9. A continuous glucose monitor measures glucose levels in the interstitial fluid rather than taking glucose readings from blood. Interstitial fluid is a thin layer of fluid that surrounds the tissue cells below the skin. As carbohydrates are digested, glucose enters the bloodstream before it is absorbed into the interstitial fluid.
10. S. O'Donnell et al. 'Evidence on User-led Innovation in Diabetes Technology (The OPEN Project): Protocol for a Mixed Methods Study' (2019) 8(11) *JMIR Research Protocols* e15368.
11. https://openaps.org/frequently-asked-questions/
12. L. Heinemann and K. Lange. 'Do It Yourself (DIY) – Automated Insulin Delivery (AID) Systems: Current Status from a German Point of View.' (2019) 14(6) *Journal of Diabetes Science and Technology* 1028–1034
13. See T. M. Hng, D. Burren, 'Do-It-Yourself Closed-loop Systems to Manage Type 1 Diabetes' (2018) 48(11) *Journal of Internal Medicine* 1400–1404 and K. Braune et al. 'Open-source Automated Insulin Delivery: International Consensus Statement and Practical Guidance for Health-care Professionals.' (2022) 10(1) *The Lancet. Diabetes & Endocrinology* 58–74.
14. T. M. Hng, D. Burren, 'Do-It-Yourself Closed-loop Systems to Manage Type 1 Diabetes' (2018) 48(11) *Journal of Internal Medicine* 1400–1404.
15. Diabetes Australia, Media Release 'Diabetes Australia Welcomes Bipartisan Commitment to CGMforAll,' 17 April 2022. www.diabetesaustralia.com.au/news/diabetes-australia-welcomes-bipartisan-commitment-to-cgmforall/
16. K. Driscoll et al. 'Fear of Hypoglycaemia in Children and Adolescents and Their Parents with Type 1 Diabetes.' (2016) 16(8) *Current Diabetes Reports* 77.
17. K. Braune, S. O'Donnell, B. Cleal, et al. 'Real-World Use of Do-It-Yourself Artificial Pancreas Systems in Children and Adolescents with Type 1 Diabetes: Online Survey and Analysis of Self-Reported Clinical Outcomes.' (2019) 7(7) *JMIR mHealth and uHealth* e14087 page 2.
18. Open-source projects or freely available material. Many modern computer systems use commercial off-the-shelf (COTS) hardware and software components, most of which are proprietary.
19. J. Roberts, V. Moore and M. Quigley. 'Prescribing Unapproved Medical Devices? The Case of DIY Artificial Pancreas Systems' (2021) 21(1) *Medical Law International* 42–68.
20. The Lancet Diabetes Endocrinology. 'Family Matters in Diabetes Care.' (2018) 6(12) *Lancet Diabetes & Endocrinology* 911.
21. K. Braune et al. 'Open-source Automated Insulin Delivery: International Consensus Statement and Practical Guidance for Health-care Professionals.' (2022) 10(1) *The Lancet. Diabetes & Endocrinology* 58–74, page 70.
22. R. Jeyaventhan, G. Gallen, P. Choudhary and S. Hussain, 'A Real-world Study of User Characteristics, Safety and Efficacy of Open-source Closed-loop Systems and Medtronic 670G.' (2021) 23(8) *Diabetes, Obesity and Metabolism* 1989–1994.
23. Z. Wu, S. Luo, X. Zheng et al. 'Use of a Do-it-yourself Artificial Pancreas System is Associated with Better Glucose Management and Higher Quality of Life among Adults with Type 1 Diabetes.' (2020) *Therapeutic Advances in Endocrinology and Metabolism* 1–11.
24. L. Petruzelkova, et al. 'Excellent Glycemic Control Maintained by Open-Source Hybrid Closed-Loop AndroidAPS During and after Sustained Physical Activity.' (2018) 20(11) *Diabetes Technology & Therapeutics* 744–750.
25. K. Braune, S. O'Donnell, B. Cleal et al. 'Real-World Use of Do-It-Yourself Artificial Pancreas Systems in Children and Adolescents with Type 1 Diabetes: Online Survey and Analysis of Self-Reported Clinical Outcomes' (2019) 7(7) *JMIR mHealth and uHealth* e14087.
26. C. Knoll et al. 'Quality of Life and Psychological Well-Being among Children with Diabetes Using Open-Source Automated Insulin Delivery Systems: Findings from a Global Survey' (2022) *American Diabetes Association 82nd Scientific Sessions* 787-P

27 S. Ahmed and S. Gallo. (2020) 'Looping with Do-It-Yourself Artificial Pancreas Systems During Ramadan Fasting in Type 1 Diabetes Mellitus: Perspectives of a User and a Physician.' (2020) 11 *Diabetes Therapy* 2453.
28 C. Johnston 'User Led Modification of Standard Medical Care for Children: An Analysis of Parents' and Healthcare Professionals' Legal Duties of Care.' (2022) 48(1) *Monash Law Review* 1–34. https://bridges.monash.edu/articles/journal_contribution/User-Led_Modification_of_Standard_Medical_Care_for_Children_An_Analysis_of_Parents_and_Healthcare_Professionals_Legal_Duties_of_Care/20521230.
29 S. McAuley et al. 'Six Months of Hybrid Closed-loop versus Manual Insulin Delivery with Fingerprick Blood Glucose Monitoring in Adults with Type 1 Diabetes: A Randomized Controlled Trial.' (2020) 43(12) *Diabetes Care* 3024–3033.
30 M. Burnside et al. (2020) 'CREATE (Community deRivEd AutomaTEd insulin delivery) Trial. Randomised Parallel Arm Open Label Clinical Trial Comparing Automated Insulin Delivery using a Mobile Controller (AnyDANA-loop) with an Open-source Algorithm with Sensor Augmented Pump Therapy in Type 1 Diabetes.' (2020) 19(2) *Journal of Diabetes & Metabolic Disorders* (2020) 1615–1629.
31 J. Schipp et al. 'We're All on the Same Team'. Perspectives on the Future of Artificial Pancreas Systems by Adults in Australia with Type 1 Diabetes using Open-Source Technologies: A Qualitative Study.' (2021) 39(5) *Diabetic Medicine* e14708.
32 K. White et al 'Motivations for Participation in an Online Social Media Community for Diabetes.' (2018) 12(3) *Journal of Diabetes Science and Technology* 712–718.
33 B. Wheeler, et al. 'Family Perceptions of Insulin Pump Adverse Events in Children and Adolescents' (2014) 16(4) *Diabetes Technology & Therapeutics* 204–207.
34 R. Jeyaventhan, G. Gallen, P. Choudhary, S. Hussain, 'A Real-world Study of User Characteristics, Safety and Efficacy of Open-source Closed-loop Systems and Medtronic 670G' (2021) 23(8) *Diabetes, Obesity and Metabolism* 1989–1994.
35 K. Braune et al. 'Open-source Automated Insulin Delivery: International Consensus Statement and Practical Guidance for Health-care Professionals' (2022) 10(1) *The Lancet. Diabetes & Endocrinology* 58–74.
36 American Diabetes Association, 'New Study Shows Open-Source Automated Insulin Delivery Is a Safe and Effective Treatment Option for People with Type 1 Diabetes,' *Press Release*, June 6, 2022 https://www.diabetes.org/newsroom/press-releases/2022/new-study-shows-opensourced-autmoated-insulin-delivery-safe-effective-treatment-option-type-1.
37 D. Lewis 'Errors of Commission or Omission: The Net Risk Safety Analysis Conversation We Should be Having Around Automated Insulin Delivery Systems.' (2022) 39(5) *Diabetic Medicine* e14687, page 1.
38 D. Lewis, 'Errors of Commission or Omission: The Net Risk Safety Analysis Conversation We Should Be Having Around Automated Insulin Delivery Systems' (2022) 39(5) *Diabetic Medicine* e14687, page 1.
39 C. Johnston and L. Gillam. 'Legal and Ethical Issues Arising from the Use of Emerging Technologies in Paediatric Type 1 Diabetes.' (2018) 18(2) *QUT Law Review* 93–110.
40 T. Beauchamp and J. Childress. *Principles of Biomedical Ethics* (8th ed., 2019 Oxford University Press, New York, NY).
41 The amount of information required to fulfill a healthcare professional's duty of care is considered in common law; see *Rogers v Whitaker* (1992) 175 CLR 479 in Australia and *Montgomery v Lanarkshire Health Board* [2015] UKSC 11in England and Wales.
42 *Gillick v West Norfolk and Wisbech Area Health Authority* [1986] AC 112.
43 C. Johnston, 'Overriding Competent Medical Treatment Refusal by Adolescents: When "No" Means "No"' (2009) 94(7) *Archives of Disease in Childhood* 487–491.
44 L. F. Ross, 'Better Than Best (Interest Standard) in Pediatric Decision Making' (2019) 30(3) *The Journal of Clinical Ethics* 183–195.
45 See K. Czapanskiy, 'Interdependencies, Families, and Children.' (1999) 39(4) *Santa Clara Law Review* 957 and J. Herring, 'The Human Rights Act and the welfare principle in family law: conflicting or complementary? (1999) 11(3) *Child and Family Law Quarterly* 223–235.

46 C. Johnston, 'Good Enough? Parental Decisions to Use DIY Looping Technology to Manage Type 1 Diabetes in Children' (2021) 39(Suppl 1) *Monash Bioethics Review* S26–S41, S32.
47 C. Auckland and I. Goold (2019) 'Parental Rights, Best Interests and Significant Harms: Who Should Have the Final Say over a Child's Medical Care?' (2019) 78(2) *Cambridge Law Journal* 287–323, page 307.
48 Re *Ashya King* [2014] EWHC 2964 (Fam) Baker J at para. 31.
49 L. Gillam, 'The Zone of Parental Discretion: An Ethical Tool for Dealing with Disagreement between Parents and Doctors about Medical Treatment for a Child.' (2016) 11(1) *Clinical Ethics* 1–8.
50 D. Diekema (2004) 'Parental Refusals of Medical Treatment: The Harm Principle as Threshold for State Intervention.' (2004) 25 *Theoretical Medicine and Bioethics* 243–264.
51 C. Auckland, I. Goold 'Parental Rights, Best Interests and Significant Harms: Who Should Have the Final Say over a Child's Medical Care?' (2019) 78(2) *Cambridge Law Journal* 287–323.
52 *Yates & Anor v Great Ormond Street Hospital for Children NHS Foundation Trust & Anor* [2017] EWCA Civ 410, para 54.
53 *Portsmouth NHS Trust v. Wyatt* [2005] EWHC 2293, Hedley J. at para. 40.
54 L. Gillam, 'The Zone of Parental Discretion: An Ethical Tool for Dealing with Disagreement between Parents and Doctors about Medical Treatment for a Child' (2016) 11(1) *Clinical Ethics* 1–8, page 4.
55 Australian Medical Association, Code of Ethics (2016) para 2.2.2.
56 www.nominet.uk/2-7m-parents-share-family-photos-complete-strangers-online, February 2018
57 S. Steinberg, 'Sharenting: Children's Privacy in the Age of Social Media.'(2017) 66 *Emory Law Journal* 839–884
58 D. Lupton, S. Pedersen and G. Thomas, 'Parenting and Digital Media: From the Early Web to Contemporary Digital Society.' (2016) 10(8) *Sociology Compass* 730–743 page 736
59 C. Johnston, 'Sharing of Children's Health Data by Health Professionals and Parents – A Consideration of Legal Suties.' (2020) 16(1) *Indian Journal of Law and Technology* 48–70 page 68.
60 S. Steinberg, 'Sharenting: Children's Privacy in the Age of Social Media' (2017) 66 *Emory Law Journal* 839–884, page 883.
61 Australian Law Reform Commission, Serious Invasions of Privacy in the Digital Era, Final Report 123 (2014).
62 Australian Law Reform Commission, Serious Invasions of Privacy in the Digital Era, Final Report 123 (2014). Des Butler, Submission 10.
63 *Breen v Williams* [1996] HCA 57, 1
64 *Norberg v Weinrib* (1992) 92 DLR (4th) 449.
65 S. Dorsett, 'Comparing Apples and Oranges: The Fiduciary Principle in Australia and Canada after Breen v Williams,' (1996) 2(3) *Bond Law Review*, 158–184 p159.
66 *Secretary, Department of Health and Community Services v J.W.B. and S.M.B. (Marion's Case)* (1992) 175 CLR 218.
67 R. Joyce (2002) 'Fiduciary Law and Non-Economic Interests' (2002) 28(2) *Monash University Law Review* 239–267, page 249.
68 S. Steinberg, 'Sharenting: Children's Privacy in the Age of Social Media' (2017) 66 *Emory Law Journal* 839–884, page 882.
69 J. Feinberg, 'The Child's Right to an Open Future' In: William Aiken and Hugh LaFollette (eds) *Whose Child?: Children's Rights, Parental Authority, and State Power* (Rowman and Littlefield, London, 1980) 124–153.
70 E. Litterbach et al. 'I Wish My Health Professionals Understood That it's Not Just all About Your HbA1C!'. Qualitative Responses from the Second Diabetes MILES – Australia (MILES-2) Study.' (2020) 37(6) *Diabetic Medicine: A Journal of the British Diabetic Association* 971–981.
71 E. Litterbach et al. "I Wish My Health Professionals Understood That It's Not Just All About Your HbA1C!'. Qualitative Responses from the Second Diabetes

MILES – Australia (MILES-2) Study' (2020) 37(6) *Diabetic Medicine: A Journal of the British Diabetic Association* 971–981.
72 J. Schipp et al. "We're All on the Same Team'. Perspectives on the Future of Artificial Pancreas Systems by Adults in Australia with Type 1 Diabetes Using Open-Source Technologies: A Qualitative Study' (2021) 39(5) *Diabetic Medicine* e14708.
73 Diabetes Australia, *People with Type 1 Diabetes and Do It Yourself (DIY) Technology Solutions* (Position Statement, August 2018) page 1.
74 L. Dowling, E. Wilmot and P. Choudhary, 'Do-it-yourself Closed-loop Systems for People Living with Type 1 Diabetes.' (2020) 37(12) *Diabetic Medicine* 1977–1980, page 1979.
75 Good Medical Practice: A Code of Conduct for Doctors in Australia, July 2009, para 1.4.
76 J. Roberts, V. Moore, M. Quigley, 'Prescribing Unapproved Medical Devices? The Case of DIY Artificial Pancreas Systems' (2021) 21(1) *Medical Law International* 42–68, page 44.
77 J. Roberts, V. Moore, M. Quigley, 'Prescribing Unapproved Medical Devices? The Case of DIY Artificial Pancreas Systems' (2021) 21(1) *Medical Law International* 42–68, page 67.
78 J. Roberts, V. Moore, M. Quigley, 'Prescribing Unapproved Medical Devices? The Case of DIY Artificial Pancreas Systems' (2021) 21(1) *Medical Law International* 42–68.
79 K. Braune et al. 'Open-source Automated Insulin Delivery: International Consensus Statement and Practical Guidance for Health-care Professionals' (2022) 10(1) *The Lancet. Diabetes & Endocrinology* 58–74, page 70.
80 K. Braune et al. 'Open-source Automated Insulin Delivery: International Consensus Statement and Practical Guidance for Health-care Professionals' (2022) 10(1) *The Lancet. Diabetes & Endocrinology* 58–74, page 64.
81 The 'Bolam test' from *Bolam v Friern Management Committee* [1957] 1 WLR 582. Australia has Civil Liability legislation, e.g. Wrongs Act 1989 (Vic) Civil Liability Act 2002 (NSW) in addition to common law.
82 A. Pease et al. 'Utilisation, Access and Recommendations Regarding Technologies for People Living with Type 1 Diabetes: Consensus Statement of the ADS/ADEA/APEG/ADIPS Working Group.' (2021) 215(10) *Medical Journal of Australia* 473–478, page 475.
83 *Bolitho v City and Hackney Health Authority* [1998] AC 232.
84 *Bolitho v City and Hackney Health Authority* [1998] AC 232, Lord Browne-Wilkinson at 241–2.
85 C. Johnston, 'User Led Modification of Standard Medical Care for Children: An Analysis of Parents' and Healthcare Professionals' Legal Duties of Care' (2022) 48(1) *Monash Law Review* 1–34, page 27.
86 R. Dickson, et al '# WeAreNotWaiting DIY Artificial Pancreas Systems and Challenges for the Law.' (2022) 39(5) *Diabetic Medicine* e14715.
87 P. Gleeson, 'The Challenge of Medicinal Cannabis to the Political Legitimacy of Therapeutic Goods Regulation in Australia.' (2019) 43(2) *Melbourne University Law Review* 558–604.
88 Therapeutic Goods Administration, Department of Health, 'ARTG ID 308140: Public ARTG Summary,' *Australian Register of Therapeutic Goods*, Web Document, August 11, 2018 https://www.ebs.tga.gov.au/servlet/xmlmillr6?dbid=ebs/PublicHTML/pdfStore.nsf&docid=A2596916D2121533CA25885500430F60&agid=(PrintDetailsPublic)&actionid=1.
89 https://androidaps.readthedocs.io/en/latest/Installing-AndroidAPS/Building-APK.html
90 Department of Health, Therapeutic Goods Administration, *Actual and Potential Harm Caused by Medical Software: A Rapid Literature Review of Safety and Performance Issues* (July 2020) 4 www.tga.gov.au/sites/default/files/actual-and-potential-harm-caused-medical-software.pdf.
91 P. Gleeson, 'The Challenge of Medicinal Cannabis to the Political Legitimacy of Therapeutic Goods Regulation in Australia' (2019) 43(2) *Melbourne University Law Review* 558–604.
92 Health, Aged Care and Sport – House of Representatives Standing Committee – The New Frontier: Delivering better health for all Australians: Inquiry into approval processes for new drugs and novel medical technologies in Australia – Report, November

2021, Mr Mike Wilson, the Chief Executive Officer of JDRF Australia, a Type 1 Diabetes group, para 4.3.
93 Health, Aged Care and Sport – House of Representatives Standing Committee – The New Frontier: Delivering better health for all Australians: Inquiry into approval processes for new drugs and novel medical technologies in Australia – Report, November 2021, Adjunct Professor John Skerritt, Therapeutic Goods Administration para 4.6.
94 'FDA Warns Against the Use of Unauthorized Devices for Diabetes Management,' *News Release*, May 17, 2019.
95 G. Alexander Fleming et al. 'Diabetes Digital App Technology: Benefits, Challenges, and Recommendations. A Consensus Report by the European Association for the Study of Diabetes (EASD) and the American Diabetes Association (ADA) Diabetes Technology Working Group' (2020) 43 *Diabetes Care* 250–260.
96 J. Schipp et al. 'We're All on the Same Team'. Perspectives on the Future of Artificial Pancreas Systems by Adults in Australia with Type 1 Diabetes Using Open-Source Technologies: A Qualitative Study' (2021) 39(5) *Diabetic Medicine* e14708.
97 S. O'Donnell et al. 'Evidence on User-led Innovation in Diabetes Technology (The OPEN Project): Protocol for a Mixed Methods Study' (2019) 8(11) *JMIR Research Protocols* e15368, page 6.
98 See S. O'Donnell et al. 'Evidence on User-led Innovation in Diabetes Technology (The OPEN Project): Protocol for a Mixed Methods Study' (2019) 8(11) *JMIR Research Protocols* e15368.

4
SMARTPHONE APPS FOR MENTAL HEALTH

Case scenario

John is 32 years old and lives alone. Last year he was diagnosed with schizophrenia and has found the diagnosis difficult to accept and the condition hard to manage. The medication he has been prescribed makes him feel lethargic, and he has put on weight. He has also been unable to work. As a result, John is isolated and has little contact with people he knows and the local community. His psychiatrist, Graham, is concerned about John's wellbeing and risks to his physical and mental health. Graham suggests that John uses an app which provides alerts for medication and will also monitor John's physical activity. This data will be useful for Graham and the clinical team to track John's progress in how he manages schizophrenia. John does use his smartphone a lot, but he is concerned that information about his mental health might be shared outside his healthcare team and make it difficult for him to ever find work because of the stigma of poor mental health.

Introduction

There is a burgeoning market in wearable devices and apps used by individuals to monitor their own health. Sensors in wearable devices, such as smart watches and bracelets, are typically connected to a smartphone which collects the information and sends it to a remote server for storage. Many apps are consumer-oriented fitness and wellbeing apps, which promote physical and mental wellbeing by tracking health-related data such as heart rate, steps walked, weight, calories, breathing rate, sleep patterns and time spent meditating. Other apps can be used as a first point of diagnosis, such as those which provide instant risk assessment of the likelihood of malignancy[1] of a skin lesion, so that medical attention can be sought for more detailed assessment (Chapter 5) and apps used to monitor fertility for the purpose of either enhancing or reducing the likelihood of pregnancy.[2] We saw during

DOI: 10.4324/9781003220190-4

the COVID-19 pandemic that a number of countries and companies developed contact tracing apps,[3] and although these raise privacy concerns, their use has been justified on the grounds of public health if there are adequate protections and governance structures to protect individual interests.[4]

Sensors in wearable devices mean that clinically relevant data can be collected outside of clinical settings. Wearable devices can be used in fall prevention among older adults – for example, gait can be measured in older adults' daily activities in an unattended home environment, providing the ability to detect and classify falls, assisting them to live independently.[5] In Chapter 3 I explore how a smartphone app and wearable glucose monitor enables people with type 1 diabetes to personalise management of that condition. Through analysis of movement, sleep duration and heart patterns collected by wearable devices, people's mental health can be monitored, as it is known that physiological and behavioural variations can be associated with psychiatric disorders.[6]

A range of terminology is used in the context of digital heath technologies. **mHealth** refers to the use of mobile technologies, such as smartphones, for remote patient monitoring or as a means for patients and health providers to communicate.[7] This might include: data collected via wearable body sensors or mobile phone apps which can be sent to the clinician; data inputted by the patient; text messaging between the patient and clinician, and automated alerts.

> Remote monitoring is typically considered to be a form of mHealth and can provide a more complete temporal picture of a patient's overall condition, giving more data points at a wider range of times during daily life, assisting in medical management.[8]

The mHealth market is projected to reach $132.2 billion by 2023.[9]

e-Mental health describes electronic interventions used specifically in the management of mental health issues, which offer the potential to provide accessible therapies and interventions outside the clinic.[10] In Chapter 7 I consider the use of telehealth, including its use in psychiatry, known as 'telepsychiatry.'

Wearable technology is the term used for accessories and clothing which incorporate computer technologies, such as smart watches and fitness trackers.[11] Sensors in wearable technologies can be connected to smartphone apps to collect data such as sleep patterns and movement, and this contextual real-time information enables estimates of disease risk and progression. Wearables are playing an increasing role in mental health, although the reliability of data depends on users wearing them over a sustained time frame.

A **smartphone** is a 'transformational technology'[12] because it "eliminates the need to carry many devices including a phone, camera, speakers, WiFi adapter, and a GPS system."[13] Although smartphone use is accepted in everyday life, it is not yet known what duration and frequency of use are problematic, and research is beginning to show the impact of smartphone addiction on daily life and on users' mental health.[14] Smartphones enable the user to download and run applications.

Smartphone programs are called **applications or 'apps'** – software for the smartphone operating system. Apps can be downloaded from an app store, and as Torous et al. note, there is "an almost infinite potential for any new idea to quickly become an 'app', which can in turn be readily proliferated across any number of users, potentially reaching billions of people across the world."[15] The number of medical and health apps is enormous and continuously growing; however, most apps are developed outside of the healthcare industry, with little or no research to evidence their utility and accuracy.[16]

Digital psychiatry refers to the use of mobile and other connected digital devices which augment mental health services.[17]

Active data is collected through smartphone-based surveys which are completed by the user "either spontaneously or in response to a prompt, and then stored while crucially time stamped (a digital record of the date and time when an item was completed) onto the collecting app."[18]

In comparison **passive data** is obtained automatically through sensors on a smartphone or via a wearable device.

Digital technology for mental health

In this chapter I focus on smartphone apps for mental health. Most of these apps are aimed at those with high-prevalence mental health issues such as anxiety and depression, although some are specifically targeted at people with psychotic disorders, including schizophrenia.

There is an increase in the prevalence of mental disorders, which has a high cost at an individual and societal level. In 2005 the World Health Organization considered the public health challenge of poor mental health and the major threat to individual and societal wellbeing from psychosocial distress.[19] Social isolation to reduce the spread of the virus during the COVID-19 pandemic exacerbated the prevalence of mental disorders,[20] and this has precipitated inquiry in, and development of, digital health technologies to support mental health and wellbeing.[21]

It has been estimated that over 50% of the population of high- and middle-income countries experiences at least one mental health disorder in their lifetime, and there is an increase in the prevalence of mental health disorders.[22] In the United States nearly one in five adults lives with a mental illness (52.9 million in 2020),[23] and in the European Union alone, approximately 5 million people (0.2%–2.6%) suffer from psychotic disorders, and patients with schizophrenia are the largest subgroup.[24] Between 30% and 50% of individuals with schizophrenia are resistant to treatment, and this generates "a high degree of suffering for patients and their families and a great financial burden on the health care system."[25] People with schizophrenia may find it challenging to get regular exercise, remember to take medication and follow a healthy diet because of the impact of their mental illness. Studies have demonstrated that smartphones can provide beneficial interventions for people with schizophrenia,[26] including monitoring symptoms and behaviours and providing mobile alerts related to patients' daily tasks, medication and medical visits.[27] The smartphone app *Actissist* provides timely intervention strategies for early psychosis by offering question-and-answer cognitive behavioural therapy–informed strategies to help people manage difficult experiences, and there is an automatic sharing of app data with the clinician.[28] The apps *FOCUS*[29] and *PRIME*[30] provide daily challenges and a way to connect virtually with other patients, potentially promoting independence of people with schizophrenia.

Digital phenotyping

Digital phenotyping is the use of data from smartphones and wearables collected in situ for capturing a digital expression of human behaviors. Digital phenotyping techniques can be used to analyze both passively (e.g., sensor) and actively (e.g., survey) collected data. Machine learning offers a possible predictive bridge between digital phenotyping and future clinical state.[31]

Some smartphone apps use artificial intelligence to track behaviours of people with mental health disorders.[32] Contemporary smartphones have sensors such as global positioning system (GPS) and microphones which collect behavioural data such as time spent at home or visiting new places, speech patterns, interactions with the phone and signals of social interactions[33] without the direct input of patients. This passive data collection creates a 'digital phenotype'[34] which provides insights into a person's mental health status. Severe mental disorders, including schizophrenia, are associated with impairments in motivation and initiative leading to decreased social engagement and mobility patterns. A study capturing geospatial data through smartphones demonstrated that study participants diagnosed with schizophrenia visited significantly fewer places and travelled significantly less often relative to age- and sex-matched healthy control subjects.[35] Passive monitoring, which detects a decrease in social interaction, may be used as "a possible early warning signal for an impending recurrent psychotic episode in an individual diagnosed with schizophrenia."[36] However, although there may be clinical utility in gathering such data, there are challenges too. The data gathered may be inaccurate. Measurement inaccuracies are frequently reported owing to high variability in embedded sensors in smartphones and wearables.[37] Constant tracking may be seen as an unacceptable infringement on the autonomy and privacy of the individual. It is also known that patients with schizophrenia may show an aversion to use of smartphones due to paranoid tendencies or cognitive impairments, and thus they may leave their smartphone at home.[38] There is a significant level of scepticism towards digital phenotyping by those with mental illness,[39] and people generally do not want to be monitored and tracked or provide private sensor-based data. Although in our case scenario John does have a smartphone, he has expressed some concerns about constant monitoring and privacy of his data.

In-person care will not be able to meet the increasing demand for mental health treatment. Even in high-income countries 35%–50% of patients do not receive treatment for their psychiatric disorder, and this increases to 76%–85% of patients in low- and middle-income countries.[40] Individuals can become more self-aware when they use apps, and this can help manage their condition. Although apps designed for mental health can augment care and provide therapeutic interventions, they do present legal, social and ethical challenges, including privacy, regulation, accessibility and acceptability.

Privacy of data

Personal information means information which is about an identified individual, or an individual who is reasonably identifiable. Information which identifies a person such as name, address and social security numbers found in medical records is known as individual or personal identifiable information but is not information about the health of the individual. Health information is "information related to the past, present and future health care or health status of the individual."[41]

Privacy regulation focusses on the collection, use and disclosure of personally identifiable information, so there is a significant incentive for organisations to assert that their data is de-identified or anonymised. Health data used in research is often de-identified as scientific researchers seek trends and correlations across broader populations, rather than conclusions about known individuals.[42] Data is nevertheless 'identifiable' when there is "some non-remote possibility of future identification",[43] and increasingly sophisticated technological ways of linking data mean that there is a risk that information that was considered non-identifying at one point in time can later be transformed into identifying information.[44] De-identification is difficult, if not impossible, for data collected through wearable sensors. The identity of an individual can be distinguished from millions of people because of the unique combination of location data and detailed behavioural data. The UK Data Protection Act 2018 and General Data Protection Regulation make it clear that one or more factors specific to the physical, physiological, genetic, mental, economic, cultural or social identity of a natural person can identify that person. In any event where apps are generating health data for the purposes of treatment, the identity of the individual is necessary to enable treatment by the clinician.

Health data illustrates correlations between incidences of diseases and use of medicines. It can assist healthcare providers in planning services and is regarded as one of the most sensitive types of personal information. It also has value for individuals, clinicians and companies that buy and sell data. Digital personal data has been described as *the* resource of the future,[45] and the 'digital economy' has developed around collecting and selling such data. Commercial companies such as Google, AOL and Yahoo! play an increasing role in providing apps, wearables and algorithms in medicine, and a market has developed in data from them. The use of digital technology, particularly in the area of mental health where health data is considered especially sensitive, raises concerns about the use and sharing of data and how much control we have over it.

The privacy and security of personal information are critical concerns for the implementation of digital health technologies. The United Nations Universal Declaration of Human Rights enshrines privacy as a fundamental human right; Article 12 states,

> No one shall be subjected to arbitrary interference with his privacy, family, home or correspondence, nor to attacks upon his honour and reputation. Everyone has the right to the protection of the law against such interference or attacks.

A working definition of a right to privacy is described as,

> Our right to keep a domain around us, which includes all those things that are part of us, such as our body, home, property, thoughts, feelings, secrets and identity. The right to privacy gives us the ability to choose which parts in this domain can be accessed by others, and to control the extent, manner and timing the using of those parts we choose to disclose.[46]

The term **e-privacy** has been coined for privacy in the digital environment. Although people say they consider privacy to be important, they often do not take action to protect their personal data, and this 'privacy paradox' is evident in the way people readily provide personal data in exchange for apps and other web-based services.[47] We may be willing to accept unfavourable or unclear conditions if that is the only way to access apps and online services (and I consider the limitations of a 'notice and consent' model in relation to data provided in exchange for use of chatbot services in Chapter 6). If a privacy policy is the only protection of the privacy interests of users of smartphone apps and wearables, we could expect it to be understandable and accessible, but some apps lack a privacy policy altogether, and others use unclear language adopting technical information and legal terminology and often written at a "post-secondary level."[48] The privacy policies for apps and wearables routinely authorise companies to "disclose, sell, and transfer consumer data to third parties."[49]

Users of wearable devices and apps may *choose* to share their personal data with others using the same app, or on social networks, for comparison and motivation, but may also feel a threat of loss of privacy knowing that data from apps may be shared with Google, Facebook and other third parties.[50] There are perhaps greater consequences of unwanted sharing of data about a person's mental health than other personal information because of the potential impact on the person's social or legal standing.[51] Increasingly data from an app may be sent to an individual's electronic health record, with their consent, but many may still be concerned that sensitive data such as mental health notes may be shared beyond their healthcare provider.

When personal data is shared inappropriately and outside privacy policies, this can impact the trust and reputation of the entity involved, yet even if there is a process providing for remedying action and compensation for the individual, it is arguably too little, too late. Mandatory notification schemes have been introduced in many countries which require the regulator and affected individual to be notified by an organisation if personal data it holds is compromised. The Notifiable Data Breaches Scheme in Australia requires an individual to be informed if there has been unauthorised access to, disclosure of or loss of personal information which is likely to result in serious harm to them. They can then take action to protect themselves, for example, by changing passwords and cancelling bank cards.[52] According to the Office of Australian Information Commissioner Notifiable Data Breaches Report for July – December 2021, the health sector remains the highest-reporting industry sector notifying 18% of all breaches, with 120 notifications of data breaches involving health information in that period.[53] But data breach schemes operate after the event, and they do not inherently improve the security of health and personal data.[54]

Promotion of autonomy and engagement with health

'Autonomy' refers to a person's capacity to think and choose for themselves and determine how they wish their life to go. An autonomous choice is predicated on having sufficient information to exercise a choice and the absence of coercing influences. The principle of *respect* for patient autonomy requires that patients be informed about healthcare choices and those choices given effect. Full autonomy is perhaps more of an ideal than reality but substantial autonomy is exercised where there is *sufficient* intentionality, understanding and provision of information.[55]

Use of wellness and health apps can be seen as empowering the individual, enabling users to make decisions about their health. But an alternative view is that they are "persuasive technology"[56] designed to influence user behaviour and decisions, and this paternalistic influence can undermine the users' autonomy. Use of apps by individuals with schizophrenia raises other concerns about autonomy. Individuals with schizophrenia may lack the cognitive ability to understand and make choices about the relative benefits and risks of using an app, so their choice may not be an exercise of even substantial autonomy. Information and alerts provided by apps should be accompanied by clear messaging about when to seek medical help to support the users' choice. Some diagnosed with mental illness may perceive monitoring of their behaviour though sensors as 'disciplinary' rather than autonomy-enhancing.[57]

Use of apps which collect data relevant to a person's mental health (digital phenotyping) and share it with the patient's doctor can allow real-time monitoring of patients. Passive monitoring for early warning signs could detect likely relapse early and enable medical intervention through telehealth or in-person consultation with a psychiatrist if needed, yet few apps can bridge from digital phenotyping to interventions, able to detect risk and respond to it in real time.

> For digital phenotyping to drive benefits in mental health and other clinical domains, serious consideration must be given to the practicalities of future

clinical application. To be used, and to be useful, digital phenotyping must fit with established norms of quality and safety, be cost-effective and feasible.[58]

Apart from the potential beneficial aspects of digital monitoring technologies, it is worth considering that patients experiencing psychosis or feelings of paranoia may liken monitoring to being under surveillance. So, the engagement and consent of patients to being monitored and sharing their data with their healthcare team are crucial to respect the autonomy of this vulnerable group of patients.

Digital technology and the therapeutic relationship

Medication reminder systems can send text messages to a smartphone, and synchronous exchanges between patient and mental health care specialists are showing increasing potential to support and manage mental health, although appropriate boundaries are needed so that a healthy therapeutic relationship is maintained. The collection of real-time data outside of the clinic means that psychiatrists will have access to unprecedented amounts of situationally relevant information, but this data will often need to be analysed and translated into actionable clinical information.[59] The potential for burnout of psychiatrists is real where data can be transmitted to them 24/7, and how digital data is to be monitored and used in the clinical setting will need to be considered.

The scope of legal duties and the standard of care will require some consideration and development. Just because a clinician has this information, is there an obligation to use it? Differentiating data depending on the nature of risk will help establish what is a reasonable response from the team providing care, rather than demanding supererogatory action. Mobile apps which provide clinically validated data directly to the clinician have implications for safeguarding and risk management and the standard of care in psychiatry, as noted by the Commission on the Future of Psychiatry (written by the World Psychiatric Association and The Lancet Psychiatry),

> As the evidence base for digital psychiatry evolves, psychiatrists need to remain up to date and educated to ensure they are practising within this evolving standard of care.[60]

If there is overall benefit to patients and society through the use of digital technologies in mental health care, then there is an ethical obligation to develop and use them.[61] Apps which support mental health are mostly identified and then used by people though their own research and initiative, and although many will derive benefit, they tend to have low ongoing engagement.[62] Where apps are recommended by healthcare professionals and used in conjunction with the clinical team, and especially if a free smartphone and data plan are provided, retention may be improved.[63] There is a balance to be struck between the benefits of digital technology through identification and management of risk factors for the patient and the harms of increased isolation and movement away from person-centred care.

The human component in mental health treatment and support is important to reduce isolation and build a relationship of trust. Pruitt and Rubin note that trust can be considered a constellation of beliefs about the extent to which others are concerned about one's personal welfare and best interests.[64] Many patients prefer direct contact with a psychiatrist, and digital technologies may in fact be a barrier to building trust if people do not understand them and have concerns that the information gathered about their mental state may be used against them.[65] Human contact in the provision of healthcare underscores the importance of the connection between patient and carer:

> When we are sick, injured, or facing an existential life crisis, our greatest human need is loving kindness and compassion in response to our vulnerability and suffering.[66]

In psychiatry, more than other fields of medicine, an effective doctor-patient relationship may be more critical to successful outcomes than it is in other medical specialties.[67] Whilst mHealth can benefit patients through ongoing monitoring and support, some reflection is necessary on the harms in the use of apps and other digital health technologies and the importance of human contact in the therapeutic relationship. Additionally, the digital divide highlights the fact that the benefits of mHealth are not universally available, requiring access to a smartphone, sufficient data and competence in using technology.[68]

Equality: access and digital skills

The utility of apps depends on access and useability. Smartphone app-based interventions for patients with schizophrenia are not feasible if a significant proportion of that group does not have access to a smartphone. Although ownership of smartphones is above 80% in the general population in the United States, access is "more likely to be lacking in those who are older, less educated, and Black or Hispanic."[69] Feasibly, the majority of the world will have access to some form of a smartphone device in the future, yet a new digital divide may arise through technology literacy.[70]

Older people tend to use a smartphone as a standard-feature phone, making calls but not downloading apps.[71] People with serious mental illness generally have lower use of smartphones than the general population,[72] and as most people with psychotic disorders have a limited income, purchase of a personal smartphone may not be an option.[73] A contributor to the *ReThink* Mental Illness survey noted that "it is a challenge to convince deprived people that investment in hardware or software will pay off for them."[74]

If apps and wearable devices are shown to be an effective form of mental health care, the mechanism to deliver it could include the cost of supplying these devices. Some anti-psychotic depot medications are extremely expensive but are justified by virtue of the need to be delivered in that mechanism due to the difficulties experienced by the patient group. We do not question the cost of this, yet would we offer a smartphone plus apps and paid for by healthcare services?

A study in South Australia of people with schizophrenia showed that about one-third of participants (n = 50) were not confident using smartphone devices.[75] One solution is to provide training on the safe use of technology for those with serious mental illness. But the same digital divide in terms of confidence and understanding of technologies may also be present among mental health professionals, many of whom started to practise before the invention of smartphones.[76]

Regulation

App stores do not themselves regulate apps for safety and effectiveness, and digital health technologies have been described as the "lawless wild west."[77]

Digital tech and the use of artificial intelligence (AI) highlight the tension between promoting innovation to improve health and wellbeing and the adequacy of regulation to avoid harm to users.[78] Rothstein et al. identify potential harms through use of smartphone health apps as including:

1   Physical and psychological harm where actions or decisions adverse to health and wellbeing are taken based on inaccurate monitoring data.
2   Dignitary harm arising from insufficient privacy protections leading to the disclosure or sale of personal information.[79]

The regulation of medical devices is perhaps "the primary basis for safety and efficacy controls over AI systems used within healthcare."[80] Regulatory bodies such as the Food and Drug Administration in the United States and the Therapeutic Goods Administration in Australia review the safety and effectiveness of medical devices and software, which is becoming increasingly important in medical devices and as a medical device in its own right, known as Software as a Medical Device (SaMD).[81] AI-powered apps used for diagnosis or treatment may qualify as 'medical devices' such as apps that calculate insulin doses based on a patient's blood glucose levels. Apps which are used as sources of information or tools to manage a healthy lifestyle, including mental health apps that assist in self-management but do not claim to diagnose or provide specific treatment suggestions, do not meet the definition of a medical device and so do not fall within the regulatory regime.[82]

Even if software does require review, under the Food and Drug Administration Digital Health Software Pre-certification Program, "the manufacturer, not the actual software product, is certified based on a company culture of software quality and commitment to patient safety,"[83] and both consumers and doctors may not realise that products have not been proven safe and effective before their release.

The International Medical Device Regulators Forum, a voluntary group of medical device regulators, proposes a risk categorisation framework for SaMD[84] and recognises the importance of greater global regulatory convergence and consistency[85]:

Ensuring the safety, quality and efficacy of these devices without impeding innovation will require suitable adapted regulatory requirements at least on the design, clinical evaluation, risk management and post market surveillance processes.[86]

If apps are to be used in a clinical context, it is important that there is a standardised and critical appraisal of evidence to demonstrate efficacy, yet this is uncommon in practice, as most app developers cannot afford controlled trials, and fixed and limited resources for a software team to deliver a digital health intervention limit their scope. In a review of 52 commercially available apps for anxiety, the majority (67.3%) were found to lack the involvement of healthcare professionals in their development.[87] Although many commercially developed mental health support apps have millions of users, very few have undergone rigorous scientific testing,[88] and even if they have, they often use a small sample size with no follow-up.[89] Sucala and colleagues note that the gold standard of research, the randomised clinical trial (RCT), typically takes 5.5 years from enrolment to publication, and "this timeline is not feasible for technology-based interventions, such as apps, as they risk that by the time they are proven to be effective, their technology has already become obsolete."[90] It has been suggested that the RCT as the primary means of evaluation should be replaced by the use of iterative participatory research.[91] New frameworks to assess the evidence base for apps and international standards for regulation will all contribute to realising the enormous potential of smartphone apps to support patients, clinicians and health services.

Conclusion

The use of digital technologies in healthcare and, more specifically in psychiatry, has been described as a 'revolution,'[92] and the empowerment and participation of individuals in their own health is to be welcomed.

Apps for mental health care, which collect data and share it with the clinical team, can bring timely personalised therapies and support to individuals outside the clinic, providing resource-effective interventions. Nevertheless, this technology should never replace human contact, which is so necessary to provide compassionate care. Collaborative development of smartphone apps, incorporating the views of patients with lived experience of mental health problems, clinicians and software developers, is key to gaining trust in the software and in the design of features which are most beneficial to this patient cohort.[93] Involvement of patients in all phases of the design, research and implementation of these technologies will be crucial for success. Whilst commercially available apps focus on the most prevalent mental disorders, there is a need to design interventions for the full breadth of mental disorders, and evidence for the feasibility of using apps to enhance the care of people with schizophrenia should be backed up with research to evidence their efficacy.[94] As the evidence base for digital psychiatry increases, so too will the need to develop standards for use of apps in mental health provision. Where their use can be shown to promote the interests of the patient, then there is an ethical imperative to use them to benefit the patient. In the future, monitoring apps may become the standard provision of care, and a failure of a health practitioner to integrate that into their practice could be considered a breach of the standard of care if a reasonably prudent practitioner would have used that app or a similar app in the circumstances.[95] What is considered a reasonable clinical response to the real-time data received from a patient's app will need to be clarified. Other issues to be resolved include the regulation of mental health apps, and an international response would ensure a consistent approach.

The potential for use of digital psychiatry in clinical care has not yet been realised, and in the future,

> actionable data from apps, both recommended by psychiatrists and selected by patients, are seamlessly returned to the EMR [electronic medical record], and data from the apps would provide clinically useful measures to the physician and immediate feedback to assist patients.[96]

The development of smartphone technology and mobile apps with users and healthcare professionals provides opportunities for new monitoring, diagnostic and treatment modalities to benefit patients with serious mental disorders.

Notes

1 N. Chuchu, Y. Takwoingi, J. Dinnes et al. 'Smartphone Applications for Triaging Adults with Skin Lesions that are Suspicious for Melanoma.' (2018) 12(2) *Cochrane Database of Systematic Reviews* CD013192.
2 M. Moglia, H. Nguyen, K. Chyjek et al, 'Evaluation of Smartphone Menstrual Cycle Tracking Applications Using an Adapted APPLICATIONS Scoring System.' (2016) 127(6) *Obstetrics & Gynecology* 1153–1160 and O. Sudjic, ' "I Felt Colossally Naïve": the Backlash against the Birth Control App', *The Guardian*, 21 July 2018.
3 P. Kostkova et al, 'Data and Digital Solutions to Support Surveillance Strategies in the Context of the COVID-19 Pandemic.' (2021) 3 *Frontiers in Digital Health*, 707902.
4 V. Xafis et al (2020) 'The Perfect Moral Storm: Diverse Ethical Considerations in the COVID-19 Pandemic.' (2020) 12(2) *Asian Bioethics Review* 65–83.
5 A. Godfrey, 'Wearables for Independent Living in Older Adults: Gait and Falls.' (2017) 100 *Maturitas* 16–26.
6 M. Sheikh, M. Qassem, P. Kyriacou, 'Wearable, Environmental, and Smartphone-Based Passive Sensing for Mental Health Monitoring.' (2021) 3 *Frontiers in Digital Health* 662811.
7 See Report by the Director-General World Health Organisation A71/20, 'mHealth Use of Appropriate Digital Technologies for Public Health' (2018) and J. Young, S. Borgetti, P. Clapham, 'Telehealth: Exploring the Ethical Issues' (2017) 19(3) *DePaul Journal of Health Care Law* 1–15.
8 J. Young, S. Borgetti, P. Clapham, 'Telehealth: Exploring the Ethical Issues' (2017) 19(3) *DePaul Journal of Health Care Law* 1–15, page 3.
9 E. Grebenshchikova, 'Digital Medicine: Bioethical Assessment of Challenges and Opportunities.' (2019) 10(1) *Jahr – European Journal of Bioethics* 211–222.
10 D. Bhugra et al. 'The WPA-Lancet Psychiatry Commission on the Future of Psychiatry.' (2017) 4(10) *The Lancet. Psychiatry* 775–818.

11 See M. Rothstein et al. 'Unregulated Health Research Using Mobile Devices: Ethical Considerations and Policy Recommendations.' (2020) 48 (1) *The Journal of Law, Medicine & Ethics* 196–226.
12 M. Bauer et al. 'Smartphones in Mental Health: A Critical Review of Background Issues, Current Status and Future Concerns.' (2020) 8:2 *International Journal of Bipolar Disorders* 2, page 1.
13 M. Bauer et al. 'Smartphones in Mental Health: A Critical Review of Background Issues, Current Status and Future Concerns' (2020) 8:2 *International Journal of Bipolar Disorders* 2, page 1.
14 E. Kim, E. Koh, 'Avoidant Attachment and Smartphone Addiction in College Students: The Mediating Effects of Anxiety and Self-esteem.' (2018) 84 *Computers in Human Behavior* 264–271.
15 J. Torous, S. Bucci, I. Bell et al. 'The Growing Field of Digital Psychiatry: Current Evidence and the Future of Apps, Social Media, Chatbots, and Virtual Reality' (2021) 20(3) *World Psychiatry* 318–335, page 319.
16 M. Bauer et al. 'Smartphones in Mental Health: A Critical Review of Background Issues, Current Status and Future Concerns' (2020) 8:2 *International Journal of Bipolar Disorders* 2.
17 D. Bhugra et al. 'The WPA-Lancet Psychiatry Commission on the Future of Psychiatry' (2017) 4(10) *The Lancet. Psychiatry* 775–818.
18 J. Torous, S. Bucci, I. Bell et al. 'The Growing Field of Digital Psychiatry: Current Evidence and the Future of Apps, Social Media, Chatbots, and Virtual Reality' (2021) 20(3) *World Psychiatry* 318–335, page 319.
19 World Health Organization, *Mental Health: Facing the Challenges, Building Solutions* (Regional Office for Europe, Brussels, 2005).
20 G. Goggin, 'COVID-19 apps in Singapore and Australia: Reimagining Healthy Nations with Digital Technology.' (2020) 177(1) *Media International Australia* 61–75.
21 M. Faurholt-Jepsen, L. Vedel Kessing, 'Apps for Mental Health Care: The Raise of Digital Psychiatry.' (2021) 47 *European Neuropsychopharmacology* 51–53.
22 I. Miralles, 'Smartphone Apps for the Treatment of Mental Disorders: Systematic Review.' (2020) 8(4) *JMIR mHealth and uHealth* e14897.
23 National Institute of Mental Health, Mental Illness, https://www.nimh.nih.gov/health/statistics/mental-illness.
24 E. Huerta Ramos, 'Measuring Users' Receptivity toward an Integral Intervention Model Based on mHealth Solutions for Patients with Treatment-Resistant Schizophrenia (m-RESIST): A Qualitative Study.' (2016) 4(3) *JMIR mHealth and uHealth* e112.
25 E. Huerta Ramos, 'Measuring Users' Receptivity toward an Integral Intervention Model Based on mHealth Solutions for Patients with Treatment-Resistant Schizophrenia (m-RESIST): A Qualitative Study.' (2016) 4(3) *JMIR mHealth and uHealth* e112.
26 D. Ben Zeev et al., 'Feasibility, Acceptability, and Preliminary Efficacy of a Smartphone Intervention for Schizophrenia.' (2014) 40(6) *Schizophrenia Bulletin* 1244–1253.
27 N. Berry et al., 'Developing a Theory-Informed Smartphone App for Early Psychosis: Learning Points from a Multidisciplinary Collaboration.' (2020) 10(11) *Frontiers in Psychiatry* 602861.
28 N. Berry et al. 'Developing a Theory-informed Smartphone App for Early Psychosis: Learning Points from a Multidisciplinary Collaboration' (2020) 10(11) *Frontiers in Psychiatry* 602861.
29 D. Ben-Zeev et al., 'Development and Usability Testing of FOCUS: A Smartphone System for Self-management of Schizophrenia.'(2013)36 *Psychiatr Rehabil J* 289–96.
30 D. Schlosser et al., 'Efficacy of PRIME, a Mobile App Intervention Designed to Improve Motivation in Young People with Schizophrenia.' (2018) 44(5) *Schizophrenia Bulletin* 1010–1020.
31 J. Benoit, H. Onyeaka, M. Keshavan, J. Torous, 'Systematic Review of Digital Phenotyping and Machine Learning in Psychosis Spectrum Illnesses. (2020) 28(5) *Harvard Review of Psychiatry*, 296–304, page 296.

32 S. D'Alfonso, M. Alvarez, '4 Ways Tech Can Help Your Mental Health' (2017) *Pursuit* 4 December.
33 M. Sheikh, M. Qassem, P. Kyriacou, 'Wearable, Environmental, and Smartphone-based Passive Sensing for Mental Health Monitoring' (2021) 3 *Frontiers in Digital Health* 662811.
34 A person's phenotype is determined by their genomic makeup (the genotype) and environmental factors.
35 N. Jongs et al. 'A Framework for Assessing Neuropsychiatric Phenotypes by Using Smartphone-based Location Data' (2020) 10(1) *Translational Psychiatry* 1–10.
36 N. Jongs et al. 'A Framework for Assessing Neuropsychiatric Phenotypes by Using Smartphone-based Location Data' (2020) 10(1) *Translational Psychiatry* 1–10.
37 T. Kuhlmann, P. Garaizar, U.-D. Reips, 'Smartphone Sensor Accuracy Varies from Device to Device in Mobile Research: The Case of Spatial Orientation' (2020) 53 *Behavior Research Methods* 22–33.
38 *ReThink* Mental Illness and Nuffield Council on Bioethics, *Summary Paper: Engaging Experts by Experience about the Role of Digital Technology in the Future of Mental Health Care* (ReThink and Nuffield Council, London, 2022).
39 *ReThink* Mental Illness and Nuffield Council on Bioethics, *Summary Paper: Engaging Experts by Experience about the Role of Digital Technology in the Future of Mental Health Care* (ReThink and Nuffield Council, London, 2022).
40 See M. Faurholt-Jepsen, L. Vedel Kessing, 'Apps for Mental Health Care: The Raise of Digital Psychiatry' (2021) 47 *European Neuropsychopharmacology* 51–53, at page 51.
41 M. Kayaalp, 'Patient Privacy in the Era of Big Data' (2018) 35 *Balkan Medical Journal* 8–17, page 9.
42 Australian Law Reform Commission (2003) Essentially yours: the protection of human genetic information in Australia (ALRC Report 96). https://www.alrc.gov.au/publications/report-96, para 3.12.
43 P. Schwartz, D. Solove, 'Reconciling Personal Information in the United States and European Union' (2014) 102(4) *California Law Review*, 877–916, page 907.
44 P. Ohm, 'Broken Promises of Privacy: Responding to the Surprising Failure of Anonymization.' (2010) 57 *UCLA Law Review*, 1701–1776.
45 K. Birch, D. Cochrane, C. Birch, 'Data as Asset? The Measurement, Governance, and Valuation of Digital Personal Data by Big Tech.' (2017) 8(1) *Big Data and Society* 1–15.
46 R. Romansky, I. Noninska, 'Challenges of the Digital Age for Privacy and Personal Data Protection.' 2020 17(5) *Mathematical Biosciences and Engineering* 5288–5303, page 5289.
47 M. van Lieshout, 'The Value of Personal Data' In: J. Camenisch, S. Fischer-Hubner, M. Hansen (eds.) *Privacy and Identity Management for the Future Internet in the Age of Globalisation* (Springer Verlag, London, 2015), 26–38.
48 M. Bauer et al. 'Smartphones in Mental Health: A Critical Review of Background Issues, Current Status and Future Concerns' (2020) 8:2 *International Journal of Bipolar Disorders* 11–19.
49 S. Elvy, 'Commodifying Consumer Data in the Era of the Internet of Things.' (2018) 59(2) *Boston College Law Review* 423–522, page 440.
50 K. Huckvale et al.,'Assessment of the Data Sharing and Privacy Practices of Smartphone Apps for Depression and Smoking Cessation.' (2019) 2(4) *JAMA Network Open* e192542
51 T. Cvrkel, 'The ethics of mHealth: Moving forward.' (2018) 74(1) *Journal of Dentistry* S15–S20.
52 M. Prictor, J. Bell, M. Taylor, 'Data Security in the Spotlight.' (2018) *Pursuit* 8 April.
53 Australian Government, Office of the Australian Information Commissioner, Notifiable Data Breaches Report, July to December 2021, 22 February 2022, page 5.
54 M. Alazab, S.-H. Hong, J. Ng, 'Louder Bark with No Bite: Privacy Protection through the Regulation of Mandatory Data Breach Notification in Australia' (2021) 116 *Future Generation Computer Systems* 22–29.
55 G. Stirrat, R. Gill, 'Autonomy in Medical Ethics after O'Neill.' (2005) 31(3) *Journal of Medical Ethics* 127–30.

56 M. Kühler, 'Exploring the Phenomenon and Ethical Issues of AI Paternalism in Health Apps.' (2022) 36(2) *Bioethics* 194–200, page 194.
57 G. Rubeis, 'iHealth: The Ethics of Artificial Intelligence and Big Data in Mental Healthcare.' (2022) 28(2) *Internet Interventions* 100518
58 K. Huckvale, S. Venkatesh, H. Christensen, 'Toward Clinical Digital Phenotyping: A Timely Opportunity to Consider Purpose, Quality, and Safety.' (2019) 2(1) *npj Digital Medicine* 1–11, page 9.
59 B. Dinesen et al., 'Personalized Telehealth in the Future: A Global Research Agenda.' (2016) 18(3) *Journal of Medical Internet Research* e53.
60 D. Bhugra et al. 'The WPA-Lancet Psychiatry Commission on the Future of Psychiatry' (2017) 4(10) *The Lancet. Psychiatry* 775–818, page 803.
61 N. Karcher, N. Presser, 'Ethical and Legal Issues Addressing the Use of Mobile Health (mHealth) as an Adjunct to Psychotherapy.' (2016) 28(1) *Ethics & Behaviour* 1–22.
62 J. Torous, S. Bucci, I. Bell et al. 'The Growing Field of Digital Psychiatry: Current Evidence and the Future of Apps, Social Media, Chatbots, and Virtual Reality' (2021) 20(3) *World Psychiatry* 318–335.
63 M. Bauer et al. 'Smartphones in Mental Health: A Critical Review of Background Issues, Current Status and Future Concerns' (2020) 8:2 *International Journal of Bipolar Disorders* 2.
64 D. Pruitt, J. Rubin, *Social Conflict Escalation, Stalemate, and Settlement* (McGraw-Hill, New York, 1986).
65 *ReThink* Mental Illness and Nuffield Council on Bioethics, *Summary Paper: Engaging Experts by Experience about the Role of Digital Technology in the Future of Mental Health Care* (ReThink and Nuffield Council, London, 2022).
66 T. Pramanik, rapid responses 'Humanising Healthcare' (2017) 355 *BMJ* i6262.
67 C. Gordon, M. Phillips, E. Beresin, 'The Doctor – Patient Relationship.' In: *Massachusetts General Hospital Handbook of General Hospital Psychiatry* (7th ed, Elsevier, London, 2017).
68 K. Wong, et al, 'Smartphone and Internet Access and Utilization by People with Schizophrenia in South Australia: Quantitative Survey Study.' 2020 7(1) *JMIR Mental Health* e11551.
69 J. Torous, S. Bucci, I. Bell et al. 'The Growing Field of Digital Psychiatry: Current Evidence and the Future of Apps, Social Media, Chatbots, and Virtual Reality' (2021) 20(3) *World Psychiatry* 318–335, page 327.
70 See J. Torous, S. Bucci, I. Bell et al. 'The Growing Field of Digital Psychiatry: Current Evidence and the Future of Apps, Social Media, Chatbots, and Virtual Reality' (2021) 20(3) *World Psychiatry* 318–335.
71 A. Berenguer, et al., 'Are Smartphones Ubiquitous?: An in-depth Survey of Smartphone Adoption by Seniors.' (2017) 6 *IEEE Consumer Electronics Magazine* 104–10.
72 A. Klee, et al.,'Interest in Technology-based Therapies Hampered by Access: A Survey of Veterans with Serious Mental Illnesses.' (2016) 39(2) *Psychiatric Rehabilitation Journal* 173–9.
73 V. Morgan et al., 'People Living with Psychotic Illness in 2010: The Second Australian National Survey of Psychosis.' (2021) 46(8) *Australian and New Zealand Journal of Psychiatry* 735–752.
74 *ReThink* Mental Illness and Nuffield Council on Bioethics, *Summary Paper: Engaging Experts by Experience about the Role of Digital Technology in the Future of Mental Health Care* (ReThink and Nuffield Council, London, 2022).
75 K. Wong et al. 'Smartphone and Internet Access and Utilization by People with Schizophrenia in South Australia: Quantitative Survey Study' 2020 7(1) *JMIR Mental Health* e11551.
76 D. Bhugra et al. 'The WPA-Lancet Psychiatry Commission on the Future of Psychiatry' (2017) 4(10) *The Lancet. Psychiatry* 775–818.
77 J. Torous, S. Bucci, I. Bell et al. 'The Growing Field of Digital Psychiatry: Current Evidence and the Future of Apps, Social Media, Chatbots, and Virtual Reality' (2021) 20(3) *World Psychiatry* 318–335, page 328.

78 D. Bates, A. Landman, D. Levine, 'Health Apps and Health Policy: What Is Needed?' (2018) 320(19) *JAMA* 1975–1976.
79 M. Rothstein et al. 'Unregulated Health Research Using Mobile Devices: Ethical Considerations and Policy Recommendations' (2020) 48(1) *The Journal of Law, Medicine & Ethics*, 196–226, page 201.
80 D. Schöberger, 'Artificial Intelligence in Healthcare: A Critical Analysis of the Legal and Ethical Implications.' (2020) 27 *International Journal of Law and Information Technology* 171–203, page 200
81 Australian Government, Department of Health and Aged Care, Therapeutic Goods Administration, 'Regulation of software based medical devices,' 17 August 2022.
82 J. Armontrout et al., 'Current Regulation of Mobile Mental Health Applications.' (2018) 46(2) *Journal of the American Academy of Psychiatry and the Law* 204–211.
83 M. Bauer et al. 'Smartphones in Mental Health: A Critical Review of Background Issues, Current Status and Future Concerns' (2020) 8:2 page 3.
84 International Medical Device Regulators Forum, 'Software as a Medical Device: Possible Framework for Risk Categorization and Corresponding Considerations' www.imdrf.org/workitems/wi-samd.asp.
85 IMDRF Management Committee, International Medical Device Regulators Forum (2020) IMDRF Strategic Plan 2021–2025.
86 IMDRF Management Committee, International Medical Device Regulators Forum (2020) IMDRF Strategic Plan 2021–2025, page 6.
87 M. Sucala et al., 'Anxiety: There is an App for that. A Systematic Review of Anxiety Apps.' (2017) 34(6) *Depress Anxiety* 518–525.
88 M. Sucala et al. 'Anxiety: There Is an App for That. A Systematic Review of Anxiety Apps' (2017) 34 4(6) *Depress Anxiety* 518–525.
89 D. Mohr et al., 'Three Problems with Current Digital Mental Health Research . . . and Three Things We Can Do About Them.' (2017) 68(5) *Psychiatric Services* 427–429.
90 M. Sucala et al. 'Anxiety: There Is an App for That. A Systematic Review of Anxiety Apps' (2017) 34 4(6) *Depress Anxiety* 518–525, page 522.
91 M. Faurholt-Jepsen, L. Vedel Kessing, 'Apps for Mental Health Care: The Raise of Digital Psychiatry' (2021) 47 *European Neuropsychopharmacology* 51–53.
92 R. Jolly, 'The e health revolution—Easier said than done'. Research Paper 3 2011–12. Canberra, Australia: Parliamentary Library.
93 M. Bauer et al. 'Smartphones in Mental Health: A Critical Review of Background Issues, Current Status and Future Concerns' (2020) 8:2 *International Journal of Bipolar Disorders* 2.
94 J. Firth, J. Torous. 'Smartphone Apps for Schizophrenia: A Systematic Review.' (2015) 3(4) *JMIR mHealth uHealth* e102.
95 T. Yang, R. Silverman, 'Mobile Health Applications: The Patchwork Of Legal And Liability Issues Suggests Strategies To Improve Oversight' (2014) 33(2) *Health Affairs* 222–27.
96 M. Bauer et al. 'Smartphones in Mental Health: A Critical Review of Background Issues, Current Status and Future Concerns' (2020) 8:2 *International Journal of Bipolar Disorders* 2, page 1.

5
AI IN THE DIAGNOSIS OF HEALTH CONDITIONS

Case scenarios

Betty is a proud Larrakia person, living in Darwin Australia. She has a mole on her leg, which she has noticed is getting darker. She visits her general practitioner (GP) to get it checked. He uses a dermatoscope, a handheld device using light, to examine the suspicious skin lesion. The GP knows that timely and accurate diagnosis is important, but he has seen very few of these skin lesions in his career. He is sufficiently concerned about the lesion to consider that a referral to a skin specialist is a prudent course of action. Betty sees a dermatologist the following month who diagnoses malignancy, and Betty is treated immediately with a good outcome. She is aware however, that her family living in remote parts of the Northern Territory may also be at high risk of skin cancer yet would be unable to access care as swiftly as she did, due to the lack of specialist provision in their locality.

Sam is a white male living in London. He has a lot of freckles and moles, and one has become sore and itchy. He speaks to a friend who is a doctor, who tells Sam that there is a specialist private dermatology clinic which has new technology that can diagnose melanoma accurately. Sam visits the clinic, and the healthcare practitioner uses Moleanalyzer-Pro, a computer-assisted diagnosis system for melanocytic lesions.[1] The artificial intelligence (AI) diagnostic system identifies a malignant lesion, and Sam receives timely treatment. His doctor friend later remarks that Sam was fortunate, because in his experience many malignant moles are difficult to identify with "old-style" observation, and he cannot understand why use of AI is not the standard of care in dermatology diagnosis.

Introduction

We are familiar with AI used in a wide range of applications in everyday activities. We may have smart hubs to control heating and lighting systems at home, our credit cards may be frozen if AI identifies fraudulent patterns of spending,

DOI: 10.4324/9781003220190-5

predictions about what we want to buy at supermarkets or online and what we watch on Netflix are powered by AI algorithms.[2] Smartphone apps can monitor our physical and mental health (Chapter 4), robotic care assistants use AI to provide care and supervision in the home (Chapter 8) and AI-powered chatbots can respond to questions about health and provide diagnosis and triage advice (Chapter 6). Companies like Google, Microsoft and IBM are providing huge investment into the development of AI for healthcare and research. DeepMind, the AI research arm of Google, has partnered with University College London Hospital to study the potential of using AI in planning radiotherapy treatment for patients with head and neck cancer. Reported results show the analysis of scans were on a par with expert clinicians but took much less time.[3] Researchers at Moorfield's Eye Hospital in London have trained machine learning technology on thousands of historical depersonalised eye scans to identify signs of eye disease, and this AI system "can recommend the correct referral decision for over 50 eye diseases with 94% accuracy, matching world-leading eye experts."[4] This technology has enabled healthcare professionals to identify conditions earlier and prioritise patients for treatment before irreversible eye damage occurs. Diagnostic AI can access information that humans are oblivious to, for example, even for clinicians who spent their whole careers looking at retinas, predicting gender from fundus photos was "inconceivable"[5] (the fundus is the inside, back surface of the eye). Yet differentiation of gender from colour fundus photography using AI has an accuracy of 91.4%.[6] Retinal biomarkers may provide information about healthy ageing and disease, so "automated machine learning may enable clinician-driven automated discovery of novel insights and disease biomarkers."[7] AI technologies thus have enormous potential to transform how healthcare is delivered; it can supplement the care provided by healthcare professionals, ease the pressure on healthcare staff and reduce costs.[8]

Terminology

'Artificial' intelligence describes the science of machines demonstrating some aspects of intelligence, mimicking human abilities and doing the tasks that humans would otherwise do.[9]

Artificial intelligence

An umbrella term used for a range of algorithm-based technologies which solve complex tasks by carrying out functions that previously required human thinking.

> AI systems, which utilise large datasets, can be designed to enhance decision-making and analytical processes while imitating human cognitive functions.[10]

Decisions made using AI are either fully automated or with a 'human in the loop.' In June 2022 a Google software engineer was suspended after claiming that the Google chatbot, LaMDA (Language Model for Dialogue Applications) had become sentient,[11] although the evidence supporting his claim was described as "about as flimsy as a film plot."[12] Sentience describes the ability to be aware of one's own existence and others, to perceive and experience sensations. Writing on the use of AI in dermatology, Tschandl states that an algorithm " 'sees' only pixels and patterns, will use whatever improves its accuracy, and has no abilities for deeper reasoning about abstract knowledge. Therefore, algorithms may not be regarded as intelligent in a human sense."[13] In the 2018 Pew Research Center report 'Artificial Intelligence and the Future of Humans' an expert considered that "by 2030, it is likely that AIs will have achieved a type of sentience, even if it is not human-like."[14]

> **Algorithm.** "A series of instructions for performing a calculation or solving a problem, especially with a computer. They form the basis for everything a computer can do and are therefore a fundamental aspect of all AI systems."[15]
> **Machine learning.** A subset of AI. Machine learning uses algorithms that make decisions and derive new knowledge based on inputted data.[16]
> **Deep learning.** The use of many layers of artificial neurons to solve difficult problems, often used to classify information from images, text or sound.

AI has used a 'rule-centric' approach, where programmers develop a logic for a machine to follow, but with machine learning; instead of being explicitly programmed, the computer system learns from previously collected examples, data and interactions in an iterative way. AI requires large amounts of data to learn from to make decisions without human control, raising concerns around fairness, transparency of AI decision making, security of the data and how it is used and shared. Given the complexity of the technology and the ability of the public to understand the way it works, patients need to trust their healthcare practitioners in the way they use AI in their diagnosis and treatment.[17]

It is important that AI is implemented and managed fairly for patients, and this can be addressed by ethical, legal and regulatory frameworks.[18] The High-Level Expert Group set up by the European Commission in 2018 noted components for trustworthy AI: that it complies with laws and regulations; that it adheres to ethical principles and values; and that decisions made are safe, accurate, reliable and reproducible.[19] In this chapter I explore the use of AI in the diagnosis of melanoma and address themes of bias and fairness in respect of 'information into' the system. If AI is shown to improve diagnosis and treatment, then should it become the standard of care, and who or what is responsible when things go wrong? I consider whether the law offers an appropriate response where harm is caused through use of AI in healthcare and address responsible regulation of AI in order to prevent harm.

AI to diagnose melanoma

AI is used in healthcare to diagnose disease and optimise treatment and has been developed in a range of specialties, including cardiology, ophthalmology and dermatology. Machine learning has been used to develop programs which are able to distinguish malignant and benign moles to a high degree of accuracy.[20]

Malignant melanoma is a relatively common but serious condition, and the prevalence of skin cancer continues to increase.[21] The risk of malignant melanoma correlates with genetic and personal characteristics and a person's ultraviolet (UV) exposure behaviour, with the highest reported rates in Australia and New Zealand.[22] If detected and treated early, mortality is reduced. "The estimated five-year survival rate for melanoma drops from over 99% if detected in its earliest stages to about 14% if detected in its latest stages."[23]

In the decision of *Coote v Kelly*,[24] the New South Wales Court of Appeal found that Dr Kelly, a GP, breached his duty of care owed to Mr Coote by failing to observe a small black mark in a lesion he presented with. A reasonably competent medical practitioner would have observed the mark and referred for further investigation. Dr Kelly diagnosed the lesion as a plantar wart on the sole of Mr Coote's left foot and treated it with liquid nitrogen. Evidence to the court showed that a complete cure is highly likely for this type of melanoma if diagnosed and removed early. The lesion metastasised and Mr Coote died. However, the claim by his widow was not successful because there was a failure to show that the breach of duty caused the harm.

Skin cancer has traditionally been diagnosed visually with aids such as a dermoscope. A comparatively new strategy is the use of convolutional neural networks (CNN), deep learning algorithms, which learn iteratively with new data inputted. A report in *Nature* in 2017 described a CNN which uses an image and can assign importance to various aspects/objects in the image trained on general skin lesions using a dataset of training and validation images and biopsy-labelled test images.[25] The authors of the report acknowledge the effectiveness of deep learning in dermatology, matching the performance of dermatologists in diagnosis. Another study compared the diagnostic accuracy of human readers of dermatoscopic images with AI for clinically relevant types of benign and malignant pigmented skin lesions.[26] Human readers, comprising certified dermatologists, dermatology residents and general practitioners, were asked to diagnose dermatoscopic images from a test set of images, and these diagnoses were compared with those of AI algorithms created by different machine learning labs. The authors concluded that "state-of-the-art machine-learning classifiers outperformed human experts in the diagnosis of pigmented skin lesions and should have a more important role in clinical practice."[27] AI in smartphone apps can be used to teach people to perform skin examinations, and they can then forward the information to their doctor.[28] The potential for machine learning algorithms to surpass the diagnostic capabilities of humans in skin cancer classification requires careful development and prospective clinical trials to validate their use,[29] and collaboration between AI developers and clinical stakeholders can ensure that AI solutions align with clinical problems to be solved.[30]

> Under the leadership of dermatologists, these tools can be designed to improve patient outcomes, root out health care disparities, bridge the gap

between a shortage of dermatologists and an abundance of patients, assist in the allocation of other limited resources, and allow increased patient traffic in our practices.[31]

However, the susceptibility for biases in machine learning algorithms, including for age, sex, ethnicity and socioeconomic status,[32] can have an impact on their accuracy for underrepresented groups, and systematic data disparities may lead to healthcare inequalities.

Ethical issues and AI

Ethical issues arising in the use of AI include protection of data, fairness, bias and the impact on the doctor-patient relationship. Various organisations have issued guidance or principles in the use of AI. Jobin, Ienca and Vayena identify that the ethical principles of transparency, justice and fairness, non-maleficence, responsibility and privacy, underpin most AI ethics guidelines.[33] One such set of principles on the use of AI is from the Organisation for Economic Co-operation and Development (OECD).[34] They include principles of *benefit* (AI should benefit people and the planet), *respect* (for the rule of law, human rights, democratic values and diversity), *transparency and responsibility*, *safety* (safeguards and management of risks) and *accountability* (of organisations and individuals developing, deploying or operating AI systems). The European Commissions' *Ethics Guidelines for Trustworthy Artificial Intelligence*[35] lists systemic, individual and societal aspects for trustworthy AI. Fairness and the avoidance of unfair bias are key ethical concerns because data used in AI systems, both for training and in its operation, may contain "inadvertent historical bias" leading to unintended prejudice and discrimination.[36]

Bias

Bias describes an unfair distortion based on arbitrary or irrelevant factors. Of course, algorithms are designed to discriminate and give priority to some factors over others in the decision-making process,[37] but they should use data which takes account of the broad population it aims to benefit. Where there is underrepresentation of certain groups in the datasets, the algorithm cannot learn and predict accurately for that group. The diagnostic accuracy of skin diseases varies between skin types,[38] yet algorithms for melanoma diagnosis are mostly learning from images of light skin with substantial under-representation of darker skin types. A systematic review of publicly available skin image datasets used to develop machine learning algorithms for skin cancer diagnosis found unequal geographical distribution of datasets . . . only one dataset originated from Asia, two from South America, and none from Africa.[39]

Melanoma can look different on diverse skin tones, and if there are insufficient images of skin lesions on dark skin inputted into the AI system, there is an unavoidable bias with a potential for significant medical harm from errors and late diagnosis.[40] It is important that these issues are addressed before AI is implemented and relied upon in clinical practice.[41] There may be a difference in the accuracy of diagnosis using an AI system to assist with diagnosis between Betty and Sam in the scenario, but biases in AI also impact society as a whole, and the implementation of AI will not be fair or effective to society if it does not take account of broad social and cultural contexts in which it operates.[42]

The ethical theory of consequentialism focusses on the outcomes of an action – whether an action is right or wrong depends solely on the consequences of performing it. A prominent consequentialist theory is utilitarianism, and the principle of utility provides that the morally right course of action is that which promotes the greatest good for the greatest number. The outcome of a dataset that is not balanced and representative is well described by Daniel Schönberger,

> From a purely utilitarian point of view, it could be argued that as long as the general population and health systems benefit overall even inherently biased systems should not be withheld from clinical practice. However, few would agree that this is a society they would want to live in, where the interests of minorities are simply rolled over. After all distributive justice requires a "fair, equitable and proportionate" distribution of the benefits and burdens any new technology entails.[43]

The European General Data Protection Regulation has provisions related to algorithmic bias and discrimination. Recital 71 states that a controller of personal data should prevent discriminatory effects on the basis of racial or ethnic origin, political opinion, religion or beliefs, trade union membership, genetic or health status or sexual orientation and this includes processing of data that has this effect.

Algorithms should not be considered in isolation, but rather as part of the decision-making process as a whole. It is not just the 'data in' that can bias the system but also how the parameters for the way the machine learns are set. Fairness is not just about more data and accurate computations, and AI systems are not necessarily objective given the inherent human qualities of AI designers and programmers. Human developers, with all their beliefs, assumptions and prejudices, may unwittingly encode human biases into algorithmic programs. The House of Lords Select Committee suggests that this sort of bias can be addressed by ensuring that developers come from diverse gender, ethnic and socioeconomic backgrounds and that they are aware of and follow ethical codes of conduct.[44] Human skills are then necessary to decide how best to respond to AI outputs, and that has impact on the doctor-patient relationship. But it is worth remembering that humans make diagnostic errors in medical practice, estimated at about 5%–15%, depending on the specialty, with cognitive biases the cause of most diagnostic errors.[45]

Doctor-patient relationship and AI

We may wonder how the use of AI in healthcare can, and will, impact the relationship between patient and healthcare professional and the legal, moral and professional obligations they owe. Stahl et al. consider that a key purpose of using AI is to promote 'human flourishing'.[46] The British Academy and the Royal Society consider the promotion of human flourishing to be the 'overarching principle' that should guide the development of systems of data governance in the use of data-enabled technologies,[47] and the UK House of Lords Select Committee reiterates the importance of education about AI to enable citizens to "flourish mentally, emotionally and economically alongside artificial intelligence."[48]

For patients, the use of AI may lead to social isolation (Chapter 8) and a depersonalisation of care (Chapter 7). In clinical practice doctors, nurses and technical staff are likely to work as a team, supporting each other in the use of AI-based systems.[49] The algorithms used to diagnose skin lesions can more efficiently and accurately manage diagnosis and complement the role of the healthcare professional, but humans should have the final judgment and thus be responsible for decision making.

But AI and the systems they generate may be so complex that they create 'black box medicine' where "the details of their contents, calculations, and procedures cannot be meaningfully understood by human practitioners."[50] If the healthcare practitioner does not understand the decision-making process behind AI, can they enter into a dialogue with the patient with sufficient understanding to convey information in order to gain informed consent? Informed consent (Chapter 6) describes the disclosure of information about the risks inherent in a procedure or intervention and possible alternative treatments the patient should be given in order to make treatment decisions, and this must conform to the legal standard. But 'patient-centred care' goes beyond the provision of facts and figures and requires that patients are treated as individuals whose values and beliefs are important. In order to give effect to such values, the patient must be heard and understood through dialogue and exchange of information (I discuss this concept in end-of-life decision making and a video format as a means by which a patient's wishes and values are expressed; Chapter 9). Bjerring and Busch state that such black box medicine is in conflict with the core ideals of patient-centred medicine,

> When the practitioner cannot make sense of the relevant medical information buried in the deep learning network, then neither can he present the information in a way that enables a patient to comprehend and process it rationally.[51]

Perhaps by trusting that AI will give a potentially superior diagnosis, medical certainty is achieved at the expense of understanding how that is achieved.

The 'doctor knows best' paternalistic model of decision making is outmoded, and as I have noted in other chapters, emerging health technologies may enable individuals to take a more active role in their health and wellbeing, for example, using apps to monitor their lifestyle (Chapter 4) and even in codesigning technology to support their health, as is apparent in the #WeAreNotWaiting movement for the management of diabetes (Chapter 3). Black box medicine may present a new type of paternalism where, rather than a deliberate withholding of information from the patient which characterised the traditional paternalistic approach, the doctor inadvertently withholds information from the patient due to a lack of awareness or understanding by the doctor themselves.

Trust and confidence are essential elements in the patient–healthcare professional relationship, and strategies for the development and use of AI systems in healthcare highlight the importance of trust.[52] The concepts of loyalty, fidelity, faith, and honour are the basic vocabulary of a fiduciary relationship[53] which arises where there is an inequality or a power differential between the parties, creating implicit dependency and vulnerability.[54] The doctor and patient relationship has been recognised as demonstrating characteristics of a fiduciary relationship; the doctor has knowledge, skills and understanding of disease and treatment options that most patients just do not have even with Dr Google on hand,[55] and the patient necessarily has to place reliance on, and have faith in, the advice of healthcare professionals. In Australia the courts have recognised that fiduciary elements exist in the doctor-patient relationship but have limited the scope of fiduciary duties owed. The High Court of Australia in *Breen v Williams*[56] recognised that whilst some aspects of the doctor-patient relationship could be fiduciary in nature, this is limited to financial matters and confidential information, and there was no aspect of the fiduciary relationship which gave rise to a right for Mrs Breen to access medical records (although a right of access is provided in legislation; Chapter 2). In Australia fiduciary obligations are viewed as limited to *avoid* a conflict between duty and personal interests, whereas in Canada the concept of fiduciary obligations is "dramatically expanded,"[57] and Canadian courts consider the fiduciary duty as a positive obligation to act in the best interests of another,[58] in other words, a *prescriptive* fiduciary obligation. Should a doctor use AI if the diagnosis rate is known to be superior and in the best interests of the patient, what information should be disclosed about the use of AI in diagnosis and treatment? Considerations on whether and how AI is used in healthcare based on a doctor's prescriptive fiduciary duty remains to be seen.

Accountability for decision making: machine or human

AI systems are not fool proof; they may malfunction, underperform and make decisions which cause harm. If a person is harmed in a healthcare setting, then they should be able to hold someone accountable for the decision made or action taken, but the responsibility for a decision where AI is involved is less clear. Who bears responsibility if an algorithmic decision leads to harm: the person who provides the data for training the algorithm; teams of developers responsible for the development and configuration of an algorithm, or the healthcare professional interpreting and using the AI outcome? The flow of data in the lifecycle of AI illustrates the ongoing and iterative AI-automated decision-making process with both a human and machine component (I use here examples from the UK Government, slightly revised, see italics, for a healthcare context),

- "A set of data (personal and non-personal) is gathered for *example photos of skin lesions* and the decisions reached as to whether they showed *malignancy*.
- A machine-learning algorithm is chosen and uses historical data (e.g. a set of past input data, the decisions reached) to build a model, optimising against a set of criteria specified by a human.
- The resulting model is then used repeatedly as part of the decision-making process, either to make an automated decision, or to offer guidance to a human making the final decision.
- New input data and associated decisions can be fed back into the dataset to enable the model to be updated (either periodically or continuously).
- The above learning process feeds on data, the machine learning algorithm and the machine learning model."[59]

Humans are thus involved in the development of an algorithm. The algorithm utilises the inputted data to identify the best action to take in each situation, but it is the healthcare professional who ultimately decides whether to use the output from the AI system. The European Group on Ethics requires 'meaningful human control'[60] is maintained, and where humans are in the loop, they can bring perspectives and contextual information which are not available to the algorithm. If humans ultimately remain in control of the decision-making process, there will always be someone on whom responsibility can be placed and who is accountable. Knowledge of and confidence in AI in dermatology can be improved through training. In a survey of 1271 dermatologists although about three-quarters of respondents agreed/strongly agreed that AI would improve dermatology, less than a quarter had either good or excellent knowledge about AI within dermatology.[61]

Regulation

Whilst a healthcare professional is liable for their decisions about interpretation and application of the output from an AI system, the producers of AI are responsible for safe and efficient functioning of the system. Regulation of AI aims to ensure that systems are as safe as possible – to take account of risks to the public and avoid harm in the first place. Regulation of AI can take different forms, including legislation, an overseeing regulatory body and self-regulation, each with their own benefits and limitations. Given the continuing and swift development of AI and the international nature of its evolution, it may be "exceptionally difficult to regulate AI as compared to other sources of public risk."[62] The challenge is to ensure effective and timely regulation in a way that does not stifle the development of innovation. Accountable algorithmic decision-making systems have been considered in the public sector, and it has been proposed that transparency and accountability of automated decision making in government could be promoted through an open register of AI systems/algorithms that make administrative decisions.[63] This may provide a fertile cross-over in the accountability of AI in healthcare.

Legislation

Legislation regulating different aspects of AI has "greater democratic legitimacy than agency rules or court decisions"[64] because a legislative body comprising elected representatives has a strong claim that it reflects public opinion. However, it can take time for legislation to be enacted, so this form of regulation may not keep pace with developments in AI.[65] Legislation is a form of ex ante regulation; that is, it sets parameters and standards *before* harm has occurred, in comparison with tort, where a claim is pursued consequent to harm occurring.

One area in which regulation of AI is paramount is the protection of patient privacy, and indeed the Office of the Australian Information Commissioner noted the significant impact that AI has on privacy.[66] The concept of privacy encompasses two main threads: protection of data from misuse and inappropriate sharing (more properly, data protection) and the control individuals have over their personal data – including having access to it. Privacy legislation protects data and facilitates appropriate access, and the trigger for its application is that personal identifying information is held about an individual. The datasets used to train and build algorithmic models and images of skin lesions may be linked with identifiable information of the individual, and datasets held by public health services may be shared with technology companies to develop AI systems. This data then is a valuable commodity.[67]

Where AI directs therapies or preventive measures that are most suited to a patient's condition, then although there are risks of abuse of patients' data, these AI applications are beneficial, both for the patient and, in principle, everyone who has an interest in a more effective and personalised treatment through the use of such data. Existing legislation on human rights, non-discrimination, equality and privacy may not explicitly mention AI, but nevertheless can be interpreted in a way that addresses relevant interests, and in their 'Review into bias in algorithmic decision-making,' the Centre for Data Ethics and Innovation did not see a need for primary legislation to address algorithmic bias.[68] Scherer argues that the legislature is best equipped to make value-laden policy decisions, but in order to regulate effectively, there must be adequate understanding of the complexities of AI, the risks it poses and the stakeholders who may be impacted, and this calls for specialist knowledge.[69] In 2021 the European Commission proposed European Union (EU) regulatory framework on AI, the Artificial Intelligence Act which has the aim of promoting the safe use of AI in high-impact sectors like healthcare and strengthening technological innovation.[70]

Regulatory agencies

Regulatory agencies have the technical expertise to respond to and deal with the safety of emerging technologies such as AI. They can formulate policy and issue guidance and can thus act to prevent harm, although sometimes the process of regulating an emerging technology can be laborious and slow (Chapter 2), and this is exacerbated by the rapid changes in AI capabilities. AI research and application are necessarily interdisciplinary. Coordinating many regulatory bodies involved in a new technology may be problematic, and partners in AI projects may be located in multiple countries with differing regulatory frameworks. Increasingly medical devices utilise AI-driven software. In Australia the Therapeutic Goods Administration (TGA), which derives its authority and power from the Therapeutic Goods Act 1989, regulates the import, supply, manufacture, export and advertising of therapeutic goods, such as medicines and medical devices. It also regulates software as a medical device (Chapter 3). In the United States the Food and Drug Administration (FDA) has issued the Artificial Intelligence/Machine Learning Action Plan.[71] The AI-driven Moleanalyzer-Pro has not been registered on the Australian Register of Therapeutic Goods or by the FDA to date, illustrating that regulation may lag behind or 'decouple' from the technology it seeks to monitor.[72]

Self-regulation

In the absence of legislation to deal with issues arising from AI, self-regulation from AI developers and industry has emerged in the form of codes of practice and standards. Indeed, self-regulation may be considered the most deft and responsive means to manage risks of AI technology, but the downside is the lack of effective enforcement, as codes only guide practice and are not obligatory.

Tort as a potential ground for a claim

Legislation and regulation through administrative agencies aim to *prevent* harm. Legislation sets the framework for the use of AI, and whilst there are currently no specific statutes relating to AI, as we have seen, privacy legislation covers the protection of data used in AI, and prevention of discrimination and protection of the dignity of patients can be addressed through equality and human rights legislation. Agencies such as the TGA and FDA that regulate medical devices set standards for safety and quality before they are supplied to the public and have a role in post-market surveillance. In contrast, courts decide matters *after* the event, and they respond only where a claim is brought by a litigant, so does the law of tort have any effective contribution to play? The tort of negligence provides legal redress for harm that has been caused by a failure to take reasonable care.[73] Liability is attributed when there is a breach of duty causing harm through a failure to meet a reasonable standard of care.

Duty of care

If a specialist uses AI in the diagnosis of melanoma for a patient and harm results, then the healthcare professional is most likely to be the subject of a legal claim (the defendant), and they will have indemnity insurance to cover any damages awarded. The first step in deciding whether behaviour amounts to a tort of negligence is to determine whether the defendant owes the patient (the claimant) a duty to take reasonable care of their interests (the duty of care). If a person sustains bodily injury as a result of a direct impact from the positive act of another, establishing a duty of care on the person who caused the harm will usually be uncontroversial. The scope of liability is based on the foreseeability of an outcome from an event – is the type of harm that eventuated foreseeable? A healthcare professional owes their patient a duty of care; there is a sufficiently proximate relationship between them; and it is reasonably foreseeable that harm may result from misuse or malfunction of a medical device which uses AI.

Standard

Liability is established based on the standard of behaviour that could be reasonably expected in the circumstances. If the healthcare professional has fallen below the standard of care, they have breached their duty of care. What is the standard of care for a dermatologist diagnosing skin lesions and melanomas? Evidence is required for AI to be used in clinical settings, so should AI be the standard provision of care if it is known to improve diagnostic accuracy, leading to better patient outcomes? The fast-paced development of AI makes it difficult to identify a standard of a particular technology or activity, as the model is constantly evolving. Although Schönberger states that "soon we may not discuss negligence in connection with the use of AI but rather with the omission to use it,"[74] we have not reached that stage with AI in the diagnosis of melanoma. Recent studies demonstrate the superiority of AI in classifying dermoscopic images of melanoma and conclude that these algorithms should assist a dermatologist's diagnoses,[75] but there would need to be more evidence of the accuracy of AI models and their effectiveness in the clinic before it could even become standard in healthcare, and there is a lot more work to be done in this space. The other challenge in requiring diagnostic techniques using AI to become standard is the cost of the AI system and its implementation. The deep learning algorithms in systems such as Moleanalyzer-Pro and DermEngine provide a risk assessment for skin lesions using AI, but whether specialist dermatologists or GPs decide to use such a system will be down to its affordability and the cost-benefit analysis. The cost-effectiveness of AI versus the current standard of care requires comparison of the costs of the AI application and the treatments following diagnosis,[76] with the accuracy of diagnosis by practitioners without AI support. But these AI systems act as an aid to clinical management decisions, and healthcare professionals who use them bear ultimate responsibility for the diagnosis and implementing treatment decisions.

The practice of medicine is described as both a science and an art,

> Diagnosis and therapy in medicine is still relatively subjective. This is why we often seek multiple opinions and host multidisciplinary meetings to discuss the large amount of digital health data available to us, suggest the most likely

diagnoses, and recommend what we think is the best therapy for the optimal outcome. Not only is this not always reproducible but the outcome for any given patient is variable.[77]

A healthcare professional is not negligent if they act in accordance with competent medical practice, i.e. in a manner widely accepted by respected practitioners in the field. The *'Bolam'* test was formulated by McNair J in the English decision of *Bolam v Friern Hospital Management Committee*.[78] In most states in Australia, legislation makes provision for the standard of care; for example, section 59 *Wrongs Act 1958* (Vic) provides that,

> a professional is not negligent if they acted in a manner that, at the time the service was provided, was widely accepted in Australia by a significant number of respected, competent practitioners in the field.

The comparable New South Wales provision is s 50 of the *Civil Liability Act 2002* (NSW).

The standards of care for claims in negligence are based on established practices that are widely accepted. It has been argued that this interpretation limits the use of innovation in healthcare and may result in innovations not being offered because of fear of legal liability.[79] Bjerring and Busch argue that when AI surpasses humans in accuracy, reliability and knowledge, "practitioners will have a prima facie epistemic and professional obligation to align their medical verdicts with those of advanced AI systems."[80] Whether a misdiagnosis constitutes a breach of duty of care is determined by a court on the basis of the admissible evidence, including expert peer professional opinion. Harm caused to patients because of erroneous prediction by an AI system may not amount to negligence on the part of the healthcare professional. It would be necessary to consider if it was reasonable for the dermatologist to use that system and whether it was being used correctly and in accordance with the regulatory framework.

Causation

To establish the defendant's liability in negligence it must be shown that the defendant breached their duty to take care and, in doing so, caused damage to the claimant that is not too remote a consequence of the breach. Did the breach of duty, the action which fails to meet the standard of care, cause harm to the claimant? It is always a challenge for a claimant to establish causation, and this is particularly true given the inherent opacity of AI systems and establishing whether the machine system was at fault or the human decision caused harm.

It is known that AI systems may develop in the future to display behaviours that are unforeseen by their creators, and even careful designers, programmers and manufacturers will not be able to control or predict what an AI system will experience after it leaves their influence.[81] Foreseeability of harm is necessary to establish liability in negligence, and AI designers may not be able to foresee how the AI system will develop and the impact on specific individuals. As Scherer notes, "if legal systems choose to view the experiences of some learning AI systems as so unforeseeable that it would be unfair to hold the systems' designers liable for harm that the systems cause, victims might be left with no way of obtaining compensation for their losses."[82]

Whilst judges have no role to play in setting policy around the use and safety of AI, tort law can influence future behaviour because of its deterrent effect, both in terms of financial compensation paid to a person who suffers harm and consequent reputational damage. The fallout from Google Deep Mind's use of medical records from the Royal Free Hospital in London and the ensuing privacy concerns was reported worldwide and impacted the reputation of Google, so we can imagine the concern where the use of AI directly harms an individual. Development of professional standards and codes of conduct for use of AI in diagnosis will enable effective regulation for patient safety and clarify legal accountability so that AI can be used innovatively and its use not restricted due to fear of liability.

Conclusion

AI-assisted decision making will have an increasing role in diagnosis and treatment. Evidence shows that AI systems can assist dermatologists in diagnosing skin diseases, although when comparing the diagnostic accuracy of deep learning algorithms and healthcare professionals in classifying diseases using medical imaging, it is important that studies make direct comparisons using the same samples. Increasingly clinicians with no coding experience can use automated deep learning to develop algorithms to do clinical classification tasks.[83]

The overall aim of AI may be to support human flourishing, but in order to do so, data used to build the system must be chosen with care. This technology could exacerbate healthcare disparities in dermatology if the data from which the machine learns does not reflect the diversity of skin types in society. Increasing use of AI-driven systems in healthcare demands that potential harms are identified and prevented before they arise. Issues of bias and data privacy may be addressed through legislation although this is currently of indirect, application to AI in healthcare. Safety standards can be set and monitored through agencies with technical expertise. The role of courts in considering claims of negligence may have a deterrent effect on designers of AI, but nevertheless operate after harm has occurred. In order to avoid a gap in accountability, humans should be ultimately responsible for healthcare decisions, and AI systems should augment, but not displace, the doctor-patient relationship. Trust in the AI system and in the healthcare professionals' use of it is fundamental to utilise its full potential, to enhance the patient experience and to improve health outcomes and reduce costs for the healthcare system.[84]

Notes

1. K. Sies, et al., 'Past and Present of Computer-assisted Dermoscopic Diagnosis: Performance of a Conventional Image Analyser versus a Convolutional Neural Network in a Prospective Data Set of 1,981 Skin Lesions.' (2020) 135, *European Journal of Cancer* 39–46.
2. See the examples in House of Lords Select Committee on Artificial Intelligence. 'AI in the UK: Ready, Willing and Able?' Report of Session 2017–19. HL Paper 100.
3. A. Hosny et al, 'AI and Radiotherapy.' (2020) 18(8) *Nature Reviews Cancer* 500–510.
4. S. Gibbs, 'Artificial intelligence tool 'as good as experts' at detecting eye problems,' The Guardian 14 August 2018 and J. De Fauw, J. Ledsam, B. Romera-Paredes, B. et al. 'Clinically applicable deep learning for diagnosis and referral in retinal disease.' (2018) 24 *Nature Medicine* 1342–1350.
5. E. Korot et al., 'Predicting Sex from Retinal Fundus Photographs using Automated Deep Learning.' (2021) 11 *Scientific Reports* 10286, page 1.
6. K. Chueh, Y. Hsieh, H. Chen, I. Ma, S. Huang, 'Identification of Sex and Age from Macular Optical Coherence Tomography and Feature Analysis Using Deep Learning. '(2022) 235 *American Journal of Ophthalmology* 221–228.
7. Korot et al. 'Predicting Sex from Retinal Fundus Photographs Using Automated Deep Learning' (2021) 11 *Scientific Reports* 10286, page 1.
8. D. Schönberger (2019) 'Artificial Intelligence in Healthcare: A Critical Analysis of the Legal and Ethical Implications.' (2019) 27(2) *International Journal of Law and Information Technology*, 71–203.
9. Academy of Royal Medical Colleges. *Artificial Intelligence in Healthcare* (Academy of Royal Medical Colleges, London, 2019).
10. T. Nadarzynski, O. Miles, A. Cowie, D. Ridge, 'Acceptability of Artificial Intelligence (AI)-Led Chatbot Services in Healthcare: A Mixed-methods Study.' (2019) 5 *Digital Health* 1–12, page 1.
11. The Economist 'Could Artificial Intelligence become Sentient?' *The Economist*, 14 June 2022 www.economist.com/the-economist-explains/2022/06/14/could-artificial-intelligence-become-sentient
12. C. Wilson, 'Is Google's AI Chatbot LaMDA Truly Self-aware, or Has it Simply Tricked Us?' (2022) *Crikey*, 13 June. www.crikey.com.au/2022/06/13/googles-ai-chatbot-lamda-truly-self-aware-or-tricked-us/
13. P. Tschandl, 'Risk of Bias and Error From Data Sets Used for Dermatologic Artificial Intelligence. (2021) 157(11) *JAMA Dermatology* 1271–1273, page 1272.
14. J. Anderson, L. Rainie, A. Luchsinger, Pew Research Center, December 2018, 'Artificial Intelligence and the Future of Humans,' page 15.
15. House of Lords Select Committee on Artificial Intelligence. 'AI in the UK: Ready, Willing and Able?' Report of Session 2017–19. HL Paper 100, page 14.
16. A. Adamson, A. Smith. 'Machine Learning and Health Care Disparities in Dermatology.' (2018) 154 (11) *JAMA Dermatology* 1247–1248.
17. Centre for Data Ethics and Innovation. *Review into Bias in Algorithmic Decision-making*. (Centre for Data Ethics and Innovation, London, 2020).
18. M. McCradden, S. Joshi, M. Mazwi, J. Anderson, 'Ethical Limitations of Algorithmic Fairness Solutions in Health Care Machine Learning.' (2020) 2(5) *Lancet Digit Health* e221–e223.
19. European Commission, 'Ethics Guidelines for Trustworthy AI,' High-level expert group on artificial intelligence, 2019.
20. A. Esteva, B. Kuprel, R. Novoa et al., 'Dermatologist-level Classification of Skin Cancer with Deep Neural Networks.' (2017) 542(7639) *Nature*. 115–118.
21. K. Urban, S. Mehrmal et al. 'The Global Burden of Skin Cancer: A Longitudinal Analysis from the Global Burden of Disease Study, 1990–2017' (2021) 2 *Journal of the American Academy of Dermatology* 98–108.

22 World Cancer Research Fund International, Skin cancer statistics, updated 23 March 2022.
23 A. Esteva, B. Kuprel, R. Novoa et al. 'Dermatologist-level Classification of Skin Cancer with Deep Neural Networks' (2017) 542(7639) *Nature*. 115–118, page 116.
24 *Coote v Kelly* [2013] NSWCA 357.
25 A. Esteva, B. Kuprel, R. Novoa et al. 'Dermatologist-level Classification of Skin Cancer with Deep Neural Networks' (2017) 542(7639) *Nature*. 115–118.
26 P. Tschandl, N. Codella, B. Akay et al. 'Comparison of the Accuracy of Human Readers Versus Machine-learning Algorithms for Pigmented Skin Lesion Classification: An Open, Web-based, International, Diagnostic Study.' (2019) 20(7) *The Lancet Oncology* 938–947.
27 P. Tschandl, N. Codella, B. Akay et al. 'Comparison of the Accuracy of Human Readers Versus Machine-learning Algorithms for Pigmented Skin Lesion Classification: An Open, Web-based, International, Diagnostic Study' (2019) 20(7) *The Lancet Oncology* 938–947, page 940.
28 K. Das, C. Cockerell, A. Patil et al., 'Machine Learning and Its Application in Skin Cancer.' (2021) 18(24) *Int J Environ Res Public Health*.13409.
29 F. Mahmood, S. Bendayan, F. Ghazawi, I. Litvinov, 'Editorial: The Emerging Role of Artificial Intelligence in Dermatology.' (2021) 8 *Frontiers in Medicine* 1–5.
30 C. González-Gonzalo, et al. 'Trustworthy AI: Closing the gap between development and integration of AI systems in ophthalmic practice.' (2021) *Progress in Retinal and Eye Research*, 101034, page 3
31 G. Zakhem, et al. 'Characterizing the Role of Dermatologists in Developing Artificial intelligence for assessment of skin cancer.' (2021) 85(6) *Journal of the American Academy of Dermatology* 1544–1556, page 1554.
32 D. Wen, et al, 'Characteristics of Publicly Available Skin Cancer Image Datasets: A Systematic Review' (2020) 4(1) *The Lancet Digital Health* e64.
33 A. Jobin, M. Ienca, E. Vayena. (2019) 'The Global Landscape of AI Ethics Guidelines.' (2019) 1 *Nature Machine Intelligence* 389–399.
34 'AI Principles, Insights from National AI Policies' OECD Digital Economy Papers June 2021 No. 311.
35 N. Smuha (2019) 'The EU Approach to Ethics Guidelines for Trustworthy Artificial Intelligence.' (2019) 20(4) *Computer Law Review International*, 97–106.
36 European Commission, 'Ethics Guidelines for Trustworthy AI,' High-level expert group on artificial intelligence, 2019, page 18, para 1.5.
37 House of Commons Science and Technology Committee, 'Algorithms in decision making', Fourth Report of Session 2017–19, 15 May 2018 (House of Commons, 2018), p 32.
38 M. Groh, C. Harris, L. Soenksen et al., 'Evaluating Deep Neural Networks Trained on Clinical Images in Dermatology with the Fitzpatrick 17k Dataset.' *2021 Proceedings of the IEEE/CVF Conference on Computer Vision and Pattern Recognition* 1820–1828.
39 D. Wen et al. 'Characteristics of Publicly Available Skin Cancer Image Datasets: A Systematic Review' (2020) 4(1) *The Lancet Digital Health* e64, page e71.
40 R. Daneshjou et al., 'Lack of Transparency and Potential Bias in Artificial Intelligence Data Sets and Algorithms A Scoping Review.' (2021) 157(11) *JAMA Dermatology* 1362–1369, page 1364.
41 A. Gomolin, E. Netchiporouk, R. Gniadecki, I. Litvinov et al., 'Artificial Intelligence Applications in Dermatology: Where do we stand?' (2020) 7 (100) *Frontiers in Medicine* 2.
42 M. Carman, B. Rosman. 'Defining What's Ethical in Artificial Intelligence Needs Input from Africans.' (2021) *The Conversation*, November 24.
43 D. Schönberger, 'Artificial Intelligence in Healthcare: A Critical Analysis of the Legal and Ethical Implications' (2019) 27(2) *International Journal of Law and Information Technology* 171–203, page 181.
44 House of Lords Select Committee on Artificial Intelligence. 'AI in the UK: Ready, Willing and Able?' Report of Session 2017–19. HL Paper 100, para 120.
45 T. Pelaccia, G. Forestier, C. Wemmert, 'Deconstructing the Diagnostic Reasoning of Human versus Artificial Intelligence.' (2019) 191 *CMAJ* e1332–5, page 1333.

46 B. Stahl et al., 'Artificial Intelligence for Human Flourishing – Beyond Principles for Machine Learning.' (2021) 124(4) *Journal of Business Review* 374–388.
47 The British Academy and The Royal Society 'Data Management and Use: Governance in the 21st Century.' (2017) https://royalsociety.org/-/media/policy/projects/data-governance/data-management-governance.pdf.
48 House of Lords Select Committee on Artificial Intelligence. 'AI in the UK: Ready, Willing and Able?' Report of Session 2017–19. HL Paper 100, para 4.17.
49 Z. Obermeyer, T. Lee, 'Lost in Thought – The Limits of the Human Mind and the Future of Medicine.' (2017) 377(13) *New England Journal of Medicine*, 1209–1211.
50 J. Christian Bjerring, J. Busch, 'Artificial Intelligence and Patient-centered Decision Making.' (2021) 34 *Philosophy & Technology* 349–371, page 349.
51 J. Christian Bjerring, J. Busch, 'Artificial Intelligence and Patient-centered Decision Making' (2021) 34 *Philosophy & Technology* 349–371, page 361.
52 E. Brattberg, R. Csernatoni, V. Rugova, *Europe and AI: Leading, Lagging Behind, or Carving Its Own Way?* (Carnegie Endowment for International Peace, Washington, DC, 2020).
53 T. Frankel, 'Fiduciary Law' (1983) 71 *California Law Review* 795–836.
54 L. Rotman, 'Fiduciary Law's 'Holy Grail': Reconciling Theory and Practice in Fiduciary Jurisprudence.' (2011) 91(3) *Boston University Law Review*, 921–971.
55 N. Van Riel, K. Auwerx, P. Debbaut, S. Van Hees B. Schoenmakers, 'The effect of Dr Google on Doctor-patient Encounters in Primary Care: A Quantitative, Observational, Cross-Sectional Study.' (2017) 1(2) *BJGP Open*, 1–10.
56 *Breen v Williams* [1996] HCA 57.
57 S. Dorsett, 'Comparing Apples and Oranges: The Fiduciary Principle in Australia and Canada after Breen v Williams.' (1996) 8(2) *Bond Law Review* 158–184, page 158.
58 *Norberg v Wynrib* (1992) 92 DLR (4th) 449, 489.
59 Department for Digital, Culture Media and Sport, 'Data: A New Direction', September 2021, page 25.
60 European Group on Ethics in Science and New Technologies, *Statement on Artificial Intelligence, Robotics and Autonomous Systems* (European Group on Ethics in Science and New Technologies, Brussels, 2018).
61 S. Polesie, M. Gillstedt, H. Kittler et al., 'Attitudes towards Artificial Intelligence within Dermatology: An International Online Survey.' (2020) 183(1) *British Journal of Dermatology* 159–161, page 161.
62 M. Scherer, 'Regulating Artificial Intelligence Systems: Risks, Challenges Competencies and Strategies.' (2016) 29(2) *Harvard Journal of Law & Technology* 354–400, page 362.
63 W. Bateman, 'Algorithmic Decision-Making and Legality: Public Law Dimensions.' (2020) 94(7) *Australian Law Journal* 520–530.
64 M. Scherer, 'Regulating Artificial Intelligence Systems: Risks, Challenges Competencies and Strategies' (2016) 29(2) *Harvard Journal of Law & Technology* 354–400, page 378.
65 M. Guihot, A. Matthew, N. Suzor, 'Nudging Robots: Innovative Solutions to Regulate Artificial Intelligence.' (2017) 20(2) *Vanderbilt Journal of Entertainment and Technology Law* 385–456.
66 Office of the Australian Information Commission, Submission to Australian Human Rights Commission, Human Rights and Technology Inquiry Issues Paper (Web page, 19 October 2018).
67 European Parliament, 'The impact of the General Data Protection Regulation (GDPR) on Artificial Intelligence.' (2020) para 4.3.1.
68 Centre for Data Ethics and Innovation, *Review into Bias in Algorithmic Decision-making* (Centre for Data Ethics and Innovation, London, 2020).
69 M. Scherer, 'Regulating Artificial Intelligence Systems: Risks, Challenges Competencies and Strategies' (2016) 29(2) *Harvard Journal of Law & Technology* 354–400.
70 The Artificial Intelligence Act - proposed European law on artificial intelligence. 'The first law on AI by a major regulator anywhere.' see https://artificialintelligenceact.eu/
71 US Food and Drug Administration, 'Artificial Intelligence/Machine Learning (AI/ML)-Based, Software as a Medical Device (SaMD) Action Plan.' (2021).

72 M. Guihot, A. Matthew, N. Suzor, 'Nudging Robots: Innovative Solutions to Regulate Artificial Intelligence' (2017) 20(2) *Vanderbilt Journal of Entertainment and Technology Law* 385–456, page 389.
73 S. Jassar, et al. 'The Future of Artificial Intelligence in Medicine: Medical-legal Considerations for Health Leaders', (2022) 35(3) *Healthcare Management Forum*, 185–189.
74 D. Schönberger (2019) 'Artificial Intelligence in Healthcare: A Critical Analysis of the Legal and Ethical Implications.' (2019) 27(2) *International Journal of Law and Information Technology*, 171–203, page 201.
75 R. Maron et al., 'Artificial Intelligence and Its Effect on Dermatologists' Accuracy in Dermoscopic Melanoma Image Classification: Web-Based Survey Study.' (2020) 22(9) *Journal of Medical Internet Research* e18091.
76 J. Gomez Rossi, N. Rojas-Perilla, J. Krois, F. Schwendicke, 'Cost-effectiveness of Artificial Intelligence as a Decision-Support System Applied to the Detection and Grading of Melanoma, Dental Caries, and Diabetic Retinopathy.' 2022 5(3) *JAMA Network Open* e220269.
77 M. Law, J. Seah, G. Shih, 'Artificial Intelligence and Medical Imaging: Applications, Challenges and Solutions, (2021) 214(10) *Medical Journal of Australia* 450–452, page 450.
78 *Bolam v Friern Hospital Management Committee* [1957] 1 WLR 582.
79 T. Keren- Paz, T. Cockburn, A.El Haj, 'Regulating Innovative Treatments: Information, Risk Allocation and Redress,' (2019) 11(1) *Law, Innovation and Technology* 1–16.
80 J. Christian Bjerring, J. Busch, 'Artificial Intelligence and Patient-centered Decision Making' (2021) 34 *Philosophy & Technology* 349–371, page 349.
81 S. Russell, S. Hauert, R. Altman, M. Veloso, 'Robotics: Ethics of Artificial Intelligence.' (2015) 521 (7553) *Nature* 415–418.
82 M. Scherer, 'Regulating Artificial Intelligence Systems: Risks, Challenges Competencies and Strategies' (2016) 29(2) *Harvard Journal of Law & Technology* 354–400, page 366.
83 L. Faes et al., 'Automated Deep Learning Design for Medical Image Classification by Health-Care Professionals with No Coding Experience: A Feasibility Study' (2019) 1(5) *The Lancet Digital Health* e232–e242.
84 E. Crigger, K. Reinbold, C. Hanson, A. Kao, K. Blake, M. Irons, 'Trustworthy Augmented Intelligence in Health Care. (2022) 46(2) *Journal of Medical Systems* 12.

6
SYMPTOM CHECKER CHATBOTS AND INFORMED CONSENT

Case scenario

Sarah is a first-time mother to Alfie, who is now two months old. Alfie has a rash on his legs, and Sarah is concerned. She has looked up symptoms on Google and is worried that the rash may be the first signs of meningitis. Her partner is away, and Sarah knows there would be a long wait for an ambulance to arrive if she called the emergency number, and she is not sure if it is an emergency anyway. So, she seeks information on what to do using a Symptom Checker chatbot, anticipating that it will recommend a course of action she should take. In response to the automated "Hello, how can I help you?" she types in information about Alfie's age, health history, current symptoms and demographic information, including their home postcode. The advice she receives is to provide plenty of fluids, monitor Alfie's temperature, take him to the general practitioner as soon as possible and, if symptoms worsen, to the nearest emergency department. Alfie seems better the next day. However, subsequently, when Sarah logs into the computer she gets pop-up advertisements for nappies and formula milk products, and she feels there is no way of shutting off completely the sense of being observed.

Symptom checker chatbots provide a digital format for individuals to input health information, such as symptom duration and severity, and receive likely diagnoses and associated triage advice – recommendations for appropriate management. Chatbots give easy and timely access to health advice and may reduce the burden on frontline care services. However, for an effective service, users are required to divulge personal information, perhaps without thinking how this information may be used and with whom it may be shared. This chapter explores the role of informed consent for the collection and sharing of a user's health information and considers the readability of terms of use and the increasing length of privacy policies. The future proliferation of chatbots as an alternative or adjunct to clinical care requires reflection on the importance of human interaction in the provision of health information and care.

DOI: 10.4324/9781003220190-6

Introduction

What are chatbots?

> A chatbot is a digital technology application powered by artificial intelligence that simulates the conversation of another person.[1]

Conversing with a machine and even developing a relationship with one may seem far-fetched, but consider the 2013 film *Her*, set in a near future, in which a lonely writer develops a relationship' with an operating system named Samantha who is designed to meet his every need.[2] It has been said that "artificial agents may be a promising source of social support for humans"[3] and chatbots provide a way to address loneliness and social isolation which, during the global COVID-19 pandemic, had a major impact on wellbeing. A study of over 7000 adults' use of chatbots as an intervention to reduce social isolation and loneliness found that chatbots were perceived positively by most participants, and "results show a pattern of personifying the chatbot and assigning human traits to it such as being helpful, caring, open to listen, and non-judgmental."[4] *Replika* is a chatbot companion powered by artificial intelligence (AI) which can engage in naturalistic human communication and learn about the user through increased interactions. It has been shown to provide a "safe space in which users can discuss any topic without the fear of judgment or retaliation, increase positive affect through uplifting and nurturing messages, and provide helpful information/advice when normal sources of informational support are not available."[5] Chatbots/chatterbots (chat robots) are commonly used in commercial settings, enhancing the customer experience and increasing sales, and in the health context they are used in health education, diagnostics and mental health. *Woebot*, a therapy chatbot designed to deliver cognitive behavioural therapy through brief, daily conversations and mood tracking, has been shown to reduce symptoms of anxiety and depression.[6] Chatbots are already being used to provide advice and to triage healthcare services[7] and may be viewed as driving efficiency and convenience and promoting equitable access to healthcare, information and support.

Conversational agents are software-based systems that interact with humans via written or spoken natural language. A personality-adaptive conversational agent can tailor conversation to the style of the user "by automatically inferring personality traits from users, giving them the ability to adapt to the changing needs and states of users when establishing a personalized interaction with them."[8] Chatbots are an example of a conversational agent – they provide text-based communication in contrast to virtual assistants that rely on voice-based interaction.[9]

Chatbots interact with humans in real time and have a particular value in providing instant responses to health-related inquiries from individuals wishing to seek medical advice and an understanding of their symptoms at any time of the day or night.

> Chatbots can provide live feedback to help patients get an overview of their symptoms, become aware of their illness, triage and manage their conditions, and ultimately improve their health.[10]

A user is prompted to enter their symptoms and health information, and a chat function provides potential diagnosis(es) and options for action. Broad triage categories for symptom checkers range from life-threatening (where medical help is required immediately), urgent (see a general practitioner [GP]/go to an urgent care facility within a time frame), non-urgent (see a healthcare provider in the near future) and self-care (stay at home and rest, see a pharmacist).[11] The responsibility is then pushed onto users, and there is no check to see if they take the recommended action. The value of a chatbot symptom checker/triage service is realised if the user follows the chatbot's suggestions, and although there is limited evidence on this, it seems that people are more likely to seek further advice for more urgent conditions.[12]

Chatbots are now mainstream in the health sector, and the global healthcare chatbots market is set to reach USD 500 million by 2025.[13] The increasing demand for healthcare services, to some extent exacerbated by an ageing population, has put a burden on healthcare providers and given rise to long wait times for health appointments. In Western medicine the first point of contact a person has with the health system is usually through primary healthcare, which encompasses a range of services delivered outside the hospital. Primary healthcare professionals include GPs, nurses and other allied health professionals. Although effective primary care can avoid unnecessary hospitalisations, limitations on timely access to GP or cost may lead individuals to seek care in an emergency department. In Australia during 2020–2021, there were 8.8 million presentations to emergency departments in public hospitals,[14] and in 2019 the Productivity Commission reported that there were almost 3 million avoidable emergency department presentations where a GP would have been the most appropriate first point of call.[15] Chatbots are considered time-saving and useful platforms for triaging users to appropriate healthcare services[16] and can fill the gaps by providing instant responses to health-related enquiries, relieving pressure on healthcare providers. There has been a proliferation of such diagnostic chatbots around the world, and this technology has been adopted by some national health organisations, for example, *Symptom Checker* in Australia and *Asia MD* in Singapore, and in the United Kingdom *Babylon Health* was set up to reduce the burden on the 111 National Health Service (NHS) telephone hotline.[17]

Chatbots to provide health information

Of course, health information can be accessed from a multitude of sources – "knowledge regarding health and well-being is cobbled together from health care professionals, family, friends, books, newspapers, magazines, educational pamphlets, radio, television, and pharmaceutical advertisements."[18] The Internet is an accessible means of finding out answers to health issues, and there is widespread use of the Google search engine ('Dr Google') for assessing symptom severity. As far back as 2003 a study estimated that globally a minimum of 6.75 million health-related searches were conducted on the Web every day,[19] and in 2013 72% of US adults looked online for health information.[20] Research published in 2020 found that "approximately 5% of all internet searches are health related."[21]

Although an online search may be faster than having to answer questions in a symptom checker,[22] it can produce huge amounts of information, which can lead to frustration.[23] Health information online can use overly technical language, and the lack of quality requirements for publishing online content means that information provided may not always be delivered from reputable or trustworthy sources and users can become misinformed through inaccurate information.[24]

Symptom checker chatbots provide a form of triage and sit between a Google search for information and seeing a primary care physician (or seeking help through an emergency department), and for many they are the first point of contact for checking symptoms. Triage chatbots can empower users by providing reassurance and support through information,[25] but this requires a certain level of health literacy. Health literacy embraces the "cognitive and social skills" to obtain, understand and utilise information to promote health.[26] Cheng and Dunne note the importance that health information is presented at a readability level that accommodates the wide range of literacy skills among the general population.[27] In their study of the readability of Australian online health information, they found that almost 80% of Australian Internet users seek out health information online, yet "the readability of Australian health websites is above the average Australian levels of reading."[28]

Medical jargon can appear in chatbot questions, and if this creates difficulty in understanding users may input unhelpful or incorrect information. A study of chatbot-based symptom checkers showed that there is a need to increase the comprehensibility of probing questions, as a number of people do not have a sufficient health literacy,[29] although young adults have high technology literacy and trust towards online platforms.[30]

Consent to use of symptom checker chatbots

In a healthcare encounter information disclosed by the patient to the healthcare professional is used to diagnose and provide a treatment plan, and the patient will be informed of the risks and benefits of different options. An aspect of the duty of care of a healthcare professional is to provide information to the patient, and a failure to disclose to the requisite standard may give rise to a claim in negligence.

> There is now agreement throughout common law jurisdictions that the failure adequately to inform a patient of the risks, benefits, and alternatives to treatment (as distinguished from the complete failure to seek any patient consent for the treatment rendered) is a species of the law of negligence, not a part of the law of battery.[31]

The healthcare professional should disclose inherent risks and consequences of a proposed treatment and alternative options, including the likely outcomes if no treatment is received. This ideal of informed consent enables the patient to be part of the decision-making process so that they can determine for themselves what course to choose.[32]

In 1992 the High Court of Australia in *Rogers v. Whitaker*[33] considered the standard of care for disclosure. Reflecting on that case, Chalmers and Schwartz note,

> On the one hand, the patient-oriented theory provides that a physician has breached his legal duty to the patient if he fails to provide the information that a reasonable patient in the position of this patient would want to know under the circumstances i.e. information that such a patient would find material to make a decision about treatment. On the other hand, the physician-oriented theory provides that a physician has breached his legal duty to the patient if he fails to provide information that reasonable physicians do, in fact, disclose under the circumstances.[34]

The High Court of Australia opted for a patient-oriented standard – patients should be informed of risks that are meaningful to them, rather than merely being informed of statistically relevant risks. The provision of information can thus be seen as a means of addressing the imbalance of power between the informed and experienced doctor and the vulnerable patient and is founded on the ethical principle of respect for patient autonomy, and the law has reiterated this justification.

In 2004 the UK House of Lords, in *Chester v Afshar*,[35] acknowledged the importance of information as a necessary precursor to the exercise of patient autonomy,

> The law is designed to require doctors properly to inform their patients of the risks attendant on their treatment and to answer questions put to them as to that treatment and its dangers, such answers to be judged in the context of good professional practice, which has tended to a greater degree of frankness over the years, with more respect being given to patient autonomy.[36]

Ten years on, the UK Supreme Court in *Montgomery v Lanarkshire Health Board* said that patients are now "widely treated as consumers exercising choices."[37]

If the purpose of informed consent in a clinical context is to protect a healthcare professional from negligence and to promote patient autonomy, what role does it have for users of symptom checker chatbots, and what information should the user be provided and agree to? Users of these chatbots resemble consumers, even where the chatbot is free, and if they are then seen by a healthcare provider, they become a patient.[38] The user of a symptom checker is providing consent, not in the traditional sense of consent to treatment, but rather consent to how that data is used. Of course, doctors collect information from their patients in return for providing services for which they are paid, so handing over personal data may be seen as just the 'price' of a receiving a service from a chatbot in the same way as from a healthcare professional. But healthcare professionals are bound by legal and professional duties of confidentiality.

Weizenbaum found that people openly disclose personal information during human-machine interactions,[39] and so a lack of clear consent for the collection of personal information and how it is retained and used is concerning. Data collected through the chatbot is not just used by the algorithm to provide information about the likely cause of symptoms and the best way to respond, the data may also be used for a commercial benefit, and it is the commodification of online data by large international companies that is of concern. The use of cookies stored on a computer, mobile phone or other device enables personalised content and target advertising, and as noted by Allsop CJ in *Facebook Inc v Australian Information Commissioner*,[40]

> the acts done to collect, store, analyse, organise, distribute and deploy the information about people and their lives are integral to the methods of monetisation or extracting commercial value from the information. The business is not about the simple sale of goods whether tangible or intangible. It is about extracting value from information about people.[41]

In order to proceed with using the chatbot services, those logging online or using an app will be asked to consent to the terms of use, including a privacy policy, which will include provisions about how the data provided may be used. The readability of such terms is important to ensure that individuals do understand what happens to their data, but this is not evident in practice. Studies have found that readability of informed consent forms used in clinical trials are too complex to be understood by the general population.[42] The terms and conditions of Amazon Kindle (a site for e-books and audio books) amounted to 73,198 words (in 2017), which the Australian consumer advocacy group Choice found would take the average person nine hours to read in full.[43] The Babylon online terms of use[44] exceed 7500 words and provide that by accessing, using or registering with the Babylon app, the user agrees to be bound by the terms of use.

The privacy policy for Babylon Health[45] outlines the sorts of information they collect, including contact information, demographic information (gender and age) and health information (symptoms, risk factors, procedures and other health-related information entered). It also states how this information is shared and used by the company. Although this is explained in a chatbot's privacy policy, consent to the terms of use and the privacy policy is often 'take it or leave it,' and individuals do not have a choice if they wish to use the chatbot.

Decades ago, Lord Denning recognised the frustration of human and machine interaction in the context of machine-operated entry to a carpark,

> He cannot refuse it. He cannot get his money back. He may protest at the machine, even swear at it; but it will remain unmoved. He is committed beyond recall.[46]

The considerable imbalance in bargaining power between digital platforms and those who use them (consumers) was recognised by the Australian Competition and Consumer Commission in its inquiry into digital platforms.[47] Features of consent processes that degrade the quality of consent provided by consumers to the use of their data include; the use of 'clickwrap agreements' (where users are requested to "provide their consent to online terms and policies without requiring them to fully engage with them"),[48] 'take-it-or-leave-it terms,' and 'bundling of consents,' (where digital platforms ask consumers to enter into contracts "without giving the individual the opportunity to choose which collections, uses and disclosures they agree to and which they do not.")[49] These approaches to consent limit the ability of people to provide well-informed and freely given consent to the use and disclosure of their data collected through digital platforms.

Narayanan describes tracking our online information for targeted advertising as "manipulative and discriminatory"[50] and reinforces harmful stereotypes, and Sarah in our case scenario would surely agree.

> The data collection that enables targeted advertising involves an opaque surveillance infrastructure to which it's impossible to give meaningfully informed consent, and the resulting databases give a few companies too much power over individuals and over democracy.[51]

In the review of the Privacy Act 1988 (Cth),[52] the Australian Competition and Consumer Commission recommended that the definition of 'consent' should be updated to require a "clear affirmative act that is freely given, specific, unambiguous and informed."[53] It is interesting to note that new definitions of 'consent' have been put forward in respect of sexual offence provisions in legislation for some states in Australia. In 2022 New South Wales and the Australian Capital Territory passed affirmative consent laws as amendments to the Crimes Act, defining consent as a free and voluntary agreement which cannot be presumed, involving ongoing, mutual communication. This new approach could raise the bar for other areas of law requiring consent, including perhaps consent to terms of use for chatbots collecting personal data.

Privacy policies are also notoriously long and difficult to understand. Research by Wagner looking at 50,000 privacy policies of some of the most visited websites in the world found that "the average privacy policy nearly quadrupled in length between 2000 and 2021"[54] at an average of 4191 words long in March 2021 and "require more access to user data for the organisations that write them."[55] Privacy laws themselves may be the reason why privacy policies have become so long and inaccessible. Wagner found that the length of privacy policies ballooned around the time the European Union's General Data Protection Regulation came into effect (May 2018) and at the start of 2020 when California introduced similar laws which in fact were designed to protect consumers' data.

The philosopher Onora O'Neill identifies informed consent procedures as allowing patients to exercise choice and providing assurance that patients and others are not deceived or coerced.[56] Individuals can decide whether or not to proceed with use of chatbots based on the terms and conditions and privacy policy offered, but this does not seem like an exercise of a "free power of choice"[57] given the potential vulnerability of those using symptom checkers and their lack of bargaining power around the use of personal data. The case scenario describes Sarah in this position – she wants quick and reliable health information to understand how to appropriately care for her son, and the options of waiting for an ambulance or a visit to the emergency department at a (local?) hospital look less appealing than a click and consent option. Where chatbot services are provided by governments as a method of triaging for treatment in a public-run health system, the consent to use of data should look less like a consumer-driven process.

Benefits and limitations of chatbots

There are many benefits to chatbots; they meet demand where there is a lack of qualified human health professionals, they provide a 24/7 service, give replicable answers (provide the same outcome in response to the same inputs) and are non-judgmental.[58] Interestingly patients commonly withhold medically relevant information from their clinicians, which may impact on the provision of best patient care.

> Patients are particularly afraid to disclose personal, sensitive or stigmatizing information. Unfortunately, such information can be the most important for them to disclose to healthcare professionals.[59]

People seem to be more willing to share personal information with a robot because they can say things without fear of negative evaluation. The anonymity of symptom checker chatbots may have some benefits where people want information on medical conditions which are perceived to have privacy issues and which carry a sense of stigma. However, chatbots may not be seen as appropriate where there is a need for empathy in response to an input of symptoms, notably in mental health.[60]

Effective communication relies on recognition of non-verbal emotional cues and may be more about *how* communication happened than *what* is communicated.[61] A machine is effective at providing information, but the development of a therapeutic alliance, which is so fundamental to the provision of medical care, relies on human openness and connection. Nevertheless, in a study that examined patients' experiences using the symptom checker *Isabel*, over 90% (274/304) reported receiving useful information for their health problems and 91.4% (278/304 reported that they would use the symptom checker again.[62] A UK-based study found that although there were no gender differences in whether individuals were more likely to use a symptom checker, there were age differences – 74% of people aged 18–24 years old would use a symptom checker compared to only 51% of those aged between 55 and 69 years, with a third of that age group stating that they would rather see a doctor or a nurse.[63]

Chatbot accuracy

There may be a belief that "algorithms can make more objective, robust and evidence-based clinical decisions (in terms of diagnosis, prognosis or treatment recommendations) compared to human healthcare providers,"[64] but what is the evidence for their accuracy? A fair assessment of the accuracy of symptom checker chatbots would be to compare them against the gold-standard performance of human doctors' history taking and diagnosis. A study of the Babylon system using case vignettes found that it was able to "produce differential diagnoses with precision and recall comparable to that of doctors, and in some cases exceeded human level performance,"[65] although this evaluation was done by the company that developed the system.[66] These findings can be compared with a study which assessed 23 free online commercial symptom checker apps using standardised patient vignettes, which highlighted significant variation in clinical accuracy.[67] The 23 symptom checkers provided the correct diagnosis first in 34% of standardized patient evaluations, and appropriate triage advice was provided in 57% of cases, illustrating deficiencies in diagnostic and triage capabilities.[68] If chatbot triage advice directs those with non-urgent ailments to hospital emergency departments unnecessarily, this "will exacerbate the unnecessary use of healthcare services."[69] The accuracy and utility of symptom checkers may depend on relevance to location; for example, Ross River virus infection is a condition specific to Australia, which is likely not programmed in a symptom checker developed overseas.[70]

Trust and chatbots

Trust from both patients and clinicians in digital health technologies such as smartphone sensor data and chatbots remains low, particularly in respect to data sharing.[71]

> Trust is an important factor that influences the use of chatbots . . . users will be reluctant to use chatbots if they do not trust them.[72]

For chatbots and any AI virtual assistant to have a positive impact on overstretched healthcare systems, they must be trusted.[73] In Australia an automated system was used to identify overpayments made to social security recipients, called *Robodebt*. Many people were incorrectly identified as having been overpaid and welfare claimants were then chased for non-existent debts and told they had to prove the calculation was incorrect. The Federal Court of Australia decided that this system was unlawful.[74] The organisation that ran the *Robodebt* program then administered Australia's national coronavirus helpline, which directed callers to medical information about COVID-19. It is key for governments, private companies and AI designers to think about trust in electronically mediated interactions; otherwise, people will not engage with them, resulting in a waste of resources.

Nissenbaum considers how trust or confidence can be engendered in an online world.[75] Although trust in the technical issues and safety of users' information is important, she argues that trust is broader than just security in an online system and encompasses social, cultural and moral issues. Luhmann sees trust as "a mechanism that reduces complexity and enables people to cope with the high levels of uncertainty and complexity of contemporary life."[76] He contends that if people were faced with a full range of alternatives and calculated all possible outcomes of all possible decision nodes, they would be overwhelmed by uncertainty and indecision. People use symptom checker chatbots to help filter out the different possibilities for their symptoms and concerns and to receive appropriate triage recommendations. The word triage comes from French, meaning to 'separate out,' and is used in military terms to assess the wounded on the battlefield. So, in this way chatbots provide this filter mechanism, and in our case scenario, Sarah is trusting that the chatbot will accurately diagnose Alfie's condition and inform her of the most appropriate action to take.

Trust or confidence is perhaps more used in the context of human relationships, and even in impersonal and formal relationships, such as that between health professionals and patients, "trust plays a critical role."[77] This is perhaps particularly true for patients, who experience physical pain, uncertainty of outcome and loss of control. Here perhaps is the double whammy of chatbots – those who use them are seeking understanding and support, like Sarah, who is in a vulnerable position vis-a-vis her lack of knowledge and her concern for her child, but they need to put their trust in the security of the system and the accuracy of any diagnosis.

A barrier to trust might be uncertainty about the identity and personal characteristics of the person we are dealing with. The first chatbot, developed in the 1960s by MIT scientist Joseph Weizenbaum, was called ELIZA based on its cinematic counterpart, Eliza Doolittle. It used a simple computer program to mimic a psychotherapist asking open-ended questions, and participants were able to converse about themselves and their lives, so that "many people actually believed that they were interacting with a live therapist."[78] Current chatbots may have features which indicate a persona – some have names such as 'Ada' and 'Health Buddy' or a virtual 'face' and where symptom checkers ask for the age and gender of the user, this can give the impression that it is more personalised. Some of the key elements for chatbots to be considered trustworthy is their ability to function effectively (with expertise) and fairly (without unjustified bias) and that the data inputted in the chatbot symptom checker is used in a manner that the user understands and consents to.

Trustworthy AI systems must be able to produce the same results under the same conditions, and it is this notion of reproducibility that could be said to put knowledge into the 'scientific' rather than 'opinion' domain.[79] Chatbots thus have rigid and formal systems and are "locked in certain a priori models of calculation."[80] Diagnosis by a doctor may be quite algorithmic in nature, such as following criteria set out in the *Diagnostic and Statistical Manual* for the diagnosis of psychological disorders, but much of clinical decision making is characterised by probabilities rather than certainty. The term 'differential diagnosis' describes a situation where symptoms indicate more than one condition and additional tests are needed to make an accurate diagnosis.

> Encountering the unexpected is an occupational hazard in clinical practice. Unlike artificial systems, experienced doctors recognise the fact that diagnoses and prognoses are always marked by varying degrees of uncertainty. They are aware that some diagnoses may turn out to be wrong or that some of their treatments may not lead to the cures expected. Thus, medical diagnosis and decision-making require "prudence."[81]

Aristotle's account of phronesis has been interpreted as "the practical wisdom needed in medicine to promote good judgement in morally complex situations."[82] A healthcare professional exercising prudence/phronesis/practical wisdom can use a flexible interpretation to determine the best course of action depending on the circumstances, and this includes the capacity to correct wrong choices and mistakes.

People increasingly take an active role in informing themselves about their health and checking symptoms online. Healthcare professionals may potentially feel threatened by patients coming in with information they have sourced online, but such information seeking is "generally seen as a way to have a more collaborative relationship with patients."[83] But who or what view takes priority? If a person gets a diagnosis from a chatbot symptom checker and their GP takes a different view, should decision making default to an algorithm? Algorithm-based triage tends to be risk averse, resulting in number of users being inappropriately advised to request an urgent appointment with their GP or seek care at an emergency unit.[84] Doctors may have to spend time convincing their patients of a chatbot misdiagnosis, potentially creating tensions in the relationship.[85]

AI must have data with which to learn from, and large amounts of data are used in training the software and development of algorithms. Symptom checker chatbots, such as the *Doctor Bot*, a mobile-based medical consultation platform, use machine learning, with data inputted from medical literature and clinical cases to process users' inquiries and provide personalised medical advice.[86] One key ethical challenge is the potential bias in AI models. Some bias may be operationally justified where it prioritises certain information as part of performing the desired task of the algorithm, and this may include information of age/frailty if this is necessary to triage for care.[87] Some chatbot symptom checkers overlook some personal information, such as race, although this may be relevant when making a diagnosis; for example, sickle cell disease is strongly correlated with certain racial groups.[88] The Correctional Offender Management Profiling for Alternative Sanctions (COMPAS) is an example of AI bias in the US justice system where racial disparities from the use of AI risk assessment tools illustrated bias connected to physical traits and postcode. As AI learns iteratively from the data inputted, if that data is biased towards certain population groups, it will not provide reliable and repeatable decisions that are of value to everyone. Biases can arise where the data used for training the AI is not representative of the target population or where data is inadequate or incomplete.[89] Any inherent bias in data it uses risks the accuracy and efficacy of the triage recommendations and can lead to medical error. As Australia's chief scientist, Dr Cathy Foley, noted, "an algorithm might be excellent at predicting heart attack survival in men in Sydney's eastern suburbs, but relatively poor at predicting risk in their female partners, or in men from Singapore or São Paulo."[90] Bias and AI is explored further in Chapter 5.

Future development of chatbots

Symptom checker chatbots process information to provide triage advice. But chatbots are being developed to provide therapeutic interventions, such as psychotherapy. Chatbots have been used in mental health care by conducting treatments such as cognitive behavioural therapy,[91] and it has been suggested that at a future time when AI is more refined, chatbots could be effectively used to triage mental health services, thereby meeting the rising demand. The chatbot would provide first-line mental healthcare services, with users of chatbots then deciding for themselves if they additionally needed to see a human therapist. But it is the personal interaction between clinician and patient that is the biggest predictor of the effectiveness in psychotherapy[92] with the need for clinical skills such as observing patient behaviour and responding to the individual needs. Those with poor mental health often lack self-advocacy to request a connection with a therapist through such a chatbot. If language is a significant means to understanding people's experiences and communicate the need for therapeutic interventions, this personalised response is currently lacking with chatbots. Brown and Halpern consider that the capacity of chatbots to tailor care to the individual's circumstances is a key challenge to the ethical principle of beneficence, which requires that clinical empathy should be maximised in all medical caregiving interactions.[93]

Conclusion

Agency and the exercise of autonomy may be compromised by illness or lack of medical knowledge. Providing information empowers people to make rational choices, and chatbots respond to users' needs and preferences, guiding the interaction and information provision. Symptom checker chatbots have the potential to reduce costs and improve access to appropriate healthcare, but their effectiveness depends on their accuracy and users' perception of them. The machine learning process of symptom checker chatbots means that their diagnostic accuracy will improve over time, and although currently some achieve a good level of accuracy, there is a wide variation between them and "overall performance is significantly below what would be accepted in any other medical field."[94] Symptom checkers should reduce the burden on healthcare services by decreasing the need for clinical care when individuals can self-manage, but the automated advice may not be safe or clinically appropriate. It seems that the AI takes a risk-adverse approach, and some chatbot symptom checkers may in fact encourage users to seek professional care where self-care would suffice, thus in fact putting pressure on an overstretched health system. Barriers for using symptom checkers includes digital literacy and trust in the way collected data is used. Readability of terms and conditions and a reframing of 'consent' to require a clear agreement to use of data is a way to rebalance the relationship between user and provider.

The social acceptability of AI systems may be compromised by the concept of 'artificial,' which may be perceived as inferior, and it has been proposed that health chatbots should be designed to take into account user experience and patients' concerns to achieve the best uptake and utilisation.[95] How the use of chatbots transforms and impacts on traditional healthcare practices remains to be seen. Currently chatbots support healthcare provision, rather than replacing experienced trained professionals, but trust and understanding flow from human interaction, and as yet, chatbots cannot be programmed to provide clinical empathy.

Notes

1. C. Grové, 'Co-developing a Mental Health and Wellbeing Chatbot with and for Young People,' (2021) 11. *Frontiers in Psychiatry* 606041, page 3.
2. The film was written, directed and co-produced by Spike Jonze and starred Joaquin Phoenix. www.imdb.com/title/tt1798709/.
3. V. Ta, C. Griffith, C. Boatfield et al. 'User Experiences of Social Support from Companion Chatbots in Everyday Contexts: Thematic Analysis' (2020) 22(3) *Journal of Medical Internet Research* e16235, page 1.
4. G. Dosovitsky, E. Bunge, 'Bonding with Bot: User Feedback on a Chatbot for Social Isolation.' (2021) 3 *Frontiers in Digital Health* 735053, page 10.
5. V. Ta, C. Griffith, C. Boatfield et al, 'User Experiences of Social Support from Companion Chatbots in Everyday Contexts: Thematic Analysis.' (2020) 22(3) *Journal of Medical Internet Research* e16235.
6. K. Kara Fitzpatrick, A. Darcy, M. Vierhile 'Delivering Cognitive Behavior Therapy to Young Adults with Symptoms of Depression and Anxiety Using a Fully Automated Conversational Agent (Woebot): A Randomized Controlled Trial.' (2017) 4(2) *JMIR Mental Health* e19.
7. J. Parviainen, J. Rantala, 'Chatbot Breakthrough in the 2020s? An Ethical Reflection on the Trend of Automated Consultations in Health Care.' (2022) 25 *Medicine, Health Care and Philosophy* 61–71.
8. R. Ahmad, D. Siemon, U. Gnewuch, S. Robra Bissantz, 'Designing Personality-Adaptive Conversational Agents for Mental Health Care.' (2022) 24 *Information Systems Frontiers* 923–943, page 924.
9. X. Fan, D. Chao, Z. Zhang, D. Wang, X. Li, F. Tian, 'Utilization of Self-Diagnosis Health Chatbots in Real-World Settings: Case Study.' (2021) 23(1) *Journal of Medical Internet Research* e19928.
10. X. Fan, D. Chao, Z. Zhang, D. Wang, X. Li, F. Tian, 'Utilization of Self-diagnosis Health Chatbots in Real-world Settings: Case Study' (2021) 23(1) *Journal of Medical Internet Research* e19928, page 2.
11. A. Baker, Y. Perov, K. Middleton et al., 'Comparison of Artificial Intelligence and Human Doctors for the Purpose of Triage and Diagnosis.' (202) 3 *Frontiers in Artificial Intelligence* 543405.
12. D. Chambers, A. Cantrell, M. Johnson et al., 'Digital and Online Symptom Checkers and Health Assessment/triage Services for Urgent Health Problems: Systematic Review.' (2019) 9 *BMJ Open* e027743.
13. Market Research Report 2021, 'Healthcare Chatbots Market, by Component (Software and Services), Deployment Model (On-premise and Cloud-based), Application and End User - Global Forecast to 2027' https://www.researchandmarkets.com/reports/5438376/healthcare-chatbots-market-by-component.
14. Australian Government, Australian Institute of Health and Welfare, Emergency department care 2020–21 Australian hospital statistics. www.aihw.gov.au/reports-data/myhospitals/sectors/emergency-department-care.
15. M. Liotta, 'New studies examine Australian ED presentations', *News GP,* 1 March 2019.
16. T. Nadarzynski, O. Miles, A. Cowie, D. Ridge, 'Acceptability of Artificial Intelligence (AI)-Led Chatbot Services in Healthcare: A Mixed-methods Study.' (2019) 5 *Digital Health* 1–12.
17. J. Turnbull, C. Pope, A. Rowsell et al., 'The Work, Workforce, Technology and Organisational Implications of the '111' Single Point of Access Telephone Number for Urgent (non-emergency) Care: A Mixed-methods Case Study.' (2014) *NIHR Journals Library*, PMID: 27466643.
18. B. Swire-Thompson, D. Lazer, 'Public Health and Online Misinformation: Challenges and Recommendations.' (2020) 41 *Annual Review of Public Health* 433–451, page 435.

19 G. Eysenbach, C. Köhler, 'What is the Prevalence of Health-related Searches on the World Wide Web? Qualitative and Quantitative Analysis of Search Engine Queries on the Internet.' (2003) *Archive of "AMIA Annual Symposium Proceedings"* 225–229.
20 S. Fox, M. Duggan, Pew Research Center, January 2013, 'Health Online 2013.' Internet and American Life Project.
21 B. Swire-Thompson, D. Lazer, 'Public Health and Online Misinformation: Challenges and Recommendations' (2020) 41 *Annual Review of Public Health* 433–451, page 435.
22 S. Aboueid, S. Meyer, J. Wallace et al., 'Young Adults' Perspectives on the Use of Symptom Checkers for Self-Triage and Self-Diagnosis: Qualitative Study.' (2021) 7(1) *JMIR Public Health and Surveillance* e22637.
23 S. LaValley, M. Kiviniemi, E. Gage-Bouchard, 'Where People Look for Online Health Information.' (2017) 34(2) *Health Information & Libraries Journal* 146–155.
24 B. Swire-Thompson, D. Lazer, 'Public Health and Online Misinformation: Challenges and Recommendations' (2020) 41 *Annual Review of Public Health* 433–451.
25 R. Pelzang, 'Time to Learn: understanding patient-centred care.'(2010) 19(14) *British Journal of Nursing*, 912–917.
26 D. Nutbeam (2000) 'Health Literacy as a Public Health Goal: A Challenge for Contemporary Health Education and Communication Strategies into the 21st Century.' (2000) 15(3) *Health Promotion International* 259–267, page 263.
27 C. Cheng, M. Dunne, 'Health Literacy and the Internet: A Study on the Readability of Australian Online Health Information.' (2015) 39 *Australian and New Zealand Journal of Public Health* 309–14.
28 C. Cheng, M. Dunne, 'Health Literacy and the Internet: A Study on the Readability of Australian Online Health Information' (2015) 39 *Australian and New Zealand Journal of Public Health* 309–314, page 309.
29 Y. You, X. Gui, 'Self-diagnosis through AI-enabled Chatbot-based Symptom Checkers: User Experiences and Design Considerations' (2020) *2020 AMIA Annual Symposium* 1354–1363.
30 S. Aboueid, S. Meyer, J. Wallace et al. "Young Adults' Perspectives on the Use of Symptom Checkers for Self-triage and Self-diagnosis: Qualitative Study' (2021) 7(1) *JMIR Public Health and Surveillance* e22637.
31 D. Chalmers, R. Schwartz, 'Rogers v. Whitaker and Informed Consent in Australia: A Fair Dinkum Duty of Disclosure.' (1993) 1(2) *Medical Law Review* 139–159, page 143.
32 C. Johnston, G. Holt, 'The Legal and Ethical Implications of Therapeutic Privilege – Is It Ever Justified to withhold Treatment Information from a Competent Patient?' 2006 1(3) *Clinical Ethics* 146–151.
33 *Rogers v Whitaker* 1992 HCA 58, (1992) CLR 479.
34 D. Chalmers, R. Schwartz, 'Rogers v. Whitaker and Informed Consent in Australia: A Fair Dinkum Duty of Disclosure' (1993) 1(2) *Medical Law Review* 139–159, page 143.
35 *Chester v Afshar* [2004] UKHL 41.
36 *Chester v Afshar* [2004] UKHL 41 Lord Steyn, para 65.
37 *Montgomery v Lanarkshire Health Board* [2015] UKSC 11, Lord Kerr and Lord Reed, para 75.
38 See General Medical Council. *Good Medical Practice* (General Medical Council, London, 2013), para 1 "Good doctors make the care of their patients their first concern."
39 J. Weizenbaum, *Computer Power and Human Reason: From Judgment to Calculation* (San Francisco, CA: W. H. Freeman & Company, 1976) at 268–69.
40 *Facebook Inc v Australian Information Commissioner* 2022 FCAFC 9.
41 *Facebook Inc v Australian Information Commissioner* 2022 FCAFC 9. Allsop CJ, para 3.
42 A. Samadi, F. Asghari, 'Readability of Informed Consent Forms in Clinical Trials Conducted in a Skin Research Center.' (2016) 3(9) *Journal of Medical Ethics and History of Medicine* 7.

43 E. Hunt, 'Amazon Kindle's Terms 'Unreasonable' and would take Nine Hours to Read,' *The Guardian*, 2017.
44 Babylon Terms of Use, Effective Date: August 22, 2022.
45 Babylon Privacy Policy 2021.
46 *Thornton v Shoe Lane Parking Ltd* 1970 EWCA Civ 2, Lord Denning MR.
47 Australian Competition and Consumer Commission, (2019) Digital Platforms Inquiry, Final Report.
48 Australian Competition and Consumer Commission, (2019) Digital Platforms Inquiry, Final Report, page 615.
49 Australian Competition and Consumer Commission, (2019) Digital Platforms Inquiry, Final Report, page 400.
50 A. Narayanan, 'When the Business model *is* the privacy violation. *Freedom to Tinker.* (Princeton Center for Information Technology Policy, Apr 12, 2018) https://freedom-to-tinker.com/2018/04/12/when-the-business-model-is-the-privacy-violation.
51 A. Narayanan, 'When the Business Model *Is* the Privacy Violation,' *Freedom to Tinker* (Princeton Center for Information Technology Policy, Apr 12, 2018) https://freedom-to-tinker.com/2018/04/12/when-the-business-model-is-the-privacy-violation.
52 The review of the Privacy Act 1988 (Cth) by the Australian Government was a response to the Australian Competition and Consumer Commission's Digital Platforms Inquiry Final Report.
  The Attorney-General's Department published the Privacy Act Review Issues Paper in 2020 outlining the terms of reference and subsequently the Privacy Act Review Discussion Paper in 2021.
53 Australian Government, Attorney-General's Department, Privacy Act Review, Discussion Paper, October 2021, page 76.
54 I. Wagner, 'Privacy Policies Get Longer and Harder to Read.'(2022) *New Scientist*, 12 February 2022, 14.
55 I. Wagner, 'Privacy Policies Get Longer and Harder to Read' (2022) *New Scientist*, 12 February 2022, 14.
56 O. O'Neill, 'Accountability, Trust and Informed Consent in Medical Practice and Research' (2004) 4(3) *Clinical Medicine* 269–276.
57 O. O'Neill, 'Accountability, Trust and Informed Consent in Medical Practice and Research' (2004) 4(3) *Clinical Medicine* 269–276, page 274.
58 See L. del Giacco, T. Anguera, S. Salcuni, 'The Action of Verbal and Non-verbal Communication in the Therapeutic Alliance Construction: A Mixed Methods Approach to Assess the Initial Interactions with Depressed Patients.' (2020) 11 *Frontiers in Psychology* 234.
59 G. Lucas, J. Gratch, A. King, L. Morency. 'It's Only a Computer: Virtual Humans Increase Willingness to Disclose,' (2014) 37 *Computers in Human Behavior* 94–100, page 94.
60 T. Nadarzynski, O. Miles, A. Cowie, D. Ridge, 'Acceptability of Artificial Intelligence (AI)-Led Chatbot Services in Healthcare: A Mixed-methods Study' (2019) 5 *Digital Health* 1–12.
61 L. del Giacco, T. Anguera, S. Salcuni, 'The Action of Verbal and Non-verbal Communication in the Therapeutic Alliance Construction: A Mixed Methods Approach to Assess the Initial Interactions with Depressed Patients' (2020) 11 *Frontiers in Psychology* 234.
62 A. Meyer, T. Giardina C. Spitzmueller et al., 'Patient Perspectives on the Usefulness of an Artificial Intelligence-Assisted Symptom Checker: Cross-Sectional Survey Study.' (2020) 22(1) *Journal of Medical Internet Research*, e14679.
63 National Reports Library, 'Using Technology to Ease the Burden on Primary Care,' *Healthwatch Enfield*, 2019.
64 J. Morley, C. Machado, C. Burr et al. 'The Debate on the Ethics of AI in Health Care: a Reconstruction and Critical Review, (2019) (Unpublished). https://philpapers.org/archive/MORTDO-58.pdf page 7.
65 A. Baker, Y. Perov, K. Middleton et al, 'A Comparison of Artificial Intelligence and Human Doctors for the Purpose of Triage and Diagnosis.' (2020) 3 *Frontiers in Artificial Intelligence* 543405 page 4.
66 'Sixty seconds on . . . GP chatbot.' *BMJ* 2018;362: k2897.

67 H. Semigran, J. Linder, C. Gidengil, A. Mehotra, 'Evaluation of Symptom Checkers for Self-Diagnosis and Triage: Audit Study.' (2015) 351 *BMJ* h3480.
68 H. Semigran, J. Linder, C. Gidengil, A. Mehotra, 'Evaluation of Symptom Checkers for Self-diagnosis and Triage: Audit Study' (2015) 351 *BMJ* h3480.
69 W. Wallace, C. Chan, S. Chidambaram et al. 'The Diagnostic and Triage Accuracy of Digital and Online Symptom Checker Tools: A Systematic Review' (2022) 5(1) *Digital Medicine* 118.
70 M. Hill, M. Sim, B. Mills, 'The Quality of Diagnosis and Triage Advice Provided by Free Online Symptom Checkers and Apps in Australia' (2020) 212(11) *Medical Journal of Australia* 514–519.
71 John Torous et al., 'The Growing Field of Digital Psychiatry: Current Evidence and the Future of Apps, Social Media, Chatbots, and Virtual Reality' (2021) 20(3) *World Psychiatry* 318–335.
72 A. Dennis, A. Kim, M. Rahimi, S. Ayabakan, 'User Reactions to COVID-19 Screening Chatbots from Reputable Providers.' (2020) 27(11) *Journal of the American Medical Informatics Association*, 1727–1731, page 1728.
73 A. Baker, Y. Perov, K. Middleton et al. 'A Comparison of Artificial Intelligence and Human Doctors for the Purpose of Triage and Diagnosis' (2020) 3 *Frontiers in Artificial Intelligence* 543405, page 1.
74 *Prygodicz v Commonwealth of Australia* [2020] FCA 1454. In August 2022, the Royal Commission into the Robodebt Scheme was established.
75 H. Nissenbaum, 'Securing Trust Online: Wisdom or Oxymoron?' (2001) 81(3) *Boston University Law Review* 101–131.
76 N. Luhmann, Trust: A Mechanism for the Reduction of Social Complexity, in Trust and Power: Two works by Niklas Luhmann 8 (photo. reprint 1988) (1979) at 25.
77 H. Nissenbaum, 'Securing Trust Online: Wisdom or Oxymoron?' (2001) 81(3) *Boston University Law Review* 101–131, page 106.
78 I. Kerr, 'Bots, Babes and the Californication of Commerce,' (2003–2004) 1 *University of Ottawa Law & Technology Journal* 285–324, footnote 92.
79 D. Matthews, 'Epistemic Humility'. In: van Gigch J.P. (eds) *Wisdom, Knowledge, and Management. C. West Churchman and Related Works Series*, vol 2 (Springer, New York, NY, 2006), page 107.
80 J. Parviainen, J. Rantala, 'Chatbot Breakthrough in the 2020s? An Ethical Reflection on the Trend of Automated Consultations in Health Care' (2022) 25 *Medicine, Health Care and Philosophy* 61–71, page 65.
81 J. Parviainen, J. Rantala, 'Chatbot Breakthrough in the 2020s? An Ethical Reflection on the Trend of Automated Consultations in Health Care' (2022) 25 *Medicine, Health Care and Philosophy* 61–71, page 62.
82 Parviainen, J. Rantala, 'Chatbot Breakthrough in the 2020s? An Ethical Reflection on the Trend of Automated Consultations in Health Care' (2022) 25 *Medicine, Health Care and Philosophy* 61–71, page 62.
83 B. Swire-Thompson, D. Lazer, 'Public Health and Online Misinformation: Challenges and Recommendations' (2020) 41 *Annual Review of Public Health* 433–451, page 443.
84 D. Chambers, A. Cantrell, M. Johnson et al. 'Digital and Online Symptom Checkers and Health Assessment/triage Services for Urgent Health Problems: Systematic Review' (2019) 9 *BMJ Open* e027743.
85 J. Parviainen, J. Rantala, 'Chatbot Breakthrough in the 2020s? An Ethical Reflection on the Trend of Automated Consultations in Health Care' (2022) 25 *Medicine, Health Care and Philosophy* 61–71.
86 X. Fan, D. Chao, Z. Zhang, D. Wang, X. Li, F. Tian, 'Utilization of Self-diagnosis Health Chatbots in Real-world Settings: Case Study' (2021) 23(1) *Journal of Medical Internet Research* e19398.
87 UK House of Lords Select Committee on Artificial Intelligence, 'AI in the UK: Ready, Willing and Able?' House of Lords Paper No 100, Session 2017–19 (2018) para 111.

88 Y. You, X. Gui, 'Self-diagnosis through AI-enabled Chatbot-based Symptom Checkers: User Experiences and Design Considerations' (2020) *2020 AMIA Annual Symposium* 1354–1363.
89 S. Reddy, S. Allan, S. Coghlan, P. Cooper, 'A Governance Model for the Application of AI in Health Care,' (2020) 27(3) *Journal of the American Medical Informatics Association* 491–497.
90 C. Foley, 'Why We Need to Think about Diversity and Ethics in AI,' 2022 *Impact Magazine*, January 2022.
91 A. Abd-alrazaq, M. Alajlani, Al. Alalwan, et al., 'An Overview of the Features of Chatbots in Mental Health: A Scoping Review.' (2019) 132 *International Journal of Medical Informatics*, 103978.
92 J. Brown, J. Halpern, 'AI Chatbots Cannot Replace Human Interactions in the Pursuit of More Inclusive Mental Healthcare.' (2021) 1 *SSM – Mental Health* 100017, page 1.
93 J. Brown, J. Halpern, 'AI Chatbots Cannot Replace Human Interactions in the Pursuit of More Inclusive Mental Healthcare' (2021) 1 *SSM – Mental Health* 100017.
94 A. Ceney, S. Tolond, A. Glowinski et al., 'Accuracy of Online Symptom Checkers and the Potential Impact on Service Utilisation.' (2021) 16(7) *PLoS ONE* e0254088, page 2 of 16.
95 T. Nadarzynski, O. Miles, A. Cowie, D. Ridge, 'Acceptability of Artificial Intelligence (AI)-Led Chatbot Services in Healthcare: A Mixed-methods Study' (2019) 5 *Digital Health* 1–12.

7
TELEHEALTH

What has been learned through the COVID-19 pandemic?

Case scenarios

Mr Robertson is a farmer living on a remote cattle station in the Northern Territory, Australia. He and his wife live hundreds of kilometres away from the nearest healthcare centre and thousands of kilometres from a public hospital. Mr Robertson was diagnosed with chronic osteoarthritis by his general practitioner (GP) during a visit to the practice five years ago, and his condition has been monitored and well managed by the GP and specialist at the hospital through telephone consultations on a regular basis since then.

Their son Archie is in his forties and lives in Western Sydney. In August 2021 during a COVID-19 lockdown, he was concerned he had contracted COVID-19 and had a video conference with his GP, who made suggestions for care and treatment. Archie's teenage daughter, Penny, has not been able to attend school or see her friends during an extended period of lockdown, and she has been feeling lonely and overwhelmed. Penny has a mental health care plan and has a series of telehealth appointments with a counsellor, which she has found helpful and supportive.

These scenarios illustrate the value of accessibility to healthcare via telehealth. Health consultations conducted remotely via telephone or video conferencing enable people to get timely support where geographical location or COVID-19 lockdowns would otherwise present barriers.

Introduction

The novel coronavirus COVID-19 was first identified in Wuhan province, China, in December 2019, and on 12 March 2020, the World Health Organization declared the COVID-19 outbreak a pandemic, leading to national lockdown policies around the world in order to minimise transmission. Before the pandemic telemedicine had been used particularly in general practice, allowing patients to consult

DOI: 10.4324/9781003220190-7

with doctors and nurses via a telephone call or through video conferencing. The uptake of telemedicine was arguably slow and fragmented[1] until the COVID-19 pandemic, which necessitated a change in the delivery of healthcare to provide continued access to care whilst complying with government lockdowns and to avoid transmission of the virus through face-to-face care. Telehealth has the potential to empower patients – they can remain in the comfort of their own home and save time and the travel costs of attending appointments. Improvements in broadband speeds and video communication technology mean that video consultations are more accessible – but not for all. Telemedicine may exacerbate inequalities in access to healthcare, and it certainly impacts on the doctor-patient relationship.

Telehealth during the COVID-19 pandemic has provided evidence of its effectiveness in delivery of timely care and reducing patient-patient and patient-clinician transmission of coronavirus, indicating the potential to embed its use post-pandemic. But the human interaction of consultation is an important part of healthcare delivery, and we may have concerns if there is a significant shift away from in-person consultations.

In this chapter I consider the meaning and use of telehealth, and my focus is on video conferencing as an example of telemedicine. I explore the benefits and disadvantages of video consultations, implications on the therapeutic relationship and the impact on health disparities for vulnerable members of society.

Telehealth: meaning and history

'Telehealth' refers to the use of technology in medicine and describes health services provided through telecommunication, including the exchange of health information.[2] 'Telemedicine' has a narrower scope and focusses on the delivery of clinical services through remote means – although the terms telemedicine and telehealth seem to be used interchangeably. The World Health Organization has adopted the following definition of telemedicine, whilst recognising that it evolves with technological advancements and the changing health needs and contexts of societies,

> The delivery of health care services, where distance is a critical factor, by all health care professionals using information and communication technologies for the exchange of valid information for diagnosis, treatment and prevention of disease and injuries, research and evaluation, and for the continuing education of health care providers, all in the interests of advancing the health of individuals and their communities.[3]

Through telemedicine medical practitioners can facilitate real-time patient care irrespective of distance. It includes live and real-time telephone and video consultations between a healthcare professional and the patient, sometimes in conjunction with other health practitioners, enabling the health provider to take a history and observe a limited physical exam conducted by the patient following directions. In the United Kingdom there is an increasing trend for general practices to use 'e-consultations,' where the patient goes logs onto their GP's website, types the health issue and then answers various questions. The computer program creates a short summary which is sent to the general practice for triage. The GP/administrative team can decide whether to invite the patient for an appointment, send a text with a plan or make a prescription. E-consultations in theory save time for GPs but in practice lead to an increase in workload.

Even as recently as 2010 the World Health Organization considered that the field of telemedicine was in its 'infancy,'[4] but this belies the long history of telehealth. The *Lancet* reported the use of the telephone to reduce unnecessary physician visits in 1878, and a tele-stethoscope was described in 1910.[5] In the United States the National Aeronautics and Space Administration recognised the need to identify and address medical issues remotely during space exploration in the 1960s,[6] and telecommunication technologies were used to monitor American astronauts. In 1993 the American Telemedicine Association was established to provide organisational focus and alliance for institutions and groups promoting telehealth.

Telemedicine was born of necessity in places where geographical remoteness gives rise to challenges to face-to-face healthcare delivery, and it is now well established in countries such as Australia. About 28% of the population (7 million people) of Australia live in rural and remote areas and often have poorer health outcomes than people living in metropolitan areas.[7] Australia has a *Digital Health Strategy* that calls for "widening access to telehealth services, especially in rural and remote Australia."[8]

In Sweden, consultations with primary care physicians using by digital platforms increased around 20% per month after its introduction in mid-2016.[9] President Obama supported increasing access to care in rural areas of the United States by promoting wider adoption of effective telecommunications and health information technologies. In the UK a poll of over 2000 adults (aged 15 and over) conducted by Ipsos MORI for the King's Fund in 2018 found that although uptake of online consultations in general practice had been low, this view was changing.[10] The majority of respondents to the poll, conducted before the COVID-19 pandemic, said that they would use video consultations to consult their GP about minor ailments (63%) and ongoing conditions or problems (55%), although only 43% of respondents would be willing to have a video consultation with their GP for immediate or emergency medical advice.[11] The National Health Service (NHS) Long Term Plan stated in 2019 that over the next five years, every patient would have the right to online 'digital' GP consultations.[12] But telemedicine also enables provision of healthcare where barriers like frailty, lack of transport or other physical or mental health conditions may make access problematic.[13] The Australian Royal Commission into Aged Care Quality and Safety recommended increased use of telehealth in residential aged care facilities.[14] So, even before the COVID-19 pandemic took hold, health systems around the world faced immense challenges due to ageing populations, financial pressures and workforce constraints, leading to the need for adoption and promotion of models of care using enabling technologies.

But of course, the pandemic brought into focus the role of telemedicine as a way of continuing the provision of care without the need for direct face-to-face contact during times of social distancing.

Telemedicine during the COVID-19 pandemic

Funding was made available for telehealth, including telephone and video consultations, at the outset of the pandemic. Medicare, the federal health insurance program in the United States, had provided funding for telehealth services only for those living in rural areas. As of February 2020, before the pandemic, only 0.1% of primary care appointments were via telehealth.[15] Restrictions on Medicare coverage of telehealth services were waived, effective from 6 March 2020, so that during the public health emergency patients in any geographic area could receive telehealth services. The US Congress passed legislation that allowed qualified providers to bill Medicare for care provided through telehealth at the same rate as for face-to-face visits.

In Australia health providers are funded by the Medicare Benefits Scheme for approved items. Prior to the pandemic, funding for virtual care was limited to; individuals living more than 15 km away from specialist care, those in aged care and those receiving care from Aboriginal medical services, and was little used. The limits on funding for video and telephone consultations were lifted when the pandemic arrived. The federal government added new telehealth items to the Medicare Benefits Schedule so that telephone and video consultations were reimbursed at the same value as the equivalent in-person consultation codes,[16] and by April 2020 when all eligibility criteria were lifted, all Australians could access Medicare-funded telehealth. In order to limit transmission of the coronavirus, telehealth consultations were encouraged to be offered in general practice and outpatient settings, and between March and the end of June 2020, "more than 7 million MBS-funded telehealth consultations had been reported, with the vast majority (91%) being done by telephone."[17] A study of experiences and opinions of telehealth delivered with a GP via video in Melbourne, Australia, during the COVID-19 pandemic showed that mental health and behavioural issues were the main reason for the consultation (38%; 241/499) and 69% (346/499).[18]

The 'Near Me' video consulting service was set up by the Scottish government in 2016, initially helping people in rural and island areas to access health services and reducing the need to travel long distances for appointments.[19] The existence of the program proved timely, because it enabled a swift scale-up of provision in response to the COVID-19 pandemic. Use of the Near Me service increased significantly from early March 2020 onwards, and between March and June 2020 there was a 50-fold increase in video consultations, from 330 per week to just under 17,000. Hospital and other community care services constituted a much higher proportion of the Near Me activity (77%) than GP services (23%).[20] In July 2020 the UK Secretary of State for Health said that NHS GPs should see patients remotely as a default position,[21] which precipitated an increase in the number of virtual GP appointments. Video consultations proved their value in avoiding direct contact with patients and thus the spread of the coronavirus. Given the heightened anxiety surrounding the impact of the virus, live video was useful for patients seeking consultation on COVID-19 symptoms,[22] and it seems that telemedicine did not compromise the health of patients with non-urgent conditions nor the quality of care.[23]

Telephone versus video consultation

Telephone consultations have been used as a viable alternative to face-to-face consultations in general practice and are considered a time-efficient way to access care for those with family responsibilities, the elderly and housebound patients.[24] Research shows that compared to face-to-face consultations, telephone consultations are "shorter, cover fewer problems, include less data gathering, less advice and rapport building, and are perceived to be suitable only for uncomplicated presentations, are less safe, and may not save time."[25] In many cases a telephone call may be sufficient and also easier, as there is no need to rely on an Internet connection and the patient does not need to have a camera phone and data. The starting point might be a phone call to see if the issue can be dealt with and then, if necessary, convert to a video call. The lack of visual clues, which can provide valuable information to the healthcare practitioner, are a disadvantage with telephone consultations.

Although there may be logistical and workflow challenges to align video consultations with appointment bookings, 'seeing' a patient during a video consultation has benefits. In Australia video conference services are the preferred approach for substituting an in person consultation, although health practitioners are funded to offer audio-only services via telephone if video is not available.[26] The Royal Australian College of General Practice Guidelines state that "the addition of visual images via a video link adds value to any telehealth consultation and can improve both quality and safety for more complex consultations."[27] In the context of telehealth in outpatient delivery of palliative care, Philip et al. note that,

> visual information allows the detection of, at least some, physical changes, provides cues to emotional responses to information, enables interactions between family members to be better understood and provides a greater sense of personal connection between patient and clinician.[28]

Video consultations may assist in determining if the patient looks unwell, and patients can be 'eyeballed' to decide whether they need urgent assessment or admission.[29] Video consultations are particularly useful to observe a child, to see if they are running around, smiling and looking well, and where the parent/carer would find the journey to the general practice difficult.

There are obviously significant limitations of video consultations impacting on the ability to perform clinical checks such as palpation of the abdomen, breast or gynaecological examinations. It is hard to assess an asthma patient by video, as the doctor cannot listen to the chest, and other checks, such as taking the pulse, will rely on the patient themselves doing it. Giving a diagnosis over the phone/video is problematic and should not be done. In comparison with telephone consultations, video consultations are considered to be better in building rapport and improving communications.

Acceptability of telemedicine during COVID-19 was high. A study in Poland suggests that the quality of teleconsultations is not inferior to the quality of consultation during a face-to-face visit and that patients surveyed indicated a high level of satisfaction regarding communication with their GP during teleconsultation.[30] However, in the survey of patients in general practice in Melbourne 11% (57/499) of the sample did not believe that video conference was as good as a face-to-face consultation.[31] A user experience survey of the Near Me platform showed that 97% of respondents would choose video consultation again and 95% of clinicians thought that video consultations should be offered to patients (when clinically appropriate).[32] Would satisfaction be so high if face-to-face and virtual healthcare are compared in a non-pandemic time? We know that video consulting is perceived by healthcare professionals and patients as beneficial, both during the COVID-19 pandemic and longer-term.[33]

Ethical issues

The American Medical Association (AMA) considers that the ethical responsibilities of doctors do not change with telemedicine. The ethical guidance formulated by the AMA focuses on the need for disclosure of financial or other interests a doctor has in the telehealth/telemedicine application or service and the security and integrity of patient information.[34] The UK Department of Health and Social Care states that use of data-driven technologies can cause unintended harm if issues such as "transparency, accountability, safety, efficacy, explicability, fairness, equity and bias" are not addressed,[35] and these issues are also covered in the UK Data Ethics Framework.[36]

Fundamental ethical principles such as respect for autonomy, beneficence, nonmaleficence and justice are relevant to telemedicine and I consider how these principles apply in an internet the setting.

Respect for autonomy

Video consultation has the potential for promoting the autonomy of patients, particularly for those patients who might find it difficult to visit a GP or health centre, such as parents with young children, wheelchair users, people with social phobia or panic disorders and individuals who might not be able to afford transport to a general practice. Patients are able to choose appointment times more easily to fit in their schedule and, for people in regional/remote areas who may have been limited to a single doctor (or none), they can now theoretically be seen by any doctor doing telehealth. Patients may feel empowered by having some control over the virtual interaction, including "how they are visually perceived, for example, through the adjustment of the camera angle, visibility of surrounding objects or brightness, and they can influence the audio transmission by technically adjusting the volume or tone of the signal."[37] They can also choose whether to include family members/carers in the consultation to provide support. This contrasts with the need to 'pay a visit' to their healthcare provider, with all the disempowerment that involves – being observed in the waiting room and then 'called in' to see the doctor, often in a non-familiar setting. So, video consultation may help reduce the inherent vulnerabilities in a traditional doctor-patient interaction.

Patients are empowered where they have, and can exercise, choice, but in the COVID-19 pandemic, face-to-face appointments, especially in general practice, were often not available. Although video consultations may not be an individual's first choice for delivery of healthcare, at least it provides continuation of medical care and so is optimal in those circumstances.

Beneficence

Patients benefit from telemedicine through real-time consultations, where they may be geographically separated from their healthcare provider and would otherwise not have reasonable access to services. Timely healthcare prevents an exacerbation of symptoms and enables appropriate treatment. This not only improves health outcomes but also patient experience and engagement. There are also economic benefits of telemedicine, including reduced travel, thereby saving time and providing environmental benefits, improved access and increased service capacity. Employers can benefit when their workforce do not have to travel or take leave to attend a health consultation, although where there is the option of telehealth perhaps employers are incentivised not to allow their staff to take leave to attend appointments, and this may cause strain on the workforce.

The use of video consultations during a pandemic reduces the reduce risk of infection from airborne viruses, and during the COVID-19 pandemic, they enabled services to continue in light of social distancing and shielding requirements. In study of acceptability of telehealth consultations in palliative care delivery (where approximately two-thirds of these telehealth consultations were by phone only), patients found this approach more acceptable than clinicians, perhaps because of the convenience of not needing to travel, find car parking and spend time in waiting rooms with the risk of COVID-19 transmission.[38] The survey of users of the Near Me platform in Scotland showed that the main benefits were saving travel time (71% of all respondents), saving time (67%), a reduced chance of catching COVID-19 (54%) and not having to take time away from work or other activities (40%).[39] It seems that the benefits of video consultations are achieved in the context of an existing doctor-patient relationship, building upon the rapport already established through previous in-person consultations.[40]

There are benefits in terms of workforce planning, and this mode of delivery is attractive for healthcare professionals who do video conferencing from home, enabling them to save travel time and be more involved in family life, thus increasing their quality of life.[41]

Non-maleficence

Meanwhile disadvantages of video consultations include connectivity and technical issues, privacy concerns, difficulty gathering information without visual clues and clinician dissatisfaction.[42] If patients are concerned about being overheard, this might limit what they feel able to discuss, particularly around sensitive issues, for example, drug and alcohol use. The changed relationship has ethical implications where a lack of physical connection may be to the detriment of the patient, and so could be said to 'harm' the patient relative to a face-to-face encounter. The information gleaned from a physical interaction may be relevant in diagnosis, particularly in psychiatry, where "the smell of perfume, alcohol, urine, working materials or lack of personal hygiene, for example, can be informative"[43] and which cannot be perceived in a video consultation. The risk of a missed diagnosis due to lack of hands-on assessment should be evaluated at the outset and a clinical decision made whether it is indeed appropriate to offer a video consultation. It would not be suitable, and could be potentially harmful, to provide health services through telemedicine where the patient has visual, auditory or communication limitations or where the presentation of the patient indicates psychosis or risk of self-harm.

Technological problems can be time consuming, stressful and have potential harms to privacy and confidentiality, and these issues have been described as 'common.'[44] In the survey of users of Near Me the majority (78%) of patients reported that consultations ran with no technical problems, but under a third (29%) of respondents reported disadvantages to video consulting, including not being able to hear the clinician properly, poor Internet connection, dislike of video calling, waiting for long periods in the virtual waiting area and requiring an extra appointment because the video consultation could not be completed.[45]

Healthcare providers bear the costs of providing hardware, software and Internet security, and testing the qualities of the technologies and setting up information governance take time.[46] Virtual care is a very different way of working and requires consideration not only how to conduct the virtual consultation but also knowing when a video consult is appropriate and when it is not sufficient and a face-to-face appointment should be offered – this all requires training.

Justice

The resources required to fund a health service include the financial cost of providing the service and the human time spent in doing so. These resources should be allocated cost-effectively, maximising the benefits achieved for the population served. This is both an economic and moral concern because "an allocation of resources that is not cost-effective produces fewer benefits than would have been possible with a different allocation."[47] So one question to be addressed is whether telemedicine, in particular video conferencing, is a cost-effective alternative to in person doctor-patient consultations. A viable telehealth service requires a commitment for ongoing governmental support and funding, and although funding was available during the extraordinary time of the COVID-19 pandemic, it remains to be seen how this is affected in the future. Perhaps the greatest ethical concerns in respect of the increased use of video consultations in primary care are widening health inequalities because of access and fundamental changes to the doctor-patient relationship.

Changes to the doctor-patient relationship

The nature of the relationship between healthcare practitioner and patient is, of course, practically altered where, instead of the patient sitting with the doctor, they are at a distance and seen through a screen.

> During face-to-face consultations, a human interaction takes place between doctor and patient which is fundamental for the therapeutic relationship. For example, GPs may notice a patient's subtle body language, make an empathetic expression after disclosure of a sensitive issue, or offer a tissue to a tearful patient. These small gestures are fundamental parts of being a caring and compassionate doctor and human-being.[48]

In some situations, physical connection is an important component of the therapeutic relationship and therapeutic effectiveness, particularly in psychiatry, where the relationship can be "particularly private, personal and highly emotional."[49] Psychiatrists in Australia have successfully provided video conference consultations since 2002, and although telepsychiatry can be useful, some patients may wish to have a face-to-face meeting, even if this requires a longer wait.[50] Social isolation during the COVID-19 pandemic and increased loneliness led to a steep increase in mental health services provided through telehealth, including video conferencing and telephone, which provided a feasible and effective means of support and treatment.[51] The assumption that conventional in-person methods are the gold standard for treatment for mental health problems is countered by evidence that 'videotherapy' (synchronous psychotherapy via video conferencing) as a treatment modality may in fact enhance outcomes for some, who may find it less confronting than in-person contact, facilitating disclosure of difficult experiences and feelings.[52] Children and teenagers who are familiar with technology for communication and gaming may find videotherapy an easier way to communicate, and in the case scenario Archie's teenage daughter, Penny, has benefitted from her telehealth appointments with a counsellor.

However, digitalised healthcare may lead to depersonalisation of medicine. We owe "duties of humanity" to each other with a recognition that we are "morally relevant and individual subjects."[53] In Chapter 8 the potential for dehumanising of the elderly when they receive care and connection through robotic care assistants is considered. Video consultations may be efficient, but people do not visit a healthcare provider just when they have symptoms; rather, the seeking of an interaction is based on a complex mix of social and psychological factors.[54] The physical sense of presence and touch of a clinician can be important for reassurance and emotional support and provide therapeutic benefit. This recognises the value that human skills bring to the innate complexity of social interactions.

> Perceptions that the use of technology in healthcare lacks privacy and is innately "cold" in nature poses a risk of depersonalizing the doctor-patient relationship, potentially damaging it irrevocably. Some have been reluctant to broaden their scope of practice to include telehealth due to valid concerns about shifting this traditionally in-person relationship to the Internet.[55]

Healthcare professionals may find video consultations quite unsatisfying in comparison to face-to-face interactions with their patients, particularly for more complex cases and where patients are unstable or experiencing deterioration. Where GPs provide telehealth from their home, there is a risk that personal/professional boundaries could become blurred.

Access and equity

Telemedicine is considered a way to reduce the cost of healthcare, and the Nuffield Council on Bioethics states that "public healthcare systems should offer telemedicine services where they can feasibly and cost-effectively help to reduce inequities in access to healthcare."[56] We may consider whether the use of telehealth exacerbates health inequalities. Telemedicine can be a way to increase empowerment and user involvement in healthcare, but this is influenced by a patient's socioeconomic status, knowledge and trust of Western medicine and technology. The greatest users of healthcare are the elderly, those who are socially and economically deprived, people with learning disabilities, those with mental health issues and individuals who do not speak English.[57] These groups need to use health services most but are also least likely to be able to use telemedicine. People with physical or cognitive impairments may find it difficult to get to grips with technology, and health inequalities may be exacerbated by a lack of access to devices, mobile data and private space at home, and this may present a barrier for our vulnerable members in society. It has been argued that broadband Internet access should be recognised as a social determinant of health and that disparities in access should be treated as a public health issue.[58] As Young, Borgetti and Clapham note, "Telehealth programs are often specifically targeted towards traditionally underserved populations, composed of persons who may have poor access to, and education regarding, the use of technology."[59] So the need for healthcare and the ability to access these telemedicine technologies may not align.

Certain population groups may be particularly impacted if video consultations are the *only* means of accessing care. During the COVID-19 pandemic migrant and asylum groups from culturally and linguistically diverse groups were particularly disadvantaged and experienced major social, economic, physical and mental health issues.[60] Even though legislation in many countries around the world enabled funding to subsidise access to medical care and advice via telehealth as a response to the pandemic, these changes did not address the underlying health issues and barriers facing many refugees and migrants. There are still "ongoing challenges in general access to telehealth and the need for greater culturally and linguistically appropriate healthcare in a multicultural Australia."[61]

Although digital technology has the potential to remove some barriers to accessing healthcare, we should ensure that they do not give rise to a widening inequity for people who lack digital literacy or access to a computer or the Internet. However, outside the extraordinary situation of lockdowns due to the coronavirus pandemic, telehealth is 'as well as,' not 'instead of.' The option of telehealth consultations does not impact on access to face-to-face consultation because practically no doctor does telehealth exclusively, and those who have issues accessing telehealth will not be denied the in-person treatment they would receive anyway.

Legal issues

Issues of informed consent, confidentiality and data protection are relevant to face-to-face care provided by a healthcare provider and require some rethinking where the interaction and exchange of information are mediated through a video consultation. Such consultations will take place in a personal space of the patient, likely in their home or office, and so discussions about the person's health concerns may be overheard by family or co-workers. Security of data which is transmitted over widely available video conferencing platforms may also be of concern.

Informed consent

For video consultations the patient needs to understand and consent to the treatment and management of their condition. It may not be appropriate to use video conferencing where there are more risks to discuss with the patient. One survey found that a majority of surgeons (53.7%) would prefer a face-to-face consultation before undertaking a procedure, particularly those procedures which are more invasive.[62]

The patient should also understand and consent to this form of telemedicine and how data will be used and stored. Guidelines suggest that recording of video meetings should be disabled[63] and personal mobile devices should not be used to record video conferences. Where a recording of a health consultation is stored by a health service, this is an act of health information collection about an individual, which would be covered by privacy laws, requiring the patient's express or implied consent.[64] The recording would form part of the medical record, and any recordings will need to be stored securely just like other medical records.

Confidentiality and privacy

I like these haikus which illustrate the comparison between confidentiality and privacy:

Confidentiality

> Keep info secret.
> Do not tell anybody.
> Or else you lose trust.

Privacy

> Collecting, using,
> disclosing and safeguarding,
> personal info.[65]

In addition to statutory protections against the misuse of personal information, healthcare professionals owe a common law (judge-made or case law) duty of confidentiality, and their use of healthcare information is also constrained by codes of practice of professional bodies, such as, for doctors, the UK General Medical Council and the Australian Medical Association, which apply whether they conduct video conferencing from home or their office. The doctor-patient relationship is one of utmost confidence and good faith, but as Gleeson CJ noted in the Australian High Court decision of *Australian Broadcasting Corporation v Lenah Game Meats Pty Ltd*,[66] it is no longer necessary for there to be a relationship of trust and confidence in order to protect confidential information; rather, the obligation of confidence is defined by reference to circumstances, not a relationship.[67] Doctors rely on full and frank disclosure from the patient in order to properly diagnose and treat patients. The Australian Medical Association's Code of Ethics states that doctors should maintain the confidentiality of the patient's personal information, including their medical records, disclosing their information to others only with the patient's express up-to-date consent or as required or authorised by law.[68]

There is a legal imperative that the use, storage and transmission of personal data, including health information, are controlled and protected. During a video consultation, health information which identifies the patient is transmitted electronically. Legislative regimes in different jurisdictions establish an individual's right to privacy and how organisations and government institutions can collect, use and/or disclose such information, including in electronic form. Video conferencing platforms such as Skype, Zoom, GoToMeeting, Facetime, WhatsApp and Webex are developed by private companies for the open community, rather than with a focus on medicine. Platforms should be compliant with relevant data protection laws such as the US Health Insurance Portability and Accountability Act and the European General Data Protection Regulation, and 'gold standard' practice points to purpose-built platforms with appropriate encryption and security of data.

Telehealth guidance for practitioners issued by the Australian Health Practitioner Regulation Agency[69] states that "free versions of applications (i.e. non-commercial versions) may not meet applicable laws for security and privacy. Practitioners must ensure that their chosen telecommunications solution meets their clinical requirements, their patient's or client's needs and satisfies privacy laws."[70] However, there may be a lack of understanding by healthcare professionals about how data is processed and stored. In a study of UK and European plastic surgeons' use of virtual consultations during the COVID-19 lockdown, the majority of respondents (97.7%) reported using virtual consultations; two-thirds used commercial platforms such as Zoom, FaceTime and Skype; and about one-third "did not know about or were unsure about adequate encryption for health care use."[71]

Speaking to a doctor in a consulting room seems very different from talking on a video call, and during the pandemic we were all aware of gaffs that happened on Zoom or other platforms. Basic checks, such as ensuring that the patient is properly identified before commencing the consultation, are important. The Royal Australian College of General Practitioners guide on telephone and video consultations advises that, on starting a telehealth consultation, the GP confirms their own identity and verifies the patient's identity (if a telephone consultation) and any necessary introductions are made if the patient has a support person present.[72] But as the patient is in control of the space where they conduct the video call, it is not possible to know if there are family members listening.

Guidance from medico-legal insurers, governments and organisations representing healthcare workers identifies the importance of setting up video conferencing to ensure confidentiality.

Standard of care: tele-negligence

Where video consultations are used, the legal obligations of healthcare professionals are the same as in normal physical consultations, however, as there are inherent limitations of telehealth, medico-legal risks may be greater including where lack of physical examination may lead to a missed diagnosis.

Healthcare practitioners owe a duty to their patients to exercise reasonable skill and care when advising and treating them. It may not be clinically appropriate to use telehealth, for example, with remote visual rather than physical examinations, and a healthcare professional may not be acting reasonably if they used telemedicine in such circumstances, although this would depend on the urgency of the need for care and the availability of other options. Guidance issued by professional bodies and organisations indicates issues to be considered so that doctors can meet a reasonable standard of care using telehealth. In the UK, the Department of Health and Social Security has provided the 'Guide to Good Practice for Digital and Data Driven Health Technologies'[73] and the Royal Australian College of General Practitioners' guide to providing telephone and video consultations in general practice covers issues such as consent, recording video consultations and information security and privacy.

Healthcare professionals must also exercise reasonable care and skill in the use of technology and security of data. There is no standard equipment or platforms that are to be used during video consultations, but nevertheless a standard of reasonableness demands that the hardware and software are fit for purpose and meet reasonable security requirements. During the COVID-19 pandemic there was adequate time to establish and refine provision of video conferencing and the attendant infrastructure, and so it would not be reasonable for sub-optimal technology to be used, which posed a risk to patients and the security of their data.

Conclusion

Around the world policy makers and governments have recognised the importance of harnessing the value of telemedicine to improve access to healthcare and are directing attention to how this can be done effectively. The World Health Organization recognises the potential of telehealth "to address some of the challenges faced by both developed and developing countries in providing accessible, cost effective, high-quality health care services."[74]

Evidence has shown that video conferencing is effective and cost-efficient. It is convenient and time saving for patients and is generally accessible. However, consulting a doctor via video does have an impact on the doctor-patient interaction, and some groups may be particularly disadvantaged through communication barriers or digital access/literacy. During the COVID-19 pandemic, in order to protect patients, healthcare workers and the public from spread of the virus, virtual consultations provided a means for continued patient access to healthcare during the pandemic. Much was learnt about telemedicine which may help to establish it more firmly post-pandemic as an important alternative (but not replacement) for health provision.

In Singapore it is expected that the telemedicine model adopted when the coronavirus spread throughout the community, which eliminated physician rounds at dialysis clinics, will be used as the new normal in a post–COVID-19 environment.[75] In Australia telehealth services introduced in response to COVID-19 will be ongoing, and eligible patients will continue to have access to GPs, nursing, midwifery and allied health services via telehealth where it is deemed clinically appropriate. In rural Australia telehealth will supersede face-to-face consultations by 2025.[76]

So, telehealth and video consultations are here to stay, requiring ongoing investment and integration within health and social care service frameworks. Ultimately, the key issues are patient choice and clinical effectiveness, and telehealth must not be seen as an alternative form of healthcare completely replacing face-to-face consultations and care.

Notes

1 M. Fisk, A. Livingstone, S. W. Pit, 'Telehealth in the Context of COVID-19: Changing Perspectives in Australia, the United Kingdom, and the United States' (2020) 22(6) *Journal of Medical Internet Research* e19264.
2 E. Grebenshchikova, 'Digital Medicine: Bioethical Assessment of Challenges and Opportunities' (2019) 10(1) *European Journal of Bioethics* 211–223.
3 World Health Organization, *A Health Telematics Policy in Support of WHO's Health-For-All Strategy for Global Health Development: Report of the WHO Group Consultation on Health Telematics* (World Health Organization, Geneva, 1998).
4 World Health Organization, 'Telemedicine: Opportunities and Developments in Member States: Report on the Second Global Survey on eHealth 2009.' (Global Observatory for eHealth Series, 2).
5 B. Dinesen, B. Nonnecke, D. Lindeman et al., 'Personalized Telehealth in the Future: A Global Research Agenda' (2016) 18(3). *Journal of Medical Internet Research* e53.
6 J. Young, S. Borgetti, P. Clapham, 'Telehealth: Exploring the Ethical Issues' (2018) 19 *DePaul Journal of Health Care Law* 1–15.
7 Australian Government, Australian Institute of Health and Welfare, Rural and Remote Health, 07 July 2022. www.aihw.gov.au/reports/australias-health/rural-and-remote-health.
8 Australia's Digital Health Strategy, 'Safe, Seamless and Secure: Evolving Health and Care to Meet the Needs of Modern Australia,' *National Digital Health Strategy and Framework for Action* (Australia's Digital Health Strategy, Brisbane, 2018).
9 C. Bjorndell, Å. Premberg, 'Physicians' Experiences of Video Consultation with Patients at a Public Virtual Primary Care Clinic: A Qualitative Interview Study,' (2021) 39(1) *Scandinavian Journal of Primary Health Care* 67–76.
10 S. Castle-Clarke, *What Will New Technology Mean for the NHS and Its Patients? Four Big Technological Trends* (The King's Fund, London, 2018).
11 S. Castle-Clarke, *What Will New Technology Mean for the NHS and Its Patients? Four Big Technological Trends* (The King's Fund, London, 2018), page 8.
12 NHS Long Term Plan, www.longtermplan.nhs.uk/
13 M. Konge Nielsen, H. Johannessen, 'Patient Empowerment and Involvement in Telemedicine.' (2019) 9(8) *Journal of Nursing Education and Practice* 54–58.
14 Royal Commission into Aged Care Quality and Safety. In: A. Government (ed.) *Final Report: Care, Dignity and Respect* (Royal Commission into Aged Care Quality and Safety, Canberra, 2020), 1–175.
15 K. Fisher, P. Magin, 'The Telehealth Divide: Health Inequity during the COVID-19 Pandemic' (2022) 39(3) *Family Practice* 547–549, page 547 and see G. Wilensky, 'Health Insurance Coverage after the COVID-19 Public Health Emergency Ends' (2022) 3(9) *JAMA Health Forum* e224207.
16 C. Snoswell, L. Caffery, H. Haydon, E. Thomas, A. Smith, 'Telehealth Uptake in General Practice as a Result of the Coronavirus (COVID-19) Pandemic' (2020) 44 *Australian Health Review* 737–740.
17 C. Snoswell, A. Smith, L. Caffrey, 'Telehealth in Lockdown Meant 7 Million Fewer Chances to Transmit the Coronavirus,' *The Conversation*, June 22, 2020.
18 J-A. Manski-Nankervis et al., 'Primary Care Consumers' Experiences and Opinions of a Telehealth Consultation Delivered via Video during the COVID-19 Pandemic,' (2022) 28(3) *Australian Journal of Primary Health* 224–231.
19 J. Wherton, T. Greenhalgh, S. Shaw, 'Expanding Video Consultation Services at Pace and Scale in Scotland During the COVID-19 Pandemic: National Mixed Methods Case Study' (2021) 23(10) *Journal of Medical Internet Research* e31374.
20 J. Wherton, T. Greenhalgh, *Evaluation of the Attend Anywhere/Near Me Video Consulting Service in Scotland during Covid-19, 2019–20* (Scottish Government, University of Oxford), page 5.
21 P. Walker, *The Guardian*, 30 Jul 2020. www.theguardian.com/society/2020/jul/30/all-gp-consultations-should-be-remote-by-default-says-matt-hancock-nhs.
22 E. Monaghesh, A. Hajizadeh, 'The Role of Telehealth during COVID-19 Outbreak: A Systematic Review based on Current Evidence,' (2020) 20 *BMC Public Health* 1193.

23 R. Bashshur, C. Doarn, J. Frenk, J. Kvedar, J. Woolliscroft, 'Telemedicine and the COVID-19 Pandemic, Lessons for the Future.' (2020) 26(5) *Telemedicine and e-Health* 571–573.
24 V. Hammersley, et al., 'Comparing the Content and Quality of Video, Telephone, and Face-to-Face Consultations: A Non-randomised, Quasi-experimental, Exploratory Study in UK Primary Care,' (2019) 69(686) *British Journal of General Practice* e595–e604.
25 V. Hammersley et al. 'Comparing the Content and Quality of Video, Telephone, and Face-to-Face Consultations: A Non-randomised, Quasi-experimental, Exploratory Study in UK Primary Care' (2019) 69(686) *British Journal of General Practice* e595–e604, page e595.
26 Medicare Benefits Schedule Temporary COVID-19 MBS Telehealth Services – Consumer Factsheet MBS Online Last updated – 18 September 2020.
27 Royal Australian College of General Practitioners, *Guide to Providing Telephone and Video Consultations in General Practice* (RACGP, East Melbourne, 2020) page 3.
28 J. Philip, O. Wawryk, L. Pasanen, A. Wong, S. Schwetlik, A. Collins, 'A. Telehealth in Outpatient Delivery of Palliative Care: A Prospective Survey Evaluation by Patients and Clinicians,' (2022) *Journal of Internal Medicine* 1–10, page 8.
29 J. Wherton, T. Greenhalgh, *Evaluation of the Attend Anywhere/Near Me Video Consulting Service in Scotland during Covid-19, 2019–20* (Scottish Government) University of Oxford, page 6.
30 M. Kludacz-Alessandri, L. Hawrysz, P. Korneta, G. Gierszewska, W. Pomaranik, R. Walczak, 'The Impact of Medical Teleconsultations on General Practitioner-Patient Communication during COVID- 19: A Case Study from Poland' (2021) 16(7) *PloS One*, e0254960.
31 J.-A. Manski-Nankervis et al. "Primary Care Consumers' Experiences and Opinions of a Telehealth Consultation Delivered via Video during the COVID-19 Pandemic' (2022) 28(3) *Australian Journal of Primary Health* 224–231.
32 J. Wherton, T. Greenhalgh, *Evaluation of the Attend Anywhere/Near Me Video Consulting Service in Scotland during Covid-19, 2019–20* (Scottish Government University of Oxford). page 31
33 V. Hammersley et al. 'Comparing the Content and Quality of Video, Telephone, and Face-to-Face Consultations: A Non-randomised, Quasi-experimental, Exploratory Study in UK Primary Care' (2019) 69(686) *British Journal of General Practice* e595–e604.
34 American Medical Association, *Code of Medica Ethics, Chapter 1: Opinions on Patient Physician Relationships*. www.ama-assn.org/system/files/code-of-medical-ethics-chapter-1.pdf
35 UK Government, Department of Health and Social Care, *Guidance A Guidance to Good Practice for Digital and Data Driven Health Technologies*. www.gov.uk/government/publications/code-of-conduct-for-data-driven-health-and-care-technology/initial-code-of-conduct-for-data-driven-health-and-care-technology#principle-1-understand-users-their-needs-and-the-context.
36 UK Government, Central Digital and Data Office, *Data Ethics Framework*, September 2020. www.gov.uk/government/publications/data-ethics-framework/data-ethics-framework-2020.
37 E-M. Frittgen, J. Haltaufderheide, "Can You Hear Me?': Communication, Relationship and Ethics in Video-based Telepsychiatric Consultations' (2022) 48(1) *Journal of Medical Ethics* 22–30, page 27.
38 J. Philip, O. Wawryk, L. Pasanen, A. Wong, S. Schwetlik, A. Collins, 'Telehealth in Outpatient Delivery of Palliative Care: A Prospective Survey Evaluation by Patients and Clinicians' (2022) *Journal of Internal Medicine* 1–10.
39 J. Wherton, T. Greenhalgh, *Evaluation of the Attend Anywhere/Near Me Video Consulting Service in Scotland during Covid-19, 2019–20* (Scottish Government University of Oxford), page 28.
40 V. Hammersley et al. 'Comparing the Content and Quality of Video, Telephone, and Face-to-Face Consultations: A Non-randomised, Quasi-experimental, Exploratory Study in UK Primary Care' (2019) 69(686) *British Journal of General Practice* e595–e604.

41 C. Bjorndell, Å. Premberg, "Physicians' Experiences of Video Consultation with Patients at a Public Virtual Primary Care Clinic: A Qualitative Interview Study' (2021) 39(1) *Scandinavian Journal of Primary Health Care* 67–76.
42 J. Philip, O. Wawryk, L. Pasanen, A. Wong, S. Schwetlik, A. Collins, 'Telehealth in Outpatient Delivery of Palliative Care: A Prospective Survey Evaluation by Patients and Clinicians' (2022) *Journal of Internal Medicine* 1–10.
43 M. Frittgen, J. Haltaufderheide, "Can You Hear Me?': Communication, Relationship and Ethics in Video-based Telepsychiatric Consultations' (2022) 48(1) *Journal of Medical Ethics* 22–30, page 25.
44 E. Donaghy et al. 'Acceptability, Benefits, and Challenges of Video Consulting: A Qualitative Study in Primary Care.' (2019) 69(686) *The British Journal of General Practice: The Journal of the Royal College of General Practitioners* e586–e594.
45 J. Wherton, T. Greenhalgh, *Evaluation of the Attend Anywhere/Near Me Video Consulting Service in Scotland, 2019–20* (Scottish Government) University of Oxford, page 28.
46 M. Fisk, A. Livingstone, S. Pit, 'Telehealth in the Context of COVID-19: Changing Perspectives in Australia, the United Kingdom, and the United States.' (2020) 22(6) *Journal of Medical Internet Research* e19264.
47 D. Brock, D. Wikler, 'Chapter 14, Ethical Issues in Resource Allocation, Research, and New Product Development,' In: D. Jamison, J. Breman, A. Measham et al. (eds) Disease Control Priorities in Developing Countries. 2nd edition. Washington (DC): (The International Bank for Reconstruction and Development, The World Bank, Oxford University Press, Washington, DC, New York, 2006). www.ncbi.nlm.nih.gov/books/NBK11739
48 Personal correspondence with Dr Selena Sellman.
49 E.-M. Frittgen, J. Haltaufderheide, "Can You Hear Me?': Communication, Relationship and Ethics in Video-based Telepsychiatric Consultations,' (2022) 48(1) *Journal of Medical Ethics* 22–30, page 24.
50 L. Newman, N. Bidargaddi, G.Schrader, 'Service Providers' Experiences of Using a Telehealth Network 12 months after Digitisation of a Large Australian Rural Mental Health Service.' (2016) 94 *International Journal of Medical Informatics* 8–20.
51 C. Snoswell, L. Caffery, H. Haydon, E. Thomas, A. Smith, 'Telehealth Uptake in General Practice as a Result of the Coronavirus (COVID-19) Pandemic' (2020) 44 *Australian Health Review* 737–740.
52 S. Simpson, L. Richardson, G. Pietrabissa, G. Castelnuovo, C. Reid, 'Videotherapy and Therapeutic Alliance in the Age of COVID-19. (2021) 28(2) *Clinical Psychology & Psychotherapy* 409–421.
53 M. Frittgen, J. Haltaufderheide, "Can You Hear Me?': Communication, Relationship and Ethics in Video-based Telepsychiatric Consultations' (2022) 48(1) *Journal of Medical Ethics* 22–30, page 28.
54 S. Campbell, M. Roland, 'Why do People Consult the Doctor?' (1996) 13 *Family Practice* 75–83.
55 J. Young, S. Borgetti, P. Clapham, 'Telehealth: Exploring the Ethical Issues' (2018) 19 *DePaul Journal of Health Care Law* 1–15, page 4.
56 Nuffield Council on Bioethics, *Medical Profiling and Online Medicine: The Ethics of 'Personalised Healthcare' in a Consumer Age* (Nuffield Council on Bioethics, London, 2010) page 198 Recommendation 21.
57 S. Campbell, M. Roland, 'Why do People Consult the Doctor?' (1996) *Family Practice* 13: 75–83.
58 N. Brenda, T. Veinot, C. Sieck, J. Ancker, 'Broadband Internet Access is a Social Determinant of Health.' (2020) 110(8) *American Journal of Public Health* 1123–1125.
59 J. Young, S. Borgetti, P. Clapham, 'Telehealth: Exploring the Ethical Issues' (2018) 19 *DePaul Journal of Health Care Law* 1–15, page 9.
60 B. O'Mara, D. Monani, G. Carey, 'Telehealth, COVID-19 and Refugees and Migrants in Australia: Policy and Related Barriers and Opportunities for More Inclusive Health and Technology Systems,' (2021) *International Journal of Health Policy and Management* 1–521.

61 B. O'Mara, D. Monani, G. Carey, 'Telehealth, COVID-19 and Refugees and Migrants in Australia: Policy and Related Barriers and Opportunities for More Inclusive Health and Technology Systems' (2021) *International Journal of Health Policy and Management* 1–5.
62 V. Sinha, M. Malik, N. Nugent, P. Drake, N. Cavale Surgeon, 'The Role of Virtual Consultations in Plastic Surgery during COVID-19 Lockdown,' (2021) 45 *Aesthetic Plastic Surgery* 777–783.
63 Australian Government, Department of Health Factsheet – Privacy Checklist for Telehealth Services, 4 August 2020.
64 M. Prictor, C. Johnston, A. Hyatt, 'Overt and Covert Recordings of Health Care Consultations in Australia: Some Legal Considerations. (2021) 214(3) M*edical Journal of Australia*, 119–123.e1.
65 S. Young, 'Privacy versus Confidentiality', 8 December 2017 Office of the Saskatchewan Privacy Commissioner accessed https://oipc.sk.ca/privacy-versus-confidentiality/
66 *Australian Broadcasting Corporation v Lenah Game Meats Pty Ltd* [2001] HCA 63.
67 *Australian Broadcasting Corporation v Lenah Game Meats Pty Ltd* [2001] HCA 63. Gummow and Hayne JJ, para 113.
68 Australian Medical Association Code of Ethics 2004. Editorially Revised 2006. Revised 2016, para 2.2.2.
69 All health practitioners in Australia must have a current registration with the Australian Health Practitioner Regulation Agency (AHPRA).
70 AHPRA Telehealth guidance for practitioners and National Boards 27 July 2020.
71 V. Sinha, M. Malik, N. Nugent, P. Drake, N. Cavale Surgeon, 'The Role of Virtual Consultations in Plastic Surgery during COVID-19 Lockdown' (2021) 45 *Aesthetic Plastic Surgery* 777–783, page 778.
72 Royal Australian College of General Practitioners, *Guide to Providing Telephone and Video Consultations in General Practice* (RACGP, East Melbourne, Vic, 2020), page 13, para 5.1.
73 UK Government, Department of Health and Social Care, *A Guidance to Good Practice for Digital and Data Driven Health Technologies*, 19 January 2021.
74 World Health Organization, 'Telemedicine: Opportunities and Developments in Member States: Report on the Second Global Survey on eHealth 2009.' (Global Observatory for eHealth Series, 2), page 6.
75 W-W. Kin (2020-05-27). Rapid Transition to a Telemedicine Service at Singapore Community Dialysis Centers During Covid-19. NEJM Catalyst. ScholarBank@NUS Repository.
76 Editorial, 'Telehealth will Supersede Face-to-Face Consultations in Rural Australia by 2025,' (2015) 23 *Australian Journal of Rural Health* 255–256.

8
ROBOTIC CARE ASSISTANTS AND OLDER ADULTS

Case scenario

June is 85 years old and lives alone in her house. Her family lives interstate and are not able to visit as often as they wish, especially during lockdowns during the COVID-19 pandemic. They have researched robotic care assistants and would like their mother to have a robot which could monitor her medication use and provide some companionship. They have spoken to June's general practitioner (GP), who has said that it would not be funded by her healthcare package. The GP also has concerns that this may in fact increase June's isolation, providing a substitute for family visits. After a recent fall at home, June's family do some further research and speak to a friend in Japan, where care robots are prevalent, to explore the cost and range of tasks a robot could provide. However, they are concerned about the impact on their mother's privacy if a robot is in her house around the clock and how it may affect her independence and sense of dignity.

I use the term 'older adults'[5] (and sometimes elderly adults) to include people 65 years and older. Robotic care assistants may be used to support people with disabilities of any age, and the same issues arise in that context, although not covered specifically here.[6]

Introduction

Robots have a wide range of applications in personal use, including for domestic tasks such as lawn mowing, vacuuming, window cleaning and for home security and surveillance.[1] The prospect of robots assisting the care of the elderly in our populations has moved from a concept to a reality. Wearable fall sensors and robots for mobility already assist older adults in nursing homes and hospitals, and companion robotic pets and personal care robots could become more frequently used in private homes.

An increase in the older population and a reduction of the number of younger people able, and willing, to provide care for them has driven interest in, and uptake

DOI: 10.4324/9781003220190-8

of, robotic care assistants in social situations and healthcare. The Czech noun 'robota' means 'labour,' and robots may undertake mundane tasks that humans do not have the time or inclination to do, providing consistent input. During the COVID-19 pandemic, robots carried out tasks such as monitoring people for a rise in temperature through heat sensors, indicating the possibility of disease, and disinfecting the home, without the risks that would arise to human carers.[2]

Robotic care may improve socialisation and autonomy of the elderly who use them, but there are also potential harms of stigmatisation, loss of dignity and concerns around privacy. Care robots do not come cheap – *Paro*, a fur seal, costs approximately around 7000 AUD,[3] and the cost to a health provider, governments, the individual or family who pay for it themselves should be justified by an overall benefit. Although it will be years before robotic care assistants are generally available, their use will have profound implications for society,[4] and regulation of the industry to ensure adequate safety and ethical use is required. Different regimes and forms of regulation have relevance, including privacy and consumer law and clinical ethics committees.

Care robots in an aging demographic

Robots have been described as "embodied technologies that contain software, or code, and move and act on other objects in real space,"[7] and a care robot is "a machine that is able to conduct tasks related to physical or emotional care either autonomously or semi-autonomously."[8] The number and range of robots used in personal care and healthcare is ever increasing, driven by a rise in the elderly population worldwide. The number of people aged 60 and older is projected to grow to nearly 2.1 billion in 2050, with most of the increase in developing countries.[9] In Australia, in June 2020, there were approximately 4.2 million people aged 65 and over, 16% of Australia's total population.[10] In the United Kingdom the number of people of pensionable age (67 years) is projected to increase by 11.3% to 1.3 million people by mid-2030.[11] Europeans are also living longer, and in some European countries, more than 40% of women aged 65 or older live alone.[12] Japan is considered to have a 'super-aged' society where people 65 and older represent about 28% of the population, and by 2036 this will amount to a third of the population.[13] The global trend for families to have fewer children impacts on interfamilial care and support for their older relatives, and this, combined with the number of people entering older age, will provide real challenges for health and social care. Over one-quarter (26.8%) of all older Australians (those aged 65 years and over) live alone.[14] More than 800,000 personal and health aides (assistants) are estimated to be required in the United States between 2014 and 2024, "yet the nature of these jobs – which often involve heavy physical demands and risk of injury, while providing relatively low wages and benefits – makes them difficult to fill and has led to concerns about an ongoing shortage in paid caregivers."[15]

Governments around the world are grappling with the use of robotic technology and how the opportunities and benefits can be harnessed whilst addressing inherent challenges such as data security and user safety. Japan is at the forefront of robot development, and the Japanese government produced a Robot Strategy in 2015, when a 'Robot Revolution Intensive Five Years Implementation Period' started, including as one priority area robot technology in nursing care.[16] Rather touchingly, the 'Message of the New Robot Strategy 2018' includes the words "robotics is like another form of life with which we share this planet, and it's growing little by little every day."[17]

In 2020 the European Parliament passed a resolution with a recommendation to the European Commission that legislation be enacted to ensure ethical use of artificial intelligence (AI) and robotics, although this does not refer specifically to robotic care assistants.[18] The UK Parliamentary Office of Science and Technology noted that while further research is needed to assess their impact in practice, use of robots automating tasks can save resources, and robotics may provide one way to improve the quality of UK social care.[19] The Australian Royal Commission into Aged Care Quality and Safety made a number of recommendations with respect to assistive technologies. These included recommendations that from 1 July 2022 the Australian government should implement an assistive technology program within aged care to provide goods, aids, equipment and services to enable independence in daily living tasks and reduce risks to living safely at home and that these technologies should be universally available and funded by the Australian government.[20] The *Assistive Technology for All* campaign, an initiative of Council on the Ageing (COTA) Victoria, noted in 2020 that "the next step is to get government to implement those recommendations."[21]

Use of robots in the care of older adults

Family and carers can monitor the elderly person remotely using a robot in the elder's home, visually checking their physical condition and daily activities. Robots also assist the elderly themselves with personal care, such as washing and eating, supervise and monitor medication and behaviour in the home and can provide cognitive support applications such as locating lost items and giving reminders of tasks.[22] Companion robots, like *Paro*, the baby seal developed in Japan, are intended to trigger positive affections and emotions in users and can encourage social behaviour and alleviate stress. Robot care assistants take many differing forms. At one end of the spectrum there are those that are simple in design and look robotic. Some have facial features and may simulate human behaviour, which is proving more acceptable to users. Some are designed for specific tasks such as feeding ('*My Spoon*') and washing, and others can be programmed for a broad range of applications. *Hobbit* can assist people to get up from a fall and notify family and emergency responders, *Care-O-bot 4* can act as a companion and helper, performing household tasks, fetching and lifting things and reminding the person of routine tasks, and it can be programmed to speak to the older person. The *Riba* robot (Robot for Interactive Body Assistance) is an adult-sized robot designed to look like a teddy bear – it can pick up and carry humans from a bed to a wheelchair. *Pearl* is a 'nursebot' reminding the user about daily activities such as eating, taking medication and exercise. *Lio* is a padded artificial leather-covered robot able to hold and move objects and complete complex tasks. These robots may support the elderly to live independently, addressing isolation and reduced physical functioning.

Robots can also facilitate telehealth. Chapter 7 explores telehealth and its application in healthcare consultations, which allows doctors to evaluate patients and detect signs of illness remotely. These teleconsultations use static computers, tablets and smartphones which are within the control of the patient. Mobile robots can provide telemedicine services that enable remote dynamic evaluation and management of patients in various settings, controlled by the clinician and in the hospital setting robots can read vital signs, use nasal and oral swabs for SARS-CoV-2 testing and place intravenous catheters.[23] The *RP-7* robot is wirelessly operated with audio visual capability, facilitating remote doctor-patient interactions and assisting in the assessment and care of patients from a distant location. It has "a digital stethoscope, privacy handset and a printer capable of providing hard copies of orders and recommendations with the digital signature of the physician conducting the remote presence clinical session."[24] The *RP-7* robot has a very high acceptance rate by patients.

Whilst they can provide enormous benefits, the interaction of personal companion robots with humans raises complex legal and ethical issues. Who do robots benefit, do the anticipated benefits outweigh potential harms from their use and what is the impact of robots on the welfare of the elderly and on society as a whole?

Harms and benefits of robotic care

The human dignity and welfare of older adults who use robotic assistants in the home provide the framing of ethical issues that arise from their use. Indeed both the United Nations Universal Declaration of Human Rights and the Treaty on European Union set out the importance of human dignity of all individuals.

Universal Declaration of Human Rights, Article 1

All human beings are born free and equal in dignity and rights. They are endowed with reason and conscience and should act towards one another in a spirit of brotherhood.

Treaty on European Union, Article 2

The Union is founded on the values of respect for human dignity, freedom, democracy, equality, the rule of law and respect for human rights, including the rights of persons belonging to minorities.

The Four Principles of Biomedical Ethics, propounded by Beauchamp and Childress,[25] are highly influential in bioethics and provide a framework to evaluate the benefits and harms of medical interventions. They include:

- Autonomy
- Non-maleficence
- Beneficence
- Justice

The literature on the use of robotic care assistants frequently utilises these four principles to explore ethical issues in their use for the elderly.

Autonomy

The concept of 'autonomy' describes the expression of individual values and choices and is considered foundational to wellbeing and human dignity. The meaning and value of autonomy are expressed by Dr Kim Atkins in this way:

> If we accept that the subjective character of experience is irreducible and that it is grounded in the particularity of our points of view, then we are bound to realise that our respect for each other's differences and autonomy embodies a respect for the particularity of each other's points of view. Respect for autonomy is at the same time recognition of the irreducible differences that separate us as subjects.[26]

Elderly users of robotic care assistants in their own homes will have different preferences about how they interact with the robots. Of key ethical concern is whether robotic care assistants enhance or reduce the autonomy of the elderly user per se and the circumstances when autonomy may be appropriately curtailed to promote other values, such as safety.

Do robotic care assistants promote autonomy?

It can be argued that robotic care assistants can increase the user's autonomy and dignity.[27] Ageing may impact the physical expression of autonomy, as an older person may have reduced mobility or not have enough strength to implement their choices. By providing assistance with tasks and medication, robotic care assistants can decrease the user's dependence on other people and can increase physical expression of autonomy, promoting independence and social contact, with the attendant psychological benefits. Autonomy is promoted where robotic technology is under the control of the user and can be programmed to respond to their commands. A robot that monitors medication could alert the user that tablets need to be taken, but then it is a choice of the user whether or not to take them. Sorell and Draper argue that the *Care-O-bot* promotes rather than impairs the user's autonomy because it "takes the user's routine and the preferences embodied in this routine as its frame of reference. This means that the user's choices are foremost and, other things being equal, are implemented unquestioningly."[28] If the programming of the robot, perhaps following the preferences of family members, resulted in limitations on when the user could leave the home, how often they are washed and what they eat, supplanting the preferences of the user, this would impair their autonomy in an unjustifiable way.

Justification for limitation of autonomy

The exercise of autonomy includes the right to make mistakes and take on the consequences of choices. But are there situations where the exercise of autonomous choice should be restricted to preserve the wellbeing of the individual? The literature uses examples of a robotic assistant programmed to predict a dangerous situation and to override the choices of the elderly user in order to prevent harm, such as turning off the cooker or "even restraining the elderly person (gently) from carrying out a potentially dangerous action such as climbing up on a chair to get something from a cupboard.[29] Whilst this may have beneficial consequences, we may question whether this is an appropriate limitation on autonomy or an unwarranted imposition on individual choice (and indeed there may be a risk that robots make incorrect decisions). Sorell and Draper consider that for users of robotic care assistants in the home, autonomy should be the "pre-eminent value," even more important than safety and social connectedness.[30] This approach is consistent with the law's respect for the exercise of autonomous choices by adults in healthcare decision making. In *Re MB (Medical Treatment)*[31] Butler-Sloss L.J. stated,

> A mentally competent patient has an absolute right to refuse to consent to medical treatment for any reason, rational or irrational, or for no reason at all, even where that decision may lead to his or her own death.[32]

There is inherent harm in overriding autonomous choice – it limits freedom and self-expression and impacts on the inherent dignity of an individual. The 19th-century philosopher John Stuart Mill considered the extent to which society has a right to control the actions and beliefs of individuals. In his famous work *On Liberty*, he argues that "the only purpose for which power can be rightfully exercised over any member of a civilized community, against his will, is to prevent harm to others."[33] However, the notion that individual liberty or autonomy has moral primacy and should be protected, unless the exercise of such interests results in harm to others, fails to appreciate the role of the community and social relationships, so important in the care of the elderly in society.

In any event the exercise of autonomy is dependent on decision-making ability,

> A person who lacks the ability to make the decisions they face in a particular domain, even when support is provided, cannot accurately be described as acting autonomously in that domain; they lack the potential for self-legislating self-determination that lies at the core of the concept of autonomy.[34]

Using Sorell and Draper's paradigm, we could conclude that the choices of an elderly person with decision-making capacity should not be overridden by a robotic care assistant even if that person is at risk of harm and no one else (such as a human carer) is at risk of harm. Elderly users of robotic care assistants may experience a decline in decision-making capacity, and although this does not mean that the preferences of a user who lacks decision-making capacity should not be considered, the obligation to protect that user from harm increases.

Beneficence

Beneficence refers to an obligation to act for the benefit of another, contributing to their welfare. Robotic care assistants do benefit the elderly user in various ways, assisting the user's ability to carry out the activities of daily living such as eating, dressing, washing, grooming and toileting[35]; providing companionship and assistance with tasks; and can have positive impacts on a user's mobility, mental health and cognitive skills. A study in the use of *Paro*, the robotic baby seal, has demonstrated that nursing home residents who held and petted it had lowered blood pressure.[36] In some care situations, for example, regarding hygiene, it may be "less stigmatising for the older adults to receive care from robots instead of humans."[37] The co-location of user and robot gives rise to what Sorell and Draper call 'presence,' a therapeutic property which means that the elderly person no longer feels alone[38] (although this could also be perceived as a type of deception of the elderly about the true nature and function of robotic care). Benefits of robotic carers also extend to the family members living apart from their elderly relative, who may feel reassured that their loved one is 'safe' with a robotic care assistant in the house. In the case scenario, June's family identify the benefits that they wish to achieve for them and June if she has a robot in her home. But these identified benefits may be realised only if the robot is programmed to provide assistance to meet those aims. June and her family can clarify if the robotic carer can provide assistance with the range of physical and social tasks they feel would be of benefit such as assisting with walking and providing reminders about eating, drinking and taking medications. Keeping the elderly well at home reduces the strain on the healthcare and social systems, with all of those attendant costs.

Best interests and use by the elderly with declining cognitive capacity

The decisions of older people should be treated with the same respect as those of other cognitively *un*impaired adults, but we know that cognitive changes occur with normal ageing, and often executive cognitive function and attention decline with age.[39] The most common cause of cognitive decline in older adults is Alzheimer disease, and the prevalence of clinically diagnosed Alzheimer disease increases exponentially with age.[40] Cognitive impairment may be significant enough to impact on the capacity of a person to make decisions, particularly pertinent for those with dementia. This presents complexity for the provision of care through a robot assistant because we should consider who is making decisions. If it is not the user themselves, then are decisions being made in their best interests? A 'decision' made by a robot may not be in the best interests of the user if the robot has not been updated to take account of new medications, diagnoses or other changes of circumstance. But in a wider context, how can we ensure that decisions of the robot such as turning the lights and TV off, opening the door for visitors and regulating the heating in the house promote the best interests of the user?

'Best interests' is the standard used in healthcare decision making for individuals who lack capacity. A key premise of the Mental Capacity Act 2005 (England and Wales), which clarifies and builds on existing principles of common law, is that any decision taken on behalf of a person who lacks capacity to make the relevant decision must be made in the best interests of the person. Best interests encompass medical, emotional and other welfare issues, and the Mental Capacity Act 2005 requires that the decision maker must consider all the relevant circumstances, and in particular the person's past and present wishes and feelings and their beliefs and values in determining best interests (s 4(6) MCA). The United Nations Convention on the Rights of Persons with Disabilities (CRPD), which came into force in 2008 and has over 160 state signatories, includes lack of legal capacity as a disability, and Article 12 highlights the importance of respecting the rights, will and preferences of the person lacking capacity. I have written elsewhere about the value of a narrative approach to help inform what the individual currently lacking capacity would now want.[41] A narrative is "an instantiation of the beliefs, values, experiences, actions, decisions, events and relationships that give meaning and coherence to a person's life."[42] The programmer of a robotic carer will not know a user's idiosyncrasies, whether they prefer to watch TV for hours on end or eat the same food every day, yet such behaviour may be an expression of their preferences and wishes. If "regard to patient narrative is congruent with an ethical obligation to respect the dignity of the patient and is consistent with patient-centeredness,"[43] then can 'artificial' decisions effected by algorithms with no knowledge of the patient ever be person centred, aligning with their individual best interests? As Ienca and others note,

> The promotion of the best interest of the user would also require a careful and continuative evaluation of their positive and negative experiences, with the knowledge that the user's preferences and experiences may change over the progression of the disease and that their ability to communicate those preferences and experiences may decrease over time.[44]

Autonomous robots have the ability to perform tasks without continuous human input or control and follow pre-programmed commands. Robots, which use AI, can learn iteratively from their environments and interaction with the user through continuous feedback. This informs the 'decisions' of robots, which although are made independently of the direction of the user, can be informed by their behaviours and interactions. This might enable decisions that are more person-centred, although potentially at a cost to the 'objective' best interests of the person – going to bed at a reasonable time, eating a varied diet, etc. At some point in future development, robots have the potential to be made intelligent and autonomous moral agents.[45] So, there is real complexity about who, or what, is making decisions in respect of the care and safety of the older user, and these may have high-stakes consequences. Should robots be programmed to always ensure the safety of the user even though such intervention would not be what the user wants, or, if the user now lacks decision-making capacity, what they would have wanted? This dilemma underscores the importance of ethical design and regulation.

Non-maleficence

The principle of non-maleficence describes an obligation not to inflict harm intentionally and includes the prevention of harm and the removal of harmful conditions. Harms arising from use of robotic care assistants include stigmatisation, enforcing the negative representations of ageing and older adults and infantilisation.[46] Research shows that patients who use *Paro* the seal treat it as if it were alive. Robots may create the perception that they have, or at least understand, emotions, with users forming emotional attachments to them. Sharkey and Sharkey consider whether interactive robots may give rise to an illusion of sentience by responding to social cues, perhaps amounting to deception about the true nature and function of robotic care.[47] Although robots may be able to provide personalised dialogue with the user and can facilitate social interactions, some consider that robotic care can result in less interaction with real people, increasing isolation and exacerbating loneliness. As Kortner notes, "the more we can communicate with robots, the less we might communicate with human beings, especially senior adults who are impaired in their mobility."[48] Reducing or depriving the elderly of human contact can be considered "unethical, and even a form of cruelty."[49] Personalised care robots should never be an alternative form of care, but rather support existing care and social structures.

> It goes without saying that most of us would enjoy the company of a living being in old age. But when human care is sparse, robots could assist the needy, or serve as companions in the many hours of loneliness.[50]

Robotic care assistants in the home also present "unprecedented intrusions" in the privacy of the user.[51] Different conceptions of privacy include *physical privacy* – the invasion of personal space, such as robots with cameras which survey elderly people in their homes to monitor for their care and security – and *information privacy*, what data is gathered and stored and who it should be shared with – family, healthcare professionals, emergency services and in what circumstances.

Article 12 of the Universal Declaration of Human Rights states: "No one shall be subjected to arbitrary interference with his privacy, family, home or correspondence, nor to attacks upon his honour and reputation. Everyone has the right to the protection of the law against such interference or attacks."

Robotic care assistants in the home are necessarily within the private space of the older person, and although they can be programmed not to go into certain areas of the home, such as the bedroom and bathroom, there remains a concern about intrusion into the private sphere of the individual. Robots with monitoring cameras and voice recognition gather personal data and can learn *from* the user and *about* the user, including information on medication use, behaviours and movement.

This information may be shared with family members who purchased the robot, and it also has value to the manufacturer, software companies or other commercial third parties. Kaminski notes that "the ability of robots to sense and record information, and likelihood that they will share that information with third parties for storage and processing purposes, are clearly legally salient features from a privacy perspective,"[52] and she asks, by consenting to have a robotic care assistant in the home do users also agree to allow them to make a recording? Privacy policies which adopt a notice and consent regime (an online "click here" to accept the terms of a provider's service and privacy policy) do not allow consumers such as June, the 85-year-old in the case scenario, to input their privacy choices on which interactions in the home are recorded and who that data is shared with. A study in France showed that a common view held by people with mild cognitive impairment was that surveillance applications in care robots could be a threat to their privacy.[53] Blake notes that,

> the thing that makes these robots useful for patients is the very thing that also makes them dangerous: patients accepting them as some version of helper and confidante and providing them sensitive information, unwitting to where that information may wind up or how it might be used.[54]

It is possible to manage harms by programming robots according to user's preferences, so that cameras can be disabled in certain locations. Consent to use of a robotic carer should clarify what data is recorded and who has access to it.[55] It could be considered a valid exercise of autonomy for an individual to choose to trade off some aspects of privacy for day-to-day assistance and care, but this depends on understanding and trust in the processes for data collection and sharing. As Kaminski notes,

> when information revealed in the home is shared and used outside of the home, people may stop trusting that the home is a private location, and may stop sharing information and conform their behavior to majority norms even within the home.[56]

Justice

The term 'distributive justice' refers to fair, equitable and appropriate distribution of resources in society, the idea that people in similar situations should be treated equally. From an ethical perspective, access to robotic assistance should be available to the elderly who need it (and want it), but this entails a large financial cost and healthcare providers may appropriately consider resources should be prioritised for other lower-cost/greater-impact care and treatment. The moral theory of utilitarianism states that the morally right action is that which maximises happiness or benefit and minimises pain or harm across society. The requirement to maximise total health benefit from a relevant budget explains why adoption of robotic care assistants at scale is slow. There may be a reluctance for governmental spending on robotic carers in return for future savings in assisted social care, although some government-funded home packages may cover robotic care assistants or companion pets. The purchase of robotic care assistants and companion pets is instead likely to be funded by the individual or their family so only those who can afford to pay can reap the benefits.

Is it ethical, then, to use robots in elder care? How we perceive the trade-off between the benefits (independent living, less social isolation, assistance with daily tasks and medication) against harms (potentially less human interaction, deception, individualised choices overridden, reduction in dignity and privacy) may change over time as we grow older and in light of our own altered circumstances. As Ipke Wachsmuth notes, "in fact some of us are likely to accept, or even prefer, a care robot's assistance, when our independence is at risk."[57]

Consent to use of a robotic care assistant

Informed consent is foundational for the exercise of autonomy and ensures that the individual who is the subject of the therapeutic intervention is aware of, understands and agrees to it. In the process of obtaining informed consent, the provider conveys the risks, benefits, burdens and alternatives of treatment and the patient gives consent for treatment. Without enough relevant information, people are unable to exercise real choice. This issue of informed consent to the use of robotic care assistants is potentially problematic (see also Chapter 6). Firstly, in the circumstances where the individual or family is instigating use of a robot in the elderly person's home, it is not the healthcare practitioner that engages in dialogue around information provision, with the attendant standards and professional framework to guide the interaction, but rather the relationship is one of consumer and product/service provider. Secondly, the elderly user may at the outset have capacity to agree to/consent for the robot to be in their home, but cognitive abilities cannot be assumed to remain at the same level as when the user provided consent, so there are implications for ongoing use in the context of dwindling capacity.

Capacity to consent to use of robot care

A study reported in 2015 found that healthy adults *with* capacity do not perceive the usefulness of robots, although caregivers do think that robotic care could alleviate their burden of providing care.[58] Older adults who are living at home and are able to manage daily tasks independently may feel this technology is unnecessary.[59] Care robots appear to be frequently provided to patients with lack of or declining cognitive ability, for example, people with dementia, both in the home and residential settings,[60] and indeed older adults with mild cognitive impairment have demonstrated the highest acceptance of robotic companionship.[61]

Interestingly "relatives have been found to be more negative towards care robots than older adults,"[62] although this depends on the particular care robot. The acceptance by June and her family to use of a robotic care assistant may then depend on the type of robotic carer, June's familiarity with technology and whether she and her family perceive that it meets their needs.

Information provision

Where a healthcare provider initiates the use of robotic care for an elderly patient, clinicians with care of the person would obtain informed consent.[63] The drive for efficiency and cost cutting in aged care and social services means that current investment in robotics leading to future savings has not been fully pursued in the public sector.[64] Given the high cost of robotic assistants and the lack of public funding, it is likely that the elderly individual, or their family, will initiate the provision of robotic care, as in the case scenario. At a minimum, the person who uses the robotic care assistant should understand the purpose of the robot, for example, whether the goal is to assist or monitor the individual and the impact on health outcomes. Sorell and Draper highlight that this goal setting may help individuals establish boundaries that they are comfortable with.[65] Information should be provided about the implications for privacy and confidentiality, such as how frequently data is obtained from the robot, what information the robot may capture and who it is shared with, including whether family members and other third parties will obtain information, as well as how long and in what manner data will be stored.[66] The enormous amount of information that could be disclosed, and the complexity of AI and decisions based on algorithms, may be beyond the understanding of the user and challenges the role and adequacy of informed consent in this setting. Rather than being able to "'lift the curtain' and receive information on who makes and owns the robot, how the robot works, what its capabilities are, and what it is really manufactured to do,"[67] perhaps it is enough that the user understands the purpose of the technology and can communicate their intentions. It would be too easy to take an ageist and paternalistic perspective, making assumptions that older people are unable to understand and engage with technology, or that they may willingly accept a certain loss of privacy in return for monitoring of their safety and improved wellbeing through interactions with a robot.[68] Meaningful consent needs to be voluntarily provided, and the subtle, or perhaps less subtle, persuasion by family members for an elderly relative to have a care robot is an issue of potential concern. Preferences may change over time, and rather than blanket consent extending to everything the robot may do, the elderly user should be able to agree to aspects of the robotic provision of care and have the option to change their mind.

Regulation of robotic care assistants

Regulation aims to protect the interests of stakeholders in society. Regulation has been defined as "any rule endorsed by government where there is an expectation of compliance,"[69] and this encapsulates regulation in the form of legislation (acts of parliament) and secondary legislation. Legislation regulates some aspects of robotic technology; for example, privacy laws deal with the way in which personal data gathered by a robotic care assistant can be used, stored and shared with others. Consumer protection laws[70] impose responsibilities on manufacturers and provide processes and remedies for defective goods. The Australian Consumer Law (which is set out in Schedule 2 of the Competition and Consumer Act 2010 Cth) provides that a manufacturer will be liable if their defective product caused an individual to suffer loss, including personal injury and death (s138). A 'state-of-the-art' defence means that manufacturers can escape liability if they can demonstrate that the defect in their product could not have been discovered because of limitations in the state of scientific knowledge at the time the goods were supplied.[71] How successfully the state-of-the-art defence may be used remains to be seen, but in the rapidly evolving field of AI and robotics, we may question whether consumer law adequately protects from harms arising.

Regulation of therapeutic goods focusses on safety issues and risks and benefits. Some robots meet the definition of a medical device, such as *Paro* the seal, which is considered a moderate-risk device by the Food and Drug Administration in the United States. An assistive care robot fulfils the requirements of a medical device according to the Australian Therapeutic Goods Act 1989 if it is "intended to be used in the treatment of dementia, such as for reducing its behavioural and psychological symptoms or assisting with functional disability or communication."[72] It can prove to be a slow and costly process to bring medical devices to market through the relevant regulatory regime.[73]

Government-endorsed regulation through legislation may assist in monitoring reports of adverse events and promulgating standards and has the advantage of ensuring compliance through the imposition of penalties. In Australia manufacturers of medical devices must demonstrate compliance with the Therapeutic Goods Administration Essential Principles,[74] which have requirements for safety and performance of a device, but it is not sufficiently responsive to keep up with fast-paced developments in technology. More flexible non-legal methods such as co-regulation and self-regulation have been proposed in the alternative.

Self-regulation

"A process whereby an organised group regulates the behaviour of its members"[75] and is characterised by industry-formulated rules and codes of conduct, with industry solely responsible for enforcement.

Co-regulation

The process where "industry develops and administers its own arrangements, but government provides legislative backing to enable the arrangements to be enforced."[76]

Responsive regulation

Authors of the report 'Robots and the Delivery of Care Services' suggest a responsive regulatory approach which "relies on actors to self and peer regulate and escalate issues as they arise upon which governments can implement regulatory efforts of different strengths."[77]

Self-regulation by AI developers has been the usual model for regulating robotics. However, such soft governance has been criticised as inadequate to protect the safety of the vulnerable and promote their interests where there are large financial returns for companies that develop them and little or no accountability for non-adherence to self-imposed rules and standards. Indeed, authors Iphofen and Kritikos argue that "policies and regulations will fail if no account is taken of the ethics of robotics."[78] They propose an 'ethics by design' principle in AI, which encompasses both the ethical reasoning capabilities of the AI system and "codes of conduct, standards and certification processes that ensure the integrity of developers and users of this technology."[79]

A framework or code of ethics is important in the development of robotics, and a report of the European Parliament Committee on Legal Affairs recommends a voluntary ethical code of conduct for robot manufacturers to guide safety. But ethical issues also arise in the everyday application and use of robotic care assistants, and one approach to address the ethical challenges arising in use of care robots in an institutional setting are ethics committees and ethical consultation services.[80]

Clinical/robot ethics committees

The focus of this chapter is use of robots in the home, not in institutions. Robots are used in healthcare institutions in surgery (for example, the da Vinci Surgical Robot), and in hospitals and care homes robots can automate mundane and routine nursing tasks and assist in moving patients.[81] Qualitative research in the emerging role of robotics in healthcare identified that

> healthcare robotic applications that were designated for particular uses (such as surgery, where they basically represented a sophisticated tool) or confined to back-office functions in controlled environments (such as pharmacy robots) were seen as less difficult to implement, as they had fewer challenging sociotechnical implications.[82]

The integration of robotics into healthcare settings may not be straightforward, raising issues about appropriate use of resources, impact on staff and acceptability by patients. Clinical/robot ethics committees can provide a valuable lens to consider the ethical use of robotic carers in a healthcare institution. Such a care robot committee could evaluate the settings and the sorts of patients where it would be appropriate to use a care robot, the extent of monitoring they provide, compliance with ethical standards and how they will be used by clinicians.[83]

A key function of clinical ethics committees/groups is to provide decision-making support to healthcare providers in ethically challenging cases through clinical case consultation. The role of an ethics committee is advisory – it does not have the remit to mandate a particular course of action.[84] Nevertheless, the process of deliberation includes discussion and application of basic concepts of ethical theory and principles, such as the Four Principles. So a clinical ethics committee would consider how the autonomy of a patient/user may be impacted by use of a robotic care assistant, the overall harms (maleficence) and benefits (beneficence) of its use, fairness (justice) in the allocation of resources for the purchase of robotic carers and the impact on the roles and continued employment of human carers. I have suggested that, a

> robot ethics committee could create hospital policies and procedures that must be followed and also provides a consultation service so that ethics advice is given in response to particular clinical situations, such as use of robotic assistants where the elderly person lacks capacity to consent, use of resources to purchase robotic carers, impact on staffing and whether the elderly person receives overall benefit.[85]

In many countries such as Australia and the United Kingdom, clinical ethics services have been developed on an ad hoc basis by interested and informed healthcare practitioners,[86] whereas in some countries clinical ethics committees have formed in response to government recommendation or requirements of regulatory authorities. In North America institutions may, in addition, use ethics consultants to provide individual support to clinicians, patients and their families. However, the purchase/use of a robotic care assistant by a family, or the elderly person themselves, to provide in-home assistance would not come within the scope of reference of a healthcare institution's ethics group.

Conclusion

The ageing population across the world is increasing, putting pressure on health and social care services and creating concerns for family members who may be unable to provide the level of care they wish because of work demands or distance from their aged relative. Robotic care assistants can provide an alternative, automated form of care, transcending human judgement, biases and inclinations. But the advantages that robots provide for an elderly person, such as the ability to live an independent life at home, come at a cost, including concerns about privacy, dignity and the exacerbation of loneliness. After all, human contact and touch are intrinsic to care.

Regulation of the ethical development of robotic carers, their safety and appropriate use demands that the welfare of the elderly user is prioritised, with an understanding that this population group may face barriers in asserting their rights because of physical limitations and cognitive decline. Regulatory frameworks also need to keep pace with the development of technology, and multiple stakeholder perspectives, including the elderly themselves, are key in the development and acceptability of robotic care assistants.

The use of robotic technologies in the health and care sectors requires further evidence, particularly in understanding the experience of users and their acceptance of robotic carers. Robotic care assistants can benefit older adults like June by helping her to live in her own home, and her family who can be reassured of her safety and wellbeing. Harms arising from unwelcome monitoring and sharing of data can be managed through meaningful consent (by the user or appropriate surrogate if the user lacks decision-making capacity) and effective regulation. The design and programming of care robots should focus on the user experience and in the future, they can be cost-effectively marketed and available for use by individuals. Whilst I recognise that an increase in the population of older adults in society, a dwindling workforce and increased health and social care costs may indicate the utility of robotic care assistants, I still feel uncomfortable about their impact on the way we perceive and value older adults.

Notes

1. N. Koceska, S. Koceski, P. Beomonte Zobel, V. Trajkovik, N. Garcia, 'A Telemedicine Robot System for Assisted and Independent Living.' (2019) 19(4) *Sensors (Basel)*. 834.
2. A. Jagan Sathyamoorthy, U. Patel, M. Paul, Y. Savle, D. Manocha, 'COVID Surveillance Robot: Monitoring Social Distancing Constraints in Indoor Scenarios,' (2021) 16(12) *PLoS ONE* e0259713
3. Alzheimer's Australia, Robotic Pets, v 2.04 2017, reviewed 3/05/17 www.dementia. org.au/sites/default/files/WA/documents/2.04%20Robotic%20Pets.pdf.
4. A. Smith, M. Anderson, Pew Research Center, October, 2017, 'Automation in Everyday Life', page 39.
5. N. Lundebjerg, D. Trucil, E. Hammond, W. Applegate, Adopts Modified American Medical Association Style.' (2017) 65(7) *Journal of the American Geriatrics Society* 1386–1388.
6. University of Melbourne, Department of Accounting & Melbourne Disability Institute, 'Assistive Technology (AT) for All: Exploring the benefits and challenges of timely access to AT when ineligible for the NDIS.' 22 April 2022.
7. M. Kaminski, 'Robots in the Home: What Will We Have Agreed To?' (2015) 51(3) *Idaho Law Review* 661–678, page 663.
8. L. Van Aerschot, J. Parviainen, 'Robots Responding to Care Needs? A Multitasking Care Robot Pursued for 25 years, Available Products Offer Simple Entertainment and Instrumental Assistance.' (2020) 22 *Ethics and Information Technology* 247–256 page 247.
9. World Health Organization, Ageing and health 1 October 2022 (Web Page). www.who.int/health-topics/ageing#tab=tab_
10. Australian Institute of Health and Welfare, 'Older Australian' *Summary* (Web Page, December 2021). www.aihw.gov.au/reports-data/population-groups/older-people/overview
11. Office for National Statistics, *Data and Analysis from Census 2021* (National Population Projections – Office for National Statistics, London)
12. World Health Organization, Ageing and health, 1 October 2022 (Web Page) www.who.int/health-topics/ageing#tab=tab_
13. European Parliament, Briefing, Continental democracies, Japan's ageing society (European Union, 2020) www.europarl.europa.eu/RegData/etudes/BRIE/2020/659419/EPRS_BRI(2020)659419_EN.pdf
14. Australian Law Reform Commission, Elder Abuse – A National Legal Response (ALRC Report 131) Who are older Australians? para 2.3, 14 June 2017.
15. A. Smith, M. Anderson, Pew Research Center, October, 2017, 'Automation in Everyday Life', page 39.

16 The Headquarters for Japan's Economic Revitalization, 'New Robot Strategy – Japan's Robot Strategy' (Online Publication, 10 February 2015). www.meti.go.jp/english/press/2015/pdf/0123_01b.pdf.
17 Ministry of Economy, Trade and Industry (METI) Government of Japan, 'Japan's New Robot Strategy,' April 2018, page 15. www.djw.de/ja/assets/media/Veranstaltungen/Symposium,%20MGV/duesseldorf-20180416/djw-symposium-duesseldorf-16.04.2018-kurihara-meti.pdf
18 European Parliament, *Framework of Ethical Aspects of Artificial Intelligence, Robotics and Related Technologies* (European Parliament, Brussels, 2020). www.europarl.europa.eu/doceo/document/TA-9-2020-0275_EN.html
19 UK Parliament, *Parliamentary Office of Science and Technology*, 'Robotics in Social Care' *POSTNOTE Number 591* (UK Parliament, London, 2018).
20 Royal Commission into Aged Care Quality and Safety, Final report, 1 March 2021, List of Recommendations, Recommendations 34 and 109.
21 Assistive Technology for All, 'AT Recommendations Included in Final Report from Royal Commission into Aged Care Quality and Safety,' December 2020.
22 A. Sharkey, N. Sharkey, 'Granny and the Robots: Ethical Issues in Robotic Care for the Elderly' (2012) 14(1) *Ethics and Information Technology* 27–40.
23 P. Chai, F. Dadabhoy, H-W. Huang, J. Chu, et al. 'Mobile Assessment of the Acceptability and Feasibility of Using Mobile Robotic Systems for Patient Evaluation.' (2021) 4(3) *JAMA Network Open* e210667.
24 I. Mendez, M. Jong, D. Keays-White, G. Turner, 'The Use of Remote Presence for Health Care Delivery in a Northern Inuit Community: A Feasibility Study.' (2013) 72(10) *International Journal of Circumpolar Health* 3402.
25 T. Beauchamp and J. Childress. Principles of Biomedical Ethics (8th ed., 2019 Oxford University Press, New York, NY).
26 K. Atkins. (2000) 'Autonomy and the Subjective Character of Experience.' (2000) 17(1) *Journal of Applied Philosophy* 71–79, page 75.
27 See UK Parliament, *Parliamentary Office of Science and Technology*, 'Robotics in Social Care' *POSTNOTE Number 591* (UK Parliament, London, 2018).
28 T. Sorell, H. Draper, 'Robot Carers, Ethics, and Older People' (2014) 16(3) *Ethics and Information Technology* 183–195, page 189.
29 A. Sharkey, N. Sharkey, 'Granny and the Robots: Ethical Issues in Robotic Care for the Elderly' (2012) 14(1) *Ethics and Information Technology* 27–40, page 33.
30 T. Sorell, H. Draper, 'Robot Carers, Ethics, and Older People' (2014) 16(3) *Ethics and Information Technology* 183–195, page 184.
31 *Re MB (Medical Treatment)* [1997] EWCA Civ 3093
32 *Re MB (Medical Treatment)* [1997] EWCA Civ 3093 para 17.
33 John Stuart Mill, *'On Liberty' Harper Collins* (Harper Collins, London, 1962).
34 W. Martin, S. Michalowski, M. Burch, Essex Autonomy Project, 'Achieving CRPD Compliance- is the Mental Capacity Act of England and Wales Compatible with the UN Convention on the Rights of Persons with Disabilities? If Not What Next? (2014) page 19.
35 L. Van Aerschot, J. Parviainen, 'Robots Responding to Care Needs? A Multitasking Care Robot Pursued for 25 Years, Available Products Offer Simple Entertainment and Instrumental Assistance' (2020) 22 *Ethics and Information Technology* 247–256.
36 H. Robinson, B. MacDonald, E. Broadbent, 'Physiological Effects of a Companion Robot on Blood Pressure of Older People in Residential Care Facility: A Pilot Study,' (2015) 34(1) *Australasian Journal on Ageing*, 27–32.
37 R-M. Johansson-Pajala et al, 'Care Robot Orientation: What, Who and How? Potential Users' Perceptions' (2020) 12(5) *International Journal of Social Robotics* 1103–1117, page 1104.
38 T. Sorell, H. Draper, 'Robot Carers, Ethics, and Older People' (2014) 16(3) *Ethics and Information Technology* 183–195, page 184.
39 D. Murman, 'The Impact of Age on Cognition.' (2015) 36(3) *Seminars in Hearing - Audiology* 111–121.
40 D. Murman, 'The Impact of Age on Cognition' (2015) 36(3) *Seminars in Hearing - Audiology* 111–121.

41 C. Johnston, N. Banner, A. Fenwick, 'Patient Narrative: An 'on-switch' for Evaluating Best Interests' (2016) 38(3) *Journal of Social Welfare and Family Law* 249–262.
42 C. Johnston, N. Banner, A. Fenwick, 'Patient Narrative: An 'On-switch' for Evaluating Best Interests' (2016) 38(3) *Journal of Social Welfare and Family Law* 249–262, page 252.
43 C. Johnston, N. Banner, A. Fenwick, 'Patient Narrative: An 'On-switch' for Evaluating Best Interests' (2016) 38(3) *Journal of Social Welfare and Family Law* 249–262, page 261.'
44 M. Ienca, F. Jotterand, C. Vic˘a, B. Elger, 'Social and Assistive Robotics in Dementia Care: Ethical Recommendations for Research and Practice.' (2016) 8 *International Journal of Social Robotics* 565–573, page 570.
45 H. Dickinson, C. Smith, N. Carey, G. Carey, *Robots and the Delivery of Care Services: What is the Role for Government in Stewarding Disruptive Innovation?* (Melbourne: ANZSOG). https://apo.org.au/node/202716
46 M. Pino, M. Boulay, F. Jouen, A. Rigaud, 'Are We Ready for Robots that Care for Us?" Attitudes and Opinions of Older Adults toward Socially Assistive Robots' (2015) 7 *Frontiers in Aging Neuroscience* 141.
47 A. Sharkey, N. Sharkey, 'Granny and the Robots: Ethical Issues in Robotic Care for the Elderly' (2012) 14(1) *Ethics and Information Technology* 27–40.
48 T. Körtner, 'Ethical Challenges in the Use of Social Service Robots for Elderly People' (2016) 49(4) *Zeitschrift für Gerontologie und Geriatrie* 303–306, page 304.
49 A. Sharkey, N. Sharkey, 'Granny and the Robots: Ethical Issues in Robotic Care for the Elderly' (2012) 14(1) *Ethics and Information Technology* 27–40, page 30.
50 I. Wachsmuth, 'Robots Like Me: Challenges and Ethical Issues in Aged Care' (2018) 9(432) *Frontiers in Psychology* 1–3, page 3.
51 V. Blake, 'Regulating Care Robots' (2020) 92(3) *Temple Law Review* 551–594, page 583.
52 M. Kaminski, 'Robots in the Home: What Will We Have Agreed To?' (2015) 51(3) *Idaho Law Review* 661–678, page 665.
53 M. Pino, M. Boulay, F. Jouen, A. Rigaud, ' "Are We Ready for Robots That Care for Us?" Attitudes and Opinions of Older Adults toward Socially Assistive Robots' (2015) 7 *Frontiers in Aging Neuroscience* 141.
54 V. Blake, 'Regulating Care Robots' (2020) 92(3) *Temple Law Review* 551–594, page 583.
55 L. Carver, D Mackinnon, 'Health Applications of Gerontechnology, Privacy, and Surveillance: A Scoping Review.' 18(2) *Surveillance & Society* 216–230.
56 M. Kaminski, 'Robots in the Home: What Will We Have Agreed to?' (2015) 51(3) *Idaho Law Review* 661–678, page 664.
57 I. Wachsmuth, 'Robots Like Me: Challenges and Ethical Issues in Aged Care' (2018) 9(432) *Frontiers in Psychology* 1–3, page3.
58 M. Pino, M. Boulay, F. Jouen, A. Rigaud, ' "Are We Ready for Robots That Care for Us?" Attitudes and Opinions of Older Adults toward Socially Assistive Robots' (2015) 7 *Frontiers in Aging Neuroscience* 141.
59 W. Koh, S. Felding, K. Budak, E. Toomey, D. Casey, 'Barriers and Facilitators to the Implementation of Social Robots for Older Adults and People with Dementia: A Scoping Review.' (2021) 21(1) *BMC Geriatrics* 351.
60 M. Ienca, F. Jotterand, C. Vicǎ, B. Elger, 'Social and Assistive Robotics in Dementia Care: Ethical Recommendations for Research and Practice' (2016) 8 *International Journal of Social Robotics* 565–573.
61 M. Pino, M. Boulay, F. Jouen, A. Rigaud, ' "Are We Ready for Robots That Care for Us?" Attitudes and Opinions of Older Adults toward Socially Assistive Robots' (2015) 7 *Frontiers in Aging Neuroscience* 141.
62 R. M. Johansson Pajala et al. 'Care Robot Orientation: What, Who and How? Potential Users' Perceptions' (2020) 12(5) *International Journal of Social Robotics* 1103–1117, page 1105.
63 *Rogers v Whitaker* (1992) 175 CLR 479.
64 H. Dickinson, C. Smith, N. Carey, G. Carey, *Robots and the Delivery of Care Services: What Is the Role for Government in Stewarding Disruptive Innovation?* (ANZSOG, Melbourne). https://apo.org.au/node/202716.
65 T. Sorell, H. Draper, 'Robot Carers, Ethics, and Older People' (2014) 16(3) *Ethics and Information Technology* 183–195.

66 T. Körtner, 'Ethical Challenges in the Use of Social Service Robots for Elderly People' (2016) 49(4) *Zeitschrift für Gerontologie und Geriatrie* 303–306.
67 V. Blake, 'Regulating Care Robots' (2020) 92(3) *Temple Law Review* 551–594, page 583.
68 E. Vaportzis, M. Clausen, A. Gow, 'Older Adults Perceptions of Technology and Barriers to Interacting with Tablet Computers: A Focus Group Study' (2017) 8 *Frontiers in Psychology* 1687.
69 The Australian Government, Department of the Prime Minister and Cabinet. 'What Do we Mean by Regulation?' www.pmc.gov.au/ria-mooc/introduction/what-do-we-mean-regulation
70 R. Leenes, E. Palmerini, B-J. Koops, A. Bertolini, P. Salvini, F. Lucivero, 'Regulatory challenges of robotics: some guidelines for addressing legal and ethical issues,' (2017) 9(1) *Law, Innovation and Technology* 1–44.
71 M. Tsui, 'The State-of-the-Art Defence: Defining the Australian Experience in the Context of Pharmaceuticals,' (2013) 13(1) *QUT Law Review* 132–157.
72 W. Moyle, 'The Promise of Technology in the Future of Dementia Care.' (2019)15 *Nature Reviews Neurology* 353–359, page 357.
73 Approval as a medical device does not guarantee safety; see the class action against Johnson & Johnson in respect of harms caused by a vaginal mesh implant. *Ethicon Sàrl v Gill* [2021] FCAFC 29.
74 Australian Government, Department of Health, Therapeutic Goods Administration, 'Consultation: Proposed changes to the medical device Essential Principles for safety and performance,' Version 1.0, September 2019.
75 N. Gunningham, D. Sinclair, Chapter 8, *Smart Regulation* in *'Regulatory Theory Foundations and Applications'* (ed P. Drahos) Australian National University Press, 2017, page 140.
76 Australian Law Reform Commission, *Classification – Content Regulation and Convergent Media* (ALRC Report 118) 1 March 2012, para 13.13.
77 H. Dickinson, C. Smith, N. Carey, G. Carey, Robots and the Delivery of Care Services: What Is the Role for Government in Stewarding Disruptive Innovation? (ANZSOG, Melbourne). https://apo.org.au/node/202716N 77, page 21.
78 R. Iphofen, M. Kritikos, 'Regulating Artificial Intelligence and Robotics: Ethics by Design in a Digital Society' (2021) 16(2) *Contemporary Social Science: Journal of the Academy of Social Sciences* 170–184, page 181.
79 R. Iphofen, M. Kritikos, 'Regulating Artificial Intelligence and Robotics: Ethics by Design in a Digital Society' (2021) 16(2) *Contemporary Social Science: Journal of the Academy of Social Sciences* 170–184, page 181.
80 A. Slowther, C. Johnston, J. Goodall, T. Hope, 'Development of Clinical Ethics Committees' (2004) 328 *BMJ* 950–952.
81 M. Saadatzi, et al., 'Acceptability of Using a Robotic Nursing Assistant in Health Care Environments: Experimental Pilot Study,' (2020) 22(11) *Journal of Medical Internet Research* e17509.
82 K. Cresswell, S. Cunningham-Burley, A. Sheikh, 'Health Care Robotics: Qualitative Exploration of Key Challenges and Future Directions,' (2018) 20(7) *Journal of Medical Internet Research* e10410.
83 V. Blake, 'Regulating Care Robots' (2020) 92(3) *Temple Law Review* 551–594, page 586.
84 A. Slowther, C. Johnston, J. Goodall, T. Hope, 'Development of Clinical Ethics Committees' (2004) 328 *BMJ* 950–952.
85 C. Johnston, 'Ethical Design and Use of Robotic Care of the Elderly' (2022) 19(1) *Journal of Bioethical Inquiry* 11–14.
86 C. Johnston, 'Online Survey of the Perceived Need for Ethics Support in a Large National Health Service Foundation Trust.' (2010) 5(4) *Clinical Ethics* 201–206.

9
A NEW USE FOR EXISTING TECHNOLOGY

Digital advance care decisions

Case scenario

Mr Chan is 67 years old and lives with his extended family in Melbourne, Australia. He has been diagnosed with dementia and is concerned about the impact that this will have on his family and his need for future care and treatment. He attended an information evening about advance care decision making at the Chinese community centre – the facilitators have said that they will provide free translation and support for those who would like to make an advance care decision. Mr Chan is keen to reduce the burden on his family of his future care, but he is unsure what information he would include in a written document, and he is reluctant to speak with his family about this because he does not want to upset and alarm them. One evening Mr Chan's grandson produces his smartphone and asks his grandfather to talk about the things he values in life and what is important to him, so that he can keep it as a record.

Introduction

A person can utilise different legal formats to support financial and health decisions for a future time when they do not have decision-making capacity. An enduring power of attorney is a legal document where a person is appointed to make financial decisions for the person who appoints them. In mental healthcare, self-binding directives can be made by people with severe episodic mental illness to instruct clinicians to overrule treatment refusal during future severe episodes of illness.[1] Do not attempt resuscitation (DNAR) orders are made by doctors, preceded by a discussion with the patient, family or surrogate decision maker, which identifies patient wishes and clinical utility of resuscitation interventions. Another type of medical order made following a discussion between seriously chronically ill patients or their surrogate and healthcare providers, the Physician Orders for Life-Sustaining Treatment (POLST), is used in some jurisdictions in Canada and the United States and, more recently, Denmark[2] to record medical orders for end-of-life treatment options. Advance care planning describes the process of discussion between an individual, their care providers and often those close to them about future treatment and care, and this discussion process may result in the person making a written document identifying their preferences for medical treatment or social aspects of care if at a future time they become unable to make decisions for themselves. Individuals on their own initiative may decide at any stage of their life to make written instructions about the treatment they wish to choose or refuse, although this is likely to be prompted by a diagnosis or anticipated deterioration in their health. Such documents have previously been known as 'living wills,' and now the terms 'advance directives,' 'advance decisions' and 'advance care decisions' are interchangeably used. In many jurisdictions there are legislative provisions which provide a framework for advance decision making, often building upon the common law recognition of advance decisions.[3] Any form of advance decision is a helpful tool to direct treatment according to the wishes of the person, but patients may not be aware of the possibility of advance decision making, and medical staff are often not familiar with the documentation and legal requirements.

It can be challenging to write an advance care decision (ACD), to grapple with regulatory requirements and address issues of illness and dying. There is low uptake of advance care decision making across the world, although research shows an increase in completion of ACD in the United States during the COVID-19 pandemic.[4] Particular barriers exist for those from culturally and linguistically diverse backgrounds or with limited literacy skills.[5]

In this chapter I explore a digital format of an ACD, a 'values video,' made on a smartphone application, that could be uploaded and stored in a national electronic health record, such as My Health Record in Australia, enabling access across all jurisdictions and at the point of treatment. Drawing on a narrative approach to medicine, values videos could provide healthcare professionals with useful information about the patient's perspective on their future care and what they would want in the event of loss of capacity. There is a lack of research evidence about whether a video recording of values and wishes could be readily made in a format that would have utility in clinical decision making, including the need for authentication of wishes and legal capacity. But if respect for patient autonomy and patient-centred care is to be taken seriously and given effect, this novel use of an existing technology is worth exploring and evaluating, and in this chapter, I consider legal and regulatory concerns which would need to be addressed to move this concept forward.

Values in healthcare decision making

There are perhaps two different aspects to decision making. One is cognitive – did the person have the capacity to make that decision, did they know and understand what the options were and could they think through and balance the pros and cons of those options to come to a decision? The other element of a decision focusses on what the person cares about, what their preferences, wishes and values are and how they impact on the decision. We can see this at play where a member of the Jehovah's Witness faith refuses blood products, or a person does not agree to limb amputation because they would "rather die with two feet than live with one."[6] The decision may not be rational or prudent according to others, but is informed by the individual's values, and respect for patient autonomy requires that such decisions should be given effect, and indeed legal frameworks around the world recognise that a competent adult can choose or refuse treatment. The law takes a different view about healthcare decisions of minors, those under 18 years. Even if a minor can demonstrate they fulfil the cognitive ingredient of the decision, there is a societal obligation to protect the best interests of the child. A court may override the decision of a minor and determine a course of treatment that promotes the overall welfare of the child.[7]

Patient-centred care is respective of, and responsive to, the preferences, needs and values of the patient, their experiences and relationships "that give meaning and coherence to a person's life."[8] Now that a person lacks capacity to make a healthcare decision, their previously stated wishes and preferences should guide clinical decisions, and written advance care plans and/or ACDs record such wishes and provide guidance for future healthcare delivery. Hurwitz, an academic and general practitioner, writes that "human beings are storytelling animals, and narrative is the most compelling form by which we recount our reality, understand events, and through which we make sense of our experiences and ourselves."[9] Narratives give expression to a person's deeply held values, and a narrative approach to medicine illuminates the patient's perspective.[10] Kuczewski considers that when an adult is unable to make healthcare decisions due to lack of capacity, the patient's story,

> has a prima facie moral claim to being finished in a way consistent with what has come before and with the values and self-conception with which the person has tried to shape it. The surviving interests of a person are interests in seeing the story carried out in a way that is meaningfully related to how it has proceeded up to the loss of decision-making capacity.[11]

Valid advance decisions provide health professionals with a type of evidence about the patient's wishes and could be seen as a way to continue the person's narrative account of themselves. But as we can observe in Margo's Logo, described later, the notion of a person's life as a continuing story neatly articulated is too simplistic – people may change their minds in response to ageing, illness and life events.

Allen Buchanan points out morally significant asymmetries between the contemporaneous choice of a competent individual and advance decisions to cover future treatment choices.[12] One concern is the amount of relevant information available at the time an advance decision is made. How can we have enough information about the effect of choices we make now for a future situation, which may look very different from the current one? In their report on ethical issues in dementia, the Nuffield Council on Bioethics acknowledges that clinical developments and new treatment options may undermine the information and rationale a person relied on in making an advance decision.[13]

Another issue is the extent to which there is a continuity of our interests and preferences over time and whether our former preferences should bind our future self.[14] This is well illustrated in the observation of Andrew Firlik in his account 'Margo's Logo.'[15] I adapt the case scenario he describes to illustrate the point about continuity of interests and advance decisions:

> Margo, a retired professor, made an advance decision stating that she would not want lifesaving treatment if she were to be diagnosed with dementia. Years later, now with Alzheimer's disease, she lives in a care home and seems to enjoy painting and reading the same pages of a book over again. She contracts pneumonia and requires antibiotics.

Should her advance decision now be respected, honouring Margo's earlier choices, or is her narrative fundamentally changed by dementia such that she may be viewed as a different person from the one who stated her wishes years earlier?[16]

The other challenge is where the prior wishes of the person, an expression of their autonomy, conflicts with the current best interests of the patient now lacking decision-making capacity. Rebecca Dresser considers reliance on advance treatment choice "misguided and morally troubling."[17]

> The person completing an advance directive seeks to commit her future impaired self, and the family, physicians, and others confronting that self, to a particular treatment approach. She believes that she is in a better position now, than others will be in the future, to make decisions about the treatment she receives as an incompetent patient.[18]

Who is in the best position to decide our future medical choices? During the debate on the Mental Capacity Bill in the UK Parliament (passed as the Mental Capacity Act 2005), it was noted that "the intention [of the Bill] is to enhance the patient's autonomy but the problem is that patients may have changed their minds and in many aspects of the legislation it is impossible to take account of that."[19]

These philosophical issues challenge the value of advance decision making. However, healthcare institutions and governmental policy promote advance decision making, which is given effect through common law or legislative frameworks in many countries around the world.

Advance care planning and advance care decisions

Advance care planning (ACP) describes a process of pre-emptive discussions and planning about healthcare, which anticipates a future loss of ability to make or communicate decisions. ACP is a process, often undertaken in discussion with family members and the support of other carers or healthcare providers, which sets out plans about where the person wants to be cared for at the end of their life, who they wish to be around and who should be consulted about their treatment. ACP can also include what sort of treatments they wish to receive or refuse. In this way ACP can reduce the burden on families who are involved in making decisions for their loved one[20]; indeed, the desire to provide guidance to family members is a key motivator for people to engage in ACP.[21] Families may be assisted in the process of bereavement where they feel they have 'done right' in articulating the care their loved one would have wanted.[22] Benefits also extend to healthcare practitioners, who feel more able to provide patient-centred care at the end of life. ACP can provide a more cost-effective direction of healthcare resources, and the UK Gold Standards framework notes that an advance care plan "becomes an action plan against which quality of care is measured."[23] The Australian Royal Commission into Aged Care Quality and Safety recommended (Recommendation 21) that as part of its review on Aged Care Quality Standards, care providers should assist people receiving care to make and update advance care plans if they wish to and ensure that those plans are followed.[24]

ACP is often considered in the context of older adults, but it may be particularly relevant and valuable at a time of diagnosis of disease and certain life stages, such as marriage or having a child, where values and perspectives may change. The UK Gold Standards Framework states that the trigger for ACP discussions with patients who have advanced disease or progressive, life-limiting conditions is "would you be surprised if the patient were to die in the next few months, weeks, days?"[25]

> Advance care planning is a process that supports adults at any age or stage of health in understanding and sharing their personal values, life goals, and preferences regarding future medical care. The goal of advance care planning is to help ensure that people receive medical care that is consistent with their values, goals and preferences during serious and chronic illness.[26]

ACP is a *process* for consideration and discussion, and one outcome may be a written ACD which documents the person's preferences, in accordance with formal requirements and sometimes in a prescribed format.

Advance decisions

Many countries around the world have legislation which sets out the framework for individuals to make an ACD. The document will become relevant when the person who made it has lost capacity or the ability to communicate their wishes, and it will be considered at the point of treatment. The Mental Capacity Act 2005, which applies in England and Wales, provides that an adult with capacity can make an advance decision to refuse treatment, and if the advance decision is a refusal of life-sustaining treatment the document must be in writing, although there is no required format. If it has been made validly and applies to the circumstances of the situation, then it is binding, and healthcare professionals must adhere to it. The ACD would not be valid if the person drafting it has subsequently done something clearly inconsistent with it remaining their fixed decision (s 25), perhaps by changing their religious beliefs where the tenet of the new faith has a different understanding about (particular) medical treatment. The legislation does not require that an ACD is renewed periodically.

In Singapore, the Advance Medical Directive Act 1996 (renewed 2020) provides that an adult aged 21 and over, who has capacity, may complete a prescribed form to refuse 'extraordinary life-sustaining treatment' if they have a terminal illness. In Australia, states and territories have different provisions (legislation, common law or policy) for ACD and the appointment of a substitute decision-maker[27] and the PEAK body Advance Care Planning Australia provides information about the different provisions. If we take the state of Victoria as an example, the Medical Treatment Planning and Decisions Act 2016 enables a person with capacity (there is no age limit[28]) to make an instructional directive, which identifies the treatments the person either consents to or refuses and which is binding on healthcare practitioners. The Act also provides for a values directive, which is a statement of a person's preferences and values as the basis on which the person would like any medical treatment decisions to be made, and this can include a statement of medical treatment outcomes that the person regards as acceptable. Examples of values statements in the Medical Treatment Planning and Decisions Act 2016 are,

> "If I am unable to recognise my family and friends, and cannot communicate, I do not want any medical treatment to prolong my life."
>
> "If a time comes when I cannot make decisions about my medical treatment, I would like to receive any life prolonging medical treatments that are beneficial. This includes receiving a medical research procedure to see if the procedure has any benefit for me." s 6(2).

As so few people make written ACDs, we could assume that those who do make them have strong views about how they want to be treated at a future time if they lose capacity, and they would expect their wishes expressed in the ACD to be followed. However, research shows that "while a majority of patients have reported that they intend for their ACD to be treated as legally binding, a majority of doctors have reported using a patient's ACD as a guide only."[29] Training for healthcare professionals can meet a gap in knowledge and reframe attitudes and experiences to advance care decision making. To have utility an ACD needs to be readily accessible, and access could be provided via an electronic health record portal.

Low uptake of advance care planning and advance care directives

Research shows low awareness and completion of ACDs around the world.[30] In 2016 Professor Kitzinger reported that uptake of advance decisions refusing treatment made in accordance with the Mental Capacity Act 2005 is estimated to be around 4% in England and just 2% in Wales.[31] In Japan, where it is expected that the population of people older than 75 years will double between 2005 and 2030, a 2017 national survey found only 8.7% of the public had made an advance decision.[32] Eighty-seven percent of older Australians live with at least one chronic condition such as cancer, cardiovascular disease and diabetes,[33] yet ACDs are underutilised in Australia, and a small retrospective medical record audit of patients with chronic conditions in hospital and community settings showed 1% (n = 10) of the patients had a legally binding ACD.[34] In a different study, an audit of 4187 health records of individuals aged 65 years or more in general practices, hospitals and residential aged care facilities showed approximately 11% of people in hospitals and 6% of people attending general practices had some form of ACD in their health record.[35] There are many reasons why people don't want to make an advance care plan or ACD. How do we know what we will want in 10 or 20 years from now, especially given the pace of medical advancement? Kuczewski points out that "it is likely that many people are not the kind of persons who will know far in advance exactly what he/she will want in new and strange situations."[36] Most individuals, including clinicians, find it difficult to think and talk about dying, and there is a reluctance to acknowledge impending mortality. Individuals may not wish to discuss end-of-life concerns with their relatives for fear of upsetting or alarming them.

One major hurdle in making an ACD is completion of the documentation, which can be "a time-consuming and psychologically challenging task."[37]

> There is little doubt that the complexity of the law and varying requirements that exist across jurisdictions for ACDs to be legally valid is a key factor which has led to this inadequate understanding on the part of healthcare practitioners and individuals.[38]

As previously noted, each state and territory in Australia has differing laws covering ACD. An individual needs to gather their thoughts about what they would want by way of care and treatment at a future time and articulate those wishes on paper, identify whether there is a required format, complete the documentation and find a witness, and in some states a healthcare practitioner is required to certify the form.

ACDs are sensitive to cultural interpretations and communication challenges.[39] Around the world, Chinese communities have low engagement with ACP services, which is "generally attributed to cultural considerations including taboos related to end-of-life consideration and the role of the collective family in decision-making or logistical considerations including health literacy, language and access to health services."[40] In Australia a low proportion of ACDs (3.5%) were completed by those born overseas,[41] and one study in the United States showed that completion of ACDs within ethnic minorities was approximately half that of Caucasian respondents.[42] Interpreters may be used to assist with understanding ACD documentation, but this adds another layer and potentially a cost to advance care decision making. Governmental bodies and health organisations can help overcome this language barrier by providing information in a range of languages and promoting ACP and ACDs amongst culturally and linguistically diverse communities. Co-design education workshops in Mandarin/Cantonese run for participants from Chinese community groups in Victoria Australia showed a modest uptake in ACP.[43] The Australian Royal Commission into Aged Care Quality and Safety recommended the need to establish culturally appropriate ACD processes, guidance material and training for aged care providers.[44]

'Values videos': digital recording of advance decisions

In an era where digital technology and apps are ubiquitous, a video recording of a patient's values, wishes and preferences for future treatment could supplement or replace written documentation. Could a digital recording of the spoken wishes of an individual provide a more accessible and useful means of informing family, carers and healthcare providers about treatment choices? Videos are used by healthcare providers to help explain medical terms and concepts such as dementia and cancer to patients, and patient-made videos can provide a narrative of their experience of illness. Health Talks Online (https://healthtalksonline.com) hosts videos, covering over 40 different conditions, providing insight and understanding of the health condition. Rosetta Life "offers those living with life-limiting conditions the creative means to explore personal narratives of illness and memory" (https://rosettalife.org). Of course, an audio recording could also serve a similar purpose – every smartphone has audio recording capability, and some people may feel uncomfortable being 'on camera.' However, the visual of a person on screen serves to authenticate identity, just as a passport and driver's licence are used to evidence identity for government services, and the nuances of behaviour observed may provide useful information, in the same manner as in video consultations in telemedicine (see Chapter 7).

The US company My Directives states that it is the "world's leading digital advance care planning platform" (https://mydirectives.com/). The webpage guides users through 'thoughtful questions, helpful tools and options' so that people can make an electronic record of their wishes; it also offers users the ability to include audio and video messages to create a 'superior' advance care plan. Another provider, 'In My Own Words,' offers an advance directive video recording service which allows the person to create a video record of their advance directive. The website (https://inmyownwords.com/) states that "nothing is more compelling than a video representation of you describing the care you want for yourself if you were to become incapacitated."

In the United States, POLST may not in fact reflect the patient's preferences for care at the end of life. An evaluation of the role of patient video testimonials found that incorporating a video testimonial or message with a written POLST can increase consensus understanding of patient goals in times of acute medical crisis.[45] So there is some evidence that a video recording of a person's wishes about treatment can be beneficial in directing patient-centred care. If so, then what would be the most appropriate format of such video recording, and how could they be used?

Format of values videos

Chan states that "one view is that a video ACD should be as short and direct as possible to include important information such as the wishes, limits to treatment and choices of substitute decision-makers."[46] Would a busy healthcare practitioner want to watch a video longer than two to three minutes, and how could the person making it convey information that would be relevant and useful? A homemade video which records a person's values and things that give pleasure, such as the video that Mr Chan's grandson in the case scenario proposes, may provide some guidance. But the real strength of a values video lies in including key information that a healthcare professional would find useful to help guide treatment decisions.

Authentication of identity

The healthcare professional viewing a values video would want to confirm the identity of the person making it. A video recording provides pictorial evidence of identity, which could be corroborated by including the full name of the person, Medicare/Medicaid/NHS ID, current address and date when the video is made.

Capacity

A person must have capacity to make an ACD, and the legislative[47] or common law framework may provide that adults are presumed to have capacity until a capacity assessment shows that they lack the ability to make one or more decisions for themselves.[48] The first principle in the Mental Capacity Act 2005 is that a person must be assumed to have capacity unless it is established that they lack capacity [the Act applies in England and Wales to individuals aged 16 and over, although only adults can make a legally binding statutory advance directive, section 24 (1)]. In different jurisdictions the definition of 'capacity' varies, but the fundamental requirements are that the person can understand information relevant to the decision, weigh and balance it in order to come to a decision and communicate the decision.[49]

If a values video is made with the assistance of a healthcare professional or during a doctor/patient consultation, they could make a statement about patient capacity. Otherwise, evidence of capacity could be drawn from the person's health records, or subsequently the person's doctor could review the video and confirm capacity. A witness to a written advance directive can make a statement about the capacity of the person making it. The Medical Treatment Planning and Decisions Act 2016 (Vic) has a requirement that one of the two witnesses to the signing of the document is a health practitioner and they certify that the person making the ACD appears to have decision-making capacity and understands the effect of statements made. In Singapore the Advance Medical Directive Act 1996 (renewed 2020) requires that a witness who is a medical practitioner take reasonable steps to ensure that the patient is not "mentally disordered" (s 4).

It would seem beneficial for healthcare professionals to be involved in assisting patients to make a video ACD – they could verify the capacity of the person making it, guide the inclusion of crucial information and provide relevant medical information and technical support. However, recording a video ACD with patients "could be time-consuming, and there may be limitations restricting doctors from participating in these sessions."[50]

Key information

There are formats and templates for written ACDs, provided by governmental or policy institutions, which direct the maker to include certain information not only verifying identity but also key information about future wishes. One study found, however, that online ACD templates have varying readability levels, can be biased either for or against medical intervention and may allow users to request or refuse medical treatment irrespective of the clinical context.[51]

If a values video is used as an alternative to a written ACD, specific information will be helpful to the person viewing it, such as:

- What treatments would the person want, and refuse, and in what circumstances?
- Who should be consulted about their care?
- Do they have any religious or cultural beliefs which inform treatment decisions?
- After death, how should the body be cared for?

A smartphone app could guide the user through questions to elicit such information, but if an app is guiding, directing or scripting the video, it may lead to the same 'biasing' issues as written ACD templates, and it would be appropriate to monitor this through research.

Legal status of values videos

The legal framework for ACDs may require that, to have binding authority, it is in written format. For example, formal requirements for making an ACD in Victoria are stated in s 16 Medical Treatment Planning and Decisions Act 2016:

> An advance care directive – (a) must be in writing in English; and (b) must include the full name, date of birth and address of the person giving it; and (c) subject to subsection (2), must be signed by the person giving it; and (d) must be witnessed and certified in accordance with the requirements set out in section 17.

If there is a written ACD in place, a compatible value videos could play a complementary role, providing further context to what is contained in the written form. Where legislation or common law states that an ACD be 'in writing,' then a video format would clearly not meet this requirement. However, a values video would have a role in informing what the patient would consider to be in their 'best interests.'

Healthcare professionals are required to make treatment decisions in the best interests of their adult patients who lack capacity (where there is no binding and relevant ACD). The UN Convention on the Rights of Persons with Disabilities (CRPD) requires signatory states to ensure the rights, will and preferences of the person lacking capacity are respected [Article 12(4)]. The Mental Capacity Act 2005 (England and Wales) provides that in determining the best interests of an adult lacking decisional capacity, their wishes, feelings, values and beliefs remain central to the decision being made. In the Supreme Court judgment in *Aintree University Hospitals NHS Foundation Trust v James*[52] Lady Hale confirmed that "the purpose of the best interests test is to consider matters from the patient's point of view."[53] Patient-centred care demands that the preferences, values and personal and social wellbeing should direct decisions about the person's medical treatment. In *Sheffield Teaching Hospitals NHS Foundation Trust v TH*[54] Mr Justice Hayden, in the Court of Protection (which deals with financial or welfare matters for people who lack mental capacity), noted that although TH (a 52-year-old man lacking capacity to give or withhold consent to his medical treatment) had made no formal advance decision to refuse treatment, "he has in so many oblique and tangential ways over so many years communicated his views so uncompromisingly and indeed bluntly that none of his friends are left in any doubt what he would want in his present situation."[55] So, a values video can draw together a compelling testimony that can have evidential weight when healthcare professionals engage in the process of best-interests decision making. Interestingly, although in an entirely different context, the Family Court of Australia considered the probative value of receiving, as evidence in a family dispute, recordings taken by a mobile telephone and from Skype conversations and found that the recordings had the quality of demonstrating issues relevant to the best interests of the children.[56]

A values video, although not complying with statutory requirements and therefore not binding, nevertheless informs a determination of best interests. So, what weight could be given to such 'evidence'? I have previously argued that a decision which fits the themes and overall direction of the patient's life story, a narrative approach, may be considered a way to promote the person's best interests, although it relies on the claim that continuing the patient's narrative coincides with what is best for them.[57] In another decision of the England and Wales Court of Protection, *Wye Valley NHS Trust v Mr B*,[58] Peter Jackson J said that there is no "theoretical limit"[59] to the weight or lack of weight that should be given to the person's wishes, feelings, values and beliefs. Strongly held values articulated before loss of capacity are at least a starting point in evaluating that person's best interests, although ultimately the patient's views are to be considered along with the harms and benefits of available medical options.[60]

Technology and older adults

Completion of an ACD in written format may be onerous for some, but would making an ACD in video format be any more accessible, resulting in greater uptake? A smartphone app could house the instructions for making a video ACD, with prompts about information to be included. Given the familiarity and use of smartphones, a video format may increase uptake of advance care decision making amongst younger generations. The paradigm group for whom ACDs may be particularly relevant are older adults, where loss of capacity, perhaps because of dementia, could be anticipated. Research shows that people with dementia want choice and control over the decisions that affect them.[61]

Authors of a study carried out in a hospital in China concluded that

> although there is an increased prevalence of electronic devices, many older people still use cheap, older phones or not so smart smartphones. Some again need support from the younger generation to purchase and use a smartphone. Many of the older people have a low level of information technology skills, often learn slowly and need someone to teach and guide them with great patience.[62]

This divide in digital literacy was a key theme in the Australian government's National Digital Health Strategy. A submission from Alzheimer's Australia (now called Dementia Australia) noted the access and navigation barriers experienced by older consumers: "they either had no access to the internet, did not have the skills necessary to navigate the website effectively, or found it too difficult to find the information that they needed."[63]

In 2019 the Australian Medical Association issued a position statement calling for innovative technologies to be co-designed with end users – older people, their families and carers and healthcare and aged care providers – to achieve the best possible outcome for older people.[64] Supporting older people with the technology to make a values ACD on a smartphone could be provided by family or healthcare professionals. Conversations about end-of-life decisions have the potential to bring up strong emotions with family members, and this may be a deterrent to family support in making a video format.[65] Additionally, there may be a concern about potential coercion where relatives support their loved one in making an ACD in video format, although at least they would know of the existence of the video, which may avoid unnecessary surprises.

Portability and accessibility

A register of advance decisions could easily be searched to find if an ACD existed at the time treatment decisions are required. In most countries there is no requirement to register an ACD, giving rise to troubling accounts of individuals being treated in contradiction to their wishes because there was no knowledge of the advance decision or it could not be found in time. One study reported that ACDs were not always actively looked for when patients presented at the hospital and that active management continued to be provided to a patient until an ACD was produced, even though a clinician was informed that a patient had one.[66]

An advantage of a values video is that its digital format enables it to be easily stored, makes it portable across borders and immediately accessible. If it is shared with family members, they can produce a copy on their phone, and the general practitioner and treating team can be sent a copy. Of course, this raises privacy concerns, as patients may lose some level of control over who has knowledge of their values video, and it could more easily be shared inappropriately. There is also the possibility of hacking and potentially manipulating the information on the video. Where there is an electronic personal health record, a values video could be uploaded and then shared with the general practitioner and healthcare providers with the agreement of the individual. This would enable transferability of the ACD between health and care sectors and accessibility at the point of care. The My Health Record (MHR) system is a shared electronic personal health record system established and operated in accordance with the My Health Records Act 2012 (Cth) in Australia. Since 2016 the legislation has allowed non-clinical ACP documents to be uploaded to the MHR system,[67] but the availability of existing ACDs within MHR is extremely low, far below the number actually made.[68] The National Digital Health Strategy will explore how ACDs can be better incorporated into MHR.

Conclusion

ACP has an important role to ensure that patient autonomy is respected at a future time when the individual does not have the capacity to make healthcare decisions themselves. Written ACDs provide a means to express treatment preferences, and if they fulfil legal requirements, healthcare professionals must adhere to them. However, there is low uptake for ACDs and challenges in making, sharing and storing them. A video format – a values video – is an alternative approach, as a stand-alone or to supplement a written format, and increasingly governments are recognising the role and importance of digital technologies to improve care and empower patients.

Empirical research is needed to evaluate whether there would be greater uptake for making an ACD in video format and their utility in clinical practice – would a visual of the patient 'speaking' from an app-based recording have greater impact than a written document? Research could consider the experience of people making a video ACD, their understanding and experience of the process (how long did it take to make it, who was involved) and then inviting healthcare practitioners to comment on their understanding of the instructions/directions in the video and whether, and if so how, it would impact their care and treatment of the patient. Of course, a statement/expression of wishes for treatment decision making in video format may be subject to the same challenges of a written document – people may not want to consider the need for medical treatment or end-of-life issues in digital format either.

If the legal framework requires that an ACD be 'in writing,' then a values video would not have binding force but could be an important tool in determining what treatment and care are in the patient's best interests, from the patient's perspective. Whether an ACD is in written or video format, its effectiveness depends on the attitudes of those interpreting them and demands greater collaboration between healthcare practitioners and their patients to provide realistic and informed choices. The co-creation of a values video with a healthcare professional would certainly assist with issues of assessment of capacity and informed decision making, but this approach is not usual in making a written ACD. Chan considers that while video ACDs may be viable alternatives to written ACDs, "they are not the panacea for the challenges involved in advance decision-making generally or written ADs specifically."[69] But as we move to greater reliance on digital technologies in healthcare, it seems possible that values videos offer promise in expanding uptake and interest in advance care decision making.

Notes

1 T. Gergel, P. Das, G. Owen et al., 'Reasons for Endorsing or Rejecting Self-binding Directives in Bipolar Disorder: A Qualitative Study of Survey Responses from UK Service Users.' (2021) 8(7) *Lancet Psychiatry* 599–609.
2 L. Tuesen, et al., 'Discussing Patient Preferences for Levels of Life-sustaining Treatment: Development and Pilot Testing of a Danish POLST Form.' (2022) 21(1) *BMC Palliative Care* 9.
3 C. Johnston, 'Advance Decision Making – Rhetoric or Reality?' (2014) 34(3) *Legal Studies* 497–514.
4 C. Auriemma, S. Halpern, J. Asch, M. Van Der Tuyn, D. Asch, 'Completion of Advance Directives and Documented Care Preferences During the Coronavirus Disease 2019 (COVID-19) Pandemic.' 202 3(7) *JAMA Network Open* e2015762.
5 K. de Vries, E. Banister, K. Dening, B. Ochieng, 'Advance Care Planning for Older People: The Influence of Ethnicity, Religiosity, Spirituality and Health Literacy.' (2019) 26(7) *Nursing Ethics* 1946–1954.
6 *Re C (Adult: Refusal of Treatment)* [1994] 1 All ER 819.
7 See *X v Sydney Children's Hospitals Network* [2013] NSWCA 320 and C. Johnston, 'Overriding Competent Medical Treatment Refusal by Adolescents: When "No" means "No" ' (2009) 94(7) *Archives of Disease in Childhood* 487–91.
8 C. Johnston, N. Banner, A. Fenwick, 'Patient Narrative: An 'On-switch' for Evaluating Best Interests,' (2016) 38(3) *Journal of Social Welfare and Family Law* 249–262, page 252.
9 B. Hurwitz, 'Narrative and the Practice of Medicine.' (2000) 356 *Lancet* 2086–89, page 2088.
10 C. Johnston, 'Lack of Capacity is Not an 'Off Switch' for Rights and Freedoms: Wye Valley NHS Trust v Mr B (By His Litigation Friend, the Official Solicitor) [2015] Ewcop 60.' (2017) 25(4) *Medical Law Review* 662–671.
11 M. Kuczewski, 'Commentary: Narrative Views of Personal Identity and Substituted Judgment in Surrogate Decision Making' (1999) 27 *The Journal of Law, Medicine & Ethics* 32–36.
12 A. Buchanan, 'Directives and the Personal Identity Problem,' (1988) 17(4) *Philosophy & Public Affairs* 277–302.
13 Nuffield Council on Bioethics, *'Dementia: Ethical Issues'* (Nuffield Council on Bioethics, London, 2009).
14 D. Parfit, *Reasons and Persons* (Oxford University Press, Oxford, 1984).
15 A. Firlik, 'A Piece of My Mind. Margo's Logo,' (1991) 265(2) *JAMA*, 201.
16 R. Dresser, 'Dworkin on Dementia: Elegant Theory, Questionable Policy Source,' (1995) 25(6) *Hastings Center Report* 32–38.
17 R. Dresser, 'Precommitment: A Misguided Strategy for Securing Death with Dignity,' (2003) 81(7) *Texas Law Review* 1823–1847, page 1823.
18 R. Dresser, 'Precommitment: A Misguided Strategy for Securing Death with Dignity' (2003) 81(7) *Texas Law Review* 1823–1847, page 1825.
19 House of Commons debate on the Mental Capacity Bill, Hansard 14th Dec 2004 col. 1540, Iain Duncan Smith.
20 D. Wendler, A. Rid, 'Systematic Review: The Effect on Surrogates of Making Treatment Decisions for Others.' (2011) 154(5) *Annals of Internal Medicine* 336–36.

21 B. Hemsley, J. Meredith, L. Bryant et al., 'An Integrative Review of Stakeholder Views on Advance Care Directives (ACD): Barriers and Facilitators to Initiation, Documentation, Storage, and Implementation.' (2019) 102(6) *Patient Education and Counseling* 1067–1079.
22 B. Hemsley, J. Meredith, L. Bryant et al. 'An Integrative Review of Stakeholder Views on Advance Care Directives (ACD): Barriers and Facilitators to Initiation, Documentation, Storage, and Implementation' (2019) 102(6) *Patient Education and Counseling* 1067–1079.
23 Gold Standard Framework Centre, Thinking Ahead' – Gold Standards Framework Advance Care Planning Discussion, 2013.
24 Australian Royal Commission into Aged Care Quality and Safety, Final Report: Care Dignity and Respect, Recommendation 21 (Australia, 2021).
25 'Matters of Life and Death, Helping People to Live Well Until They Die', General Practice Guidance for Implementing the RCGP/RCN End of Life Care Patient Charter (Matters of Life and Death, London, 2012).
26 R. Sudore et al., 'Defining Advance Care Planning for Adults: A Consensus Definition from a Multidisciplinary Delphi Panel.' (2017) 53(5) *Journal of Pain and Symptom Management* 821–832, page 822.
27 See R. Carter, K. Detering, W. Silvester, E. Sutton, 'Advance Care Planning in Australia: What Does the Law Say?' (2015) 40(4) *Australian Health Review* 405–414 and S. Fountain, L. Nolte, M. Wills, H. Kelly, K. Detering, *Review of Advance Care Planning Laws across Australia: Short Report* (Advance Care Planning Australia, Austin Health, Melbourne, 2018).
28 C. Johnston, 'Children Can Decide Their Medical Treatments under Victoria's Unique Advance Directive Laws,' (2017) *The Conversation*, October 4.
29 S. McCarthy, J. Meredith, L. Bryant, B. Hemsley (2017) 'Legal and Ethical Issues Surrounding Advance Care Directives in Australia: Implications for the Advance Care Planning Document in the Australian My Health Record,' (2017) 25(1) *The Journal of Law, Medicine & Ethics* 136–149, page 143.
30 J. Friend, D. Alden, 'Improving Patient Preparedness and Confidence in Discussing Advance Directives for End-of-Life Care with Health Care Providers in the United States and Japan.' (2021) 41(1) *Medical Decision Making* 60–73.
31 J. Kitzinger, C. Kitzinger, 'Increasing Understanding and Uptake of Advance Decisions in Wales,' (2016). Public Policy Institute for Wales, page 6. www.wcpp.org.uk/wp-content/uploads/2018/04/PPIW-Report-Increasing-the-awareness-and-uptake-of-Advance-Decisions.pdf.
32 K. Iijima, H. Arai, M. Akishita, et al., 'Toward the Development of a Vibrant, Superaged Society: The Future of Medicine and Society in Japan.' (2021) 21(8) *Geriatrics & Gerontology International* 601–613.
33 S. Jeong, T. Barrett, S. Ohr, et al. 'Prevalence of Advance Care Planning Practices among People with Chronic Diseases in Hospital and Community Settings: A Retrospective Medical Record Audit.' (2021) 303 *BMC Health Services Research* 1–8.
34 S. Jeong, T. Barrett, S. Ohr et al. 'Prevalence of Advance Care Planning Practices among People with Chronic Diseases in Hospital and Community Settings: A Retrospective Medical Record Audit' (2021) 303 *BMC Health Services Research* 1–8.
35 K. Buck, K. Detering, M. Sellars, R. Ruseckaite, H. Kelly, L. Nolte, *Prevalence of Advance Care Planning Documentation in Australian Health and Residential Aged Care Services, Short Report* (Advance Care Planning Australia, Austin Health, Melbourne, 2017).
36 M. Kuczewski, 'Commentary: Narrative Views of Personal Identity and Substituted Judgment in Surrogate Decision Making' (1999) 27 *The Journal of Law, Medicine & Ethics* 32–36, page 33.
37 R. Dresser, 'Precommitment: A Misguided Strategy for Securing Death with Dignity' (2003) 81(7) *Texas Law Review* 1823–1847, page 1830.
38 S. McCarthy, J. Meredith, L. Bryant, B. Hemsley 'Legal and Ethical Issues Surrounding Advance Care Directives in Australia: Implications for the Advance Care Planning

Document in the Australian My Health Record' (2017) 25(1) *The Journal of Law, Medicine & Ethics* 136–149, page 142.
39 *Advance Care Planning in End-of-Life Care* (eds K. Thomas, B. Lobo, Oxford University Press, Oxford, 2011).
40 S. Yap, K. Shen, K. Detering, S. Fraser 'Exploring the Knowledge, Attitudes and Needs of Advance Care Planning in Older Chinese Australians' (2018) 27(17–18) *Journal of Clinical Nursing* 3298–3306, page 3304.
41 A. Wong, A. Collins, A. Ng, L. Buizen, J. Philip, B. Le, 'Evaluation of a Large-Scale Advance Care Planning Co-Design Education Program for Chinese-Speaking People in Australia.' (2022) 39(2) *American Journal of Hospice and Palliative Medicine* 178–183.
42 J. Rao, L. Anderson, F-C Lin, J. Laux, 'Completion of Advance Directives among U.S. Consumers.' (2014) 46(1) *American Journal of Preventive Medicine* 65–70.
43 A. Wong, A. Collins, A. Ng, L. Buizen, J. Philip, B. Le, 'Evaluation of a Large-scale Advance Care Planning Co-design Education Program for Chinese-speaking People in Australia' (2022) 39(2) *American Journal of Hospice and Palliative Medicine* 178–183.
44 Australian Royal Commission into Aged Care Quality and Safety, Final Report: Care Dignity and Respect, Recommendation 48:Cultural Safety (Australia, 2021).
45 F. Mirarchi, T. Cooney, A. Venkat et al. '*TRIAD VIII: Nationwide Multicenter Evaluation to Determine Whether Patient Video Testimonials Can Safely Help Ensure Appropriate Critical Versus End-of-Life Care.*' (2017) 13(2) *Journal of Patient Safety* 51–61.
46 H. Y. Chan, 'Video Advance Directives: A Turning Point for Advance Decision-Making? A Consideration of Their Roles and Implications for Law and Practice,' (2020) 41 *Liverpool Law Review* 1–26, page 18.
47 S. Menon, C. Ho, 'Decision-making for Adults Lacking the Capacity to Consent' in J. Chin, N. Berlinger, M. Dunn, M. Gusmano (eds.), *A Singapore Bioethics Casebook*, 2 vols (Singapore: National University of Singapore, 2017).
48 C. Johnston, J. Liddle, 'The Mental Capacity Act 2005: A New Framework for Healthcare Decision Making'. (2007) 33(2) *Journal of Medical Ethics* 94–97.
49 The Medical Treatment Planning and Decisions Act 2016 in Victoria Australia, mirrors the wording of the Mental Capacity Act 2005 in England & Wales.
50 H. Y. Chan, 'Video Advance Directives: A Turning Point for Advance Decision Making? A Consideration of Their Roles and Implications for Law and Practice' (2020) 41 *Liverpool Law Review* 1–26, page 18.
51 T. Luckett et al., 'Advance Care Planning in 21st Century Australia: A Systematic Review and Appraisal of Online Advance Care Directive Templates against National Framework Criteria.' (2015) 39 *Australian Health Review* 552–560.
52 *Aintree University Hospitals NHS Foundation Trust v James* [2013] UKSC 67.
53 *Aintree University Hospitals NHS Foundation Trust v James* [2013] UKSC 67 para 45.
54 *Sheffield Teaching Hospitals NHS Foundation Trust v. TH* [2014] EWCOP 4.
55 *Sheffield Teaching Hospitals NHS Foundation Trust v. TH* [2014] EWCOP 4, Hayden J para 53.
56 *Gin & Hing* [2019] Fam- CA 779.
57 C. Johnston, 'The Weight Attributed to Patient Values in Determining Best Interests,' (2013) 39(9) *Journal of Medical Ethics* 562–564.
58 *Wye Valley NHS Trust v B* [2015] EWCOP 60.
59 *Wye Valley NHS Trust v B* [2015] EWCOP 60, Peter Jackson J. para 10.
60 *Sheffield Teaching Hospitals NHS Foundation Trust v. TH* [2014] EWCOP 4, Hayden J para 56.
61 Dementia Action Alliance *UK Dementia* (Dementia Action Alliance, London, 2014).
62 J. Tu, M. Shen, J. Zhong, G. Yuan, M. Chen, 'The Perceptions and Experiences of Mobile Health Technology by Older People in Guangzhou, China: A Qualitative Study.' (2021) 9 *Frontiers in Public Health* 683712.
63 Australia's Digital Health Strategy, 'Safe, Seamless and Secure: Evolving Health and Care to Meet the Needs of Modern Australia,' *National Digital Health Strategy and Framework for Action* (Australia's Digital Health Strategy, Brisbane, 2018), page 50.

64 Australian Medical Association, *Position Statement on Innovation in Aged Care* (Australian Medical Association, Barton, ACT, 2019).
65 C. Bernard, A. Tan, M. Slaven, et al., 'Exploring Patient-reported Barriers to Advance Care Planning in Family Practice.' (2020) 21(94) *BMC Family Practice* 1–10.
66 C. Johnson, R. Singer, M. Masso, M. Sellars, W. Silvester, 'Palliative Care Health Professionals' Experiences of Caring for Patients with Advance Care Directives.' (2015) 39(2) *Australian Health Review* 154–159.
67 S. McCarthy, J. Meredith, L. Bryant, B. Hemsley, 'Legal and Ethical Issues Surrounding Advance Care Directives in Australia: Implications for the Advance Care Planning Document in the Australian My Health Record' (2017) 25(1) *The Journal of Law, Medicine & Ethics* 136–149.
68 S. McCarthy, J. Meredith, L. Bryant, B. Hemsley, 'Legal and Ethical Issues Surrounding Advance Care Directives in Australia: Implications for the Advance Care Planning Document in the Australian My Health Record' (2017) 25(1) *The Journal of Law, Medicine & Ethics* 136–149.
69 H. Y. Chan, 'Video Advance Directives: A Turning Point for Advance Decision Making? A Consideration of Their Roles and Implications for Law and Practice' (2020) 41 *Liverpool Law Review* 1–26, page 15.

INDEX

10K Project 13–14

access: to genomic data 16–20; to healthcare 1, 82, 98, 107, 111; to personal data, privacy and 18–19; smartphone 55–56; to telemedicine 107–108
accountability: AI ethics 67; for decision making 70–71; human control 65
accuracy: AI diagnosis 64–68, 74–76; chatbot 88–92; smartphone apps 49
Actissit (app) 50
active data 49
advance care decision (ACD) 8, 135–148; key information 144; legal framework 144–145; legislation 139–141, 147; low uptake of 140–142; portability and accessibility 146–147; privacy 146–147; technology and older adults 145–146; values video 8, 136, 142–145
advance care directive *see* advance care decision (ACD)
advance care planning (ACP) 136, 138–142; autonomy 138, 147; low uptake of 140–142; overview 138–139
Advance Care Planning Australia 140
Advance Medical Directive Act (Singapore) 140, 143
advertising: pop-up advertisements 81; targeted 87
aging demographic, care robots in 117–118
AI *see* artificial intelligence (AI)

AID (automated insulin delivery) system 29, 37, 40
algorithm: bias 6, 67–68, 72; deep learning 66, 74, 76; definition of 65; machine learning 65–68, 71
Allsop, CJ 86
Alzheimer disease 122, 138
Amazon Kindle, terms and conditions 86
AndroidAPS 30–31, 39
apps/mobile applications: contact tracing 48; digital phenotyping 53–54; as first point of diagnosis 47; overview 49; persuasive technology 53; privacy policies 52; smartphone for mental health 5–6, 47–58
APS (artificial pancreas system) 29, 37–38
Aristotle 90
artificial intelligence (AI): accountability 70–72; applications in everyday activities 63–64; bias 72; decision making 64–65, 67–72, 76; in diagnosis of health conditions 6, 63–76; doctor-patient relationship 69–70; ethical issues 67; ethics by design principle 129; harm 71–76; human in the loop 64; legislation regulating 72; melanoma diagnosis 65–68; privacy, impact on 72; regulation of 71–73; regulatory agencies 72–73; robot use 123; sentience 65; standard of care 74–75; terminology 64–65; trust in 70, 76; trustworthy 65, 67, 90
Artificial Intelligence Act (EU) 72

Index

Artificial Intelligence/Machine Learning Action Plan (Food and Drug Administration) 73
artificial pancreas system (APS) 29, 37–38
Asia MD (Singapore) 83
assistive technologies, for aged care 118
Assistive Technology for All campaign 118
Atkins, Kim 120
Australian Competition and Consumer Commission 86–87
Australian Health Practitioner Regulation Agency 110
Australian Law Reform Commission 36
Australian Medical Association 37, 109, 146
Australian Register of Therapeutic Goods (ARTG) 39
Australian Royal Commission into Aged Care Quality and Safety 139, 142
authentication of identity 143
automated insulin delivery (AID) system 29, 37, 40
autonomy 23; advance care planning (ACP) 147; constant tracking as infringement 50; dependent on decision-making ability 121; health apps 53; individuality 8; information as necessary precursor to 85; information sharing 21; justification for limitation of 121–122; meaning and value of 120; parental 33, 36; respect for patient 41, 53–54, 85, 103–104, 136–137; return of raw genomic data 16; rights-in-trust of children 36; robotic care assistants 120–122

Babylon Health (UK) 83, 86, 89
Baker, J 34
BAM (Binary Alignment Map) files 16
beneficence 23, 104–105; elderly with declining cognitive capacity 122–124; robotic care assistants 122–124
benefit, and AI ethics 67
best interests standard: DIY looping 33–34, 37; elderly with declining cognitive capacity 122–124; prescriptive fiduciary obligation 70
bias 2, 6, 65, 76, 90–91, 103, 130, 144; algorithmic 72; artificial intelligence 72; machine learning algorithms 67–68; as source of diagnostic errors 68
biobank: disease-agnostic 13; obligations of researchers 12–14; right not to know 14–16; sharing information from research 12–16

biosamples, and property rights 17–18
black box medicine 69–70
BRCA1 12, 14, 18
BRCA2 12, 14, 18
Buchanan, Allen 137
Butler-Sloss, L.J. 121

Cambridge Analytica 2
capacity: advance care decision (ACD) and 143; to consent 126–127; definition 143
Care-O-bot (robotic care assistant) 118, 120
care robots *see* robotic care assistant(s)
case scenario: advance care decision 135–148; AI diagnosis 63–76; DIY diabetes management 28–41; right to access genomic data 16–20; robotic care assistants and older adults 116–131; sharing information from research biobanks 12–16; sharing information with genetic relatives 20–24; smartphone apps for mental health 47–58; symptom checker chatbots 81–93; telehealth 98–111
causation 75–76
CGM (continuous glucose monitor) 28–30, 32, 37
chatbots 81–93; accuracy 88–89, 92; benefits and limitations 88, 92; consent to use 84–88; global healthcare chatbots market 83; overview of 82–83; privacy policy 86; to provide health information 83–84; triage 82–85, 89, 90; trust 89–91
children: DIY diabetes management by parents 28–41; healthcare decisions of minors 137; rights-in-trust of 36; right to open future 36–37; United Nations Convention on the Rights of the Child 33
clickwrap agreements 86–87
clinical/robot ethics committees 129–130
cognitive behavioural therapy 50, 82, 91–92
cognitive impairment, elderly with 122–124, 126
commodification of online data 86
Commonwealth Privacy Act (Australia) 2, 19, 22
companion robots 118–119
competence 33, 55
confidence: engendered in online world 89; in managing own care 37; patient–healthcare professional relationship 70, 90, 109; in smartphone use 56
confidentiality: duty of 20–21, 23–24; genetic counsellors 20–21; haiku 109;

healthcare professionals 84; joint account model 22–23; legal issues 109; personal account model 22; video conferencing 109–110
consent: capacity to consent 126–127; to data sharing 2–3; Gillick-competence 33; new definitions of 87; parental choice 33; readability of terms 86, 92; right to refuse 121; robotic care assistant 7, 125, 126–127; sharing genetic information 21; symptom checker chatbots 84–88; *see also* informed consent
consequentialism 68
consumer protection laws 128
continuous glucose monitor (CGM) 28–30, 32, 37
conversational agents 82
convolutional neural networks 66
cookies 86
Council on the Ageing (COTA) Victoria 118
COVID-19 pandemic: contact tracing apps 48; robot use during 117; social isolation during 49, 82, 106; telehealth 7, 98–111
CREATE (Community deRivEd AutomaTEd insulin delivery) clinical trial 32
cultural context/considerations 3, 51, 68, 89, 141, 144

Danish Council of Ethics 15
data: active 49; collection (*see* data collection); commodification of online 86; genomic (*see* genomic data); mandatory notification schemes for compromised 53; passive 49, 53; privacy (*see* data privacy); property rights 18; sharing (*see* data sharing)
data breaches involving health information 53
data collection: chatbot 85–87; outside hospital or healthcare provider 6; robotic care assistant 127; targeted advertising 87
Data Ethics Framework (UK) 103
data lifecycle 70
data privacy 2; artificial intelligence 72; health data 51–53; personally identifiable information 51; smartphone app tracking 50; *see also* privacy
Data Protection Act (UK) 18, 51
datasets: applicability of 2; underrepresentation of certain groups 67
data sharing: by apps 52; artificial intelligence 72; consent 2–3; genomic 10–24, 18; harm of 36; limits on sharing child's health data 31, 36–37; public good 3; robotic care assistant 127; sharenting 31, 35–37; trust and chatbots 89
decision making: accountability 70–71; advance care decisions 135–138, 140–141, 143, 145, 147–148; artificial intelligence (AI) 64–65, 67–72, 76; bias 67; end-of-life 69; human control in 71; paternalistic model of 69–70; philosophical issues challenging value of advance 138; values in healthcare 136–138
deep learning 65; algorithm 66, 74, 76; network 69
DeepMind 2, 64, 76
de-identification of data 2, 51
dementia 122, 126, 128, 135, 137–138, 142, 146
Dementia Australia 146
Denning, Lord 86
depersonalisation of care 69, 106–107
dermatology 6, 63, 65–66, 71, 76
DermEngine 74
device failure, risk of 32
diabetes, DIY management of 28–41
diagnostic AI 63–76
differential diagnosis 90
digital advance care decisions 135–148
digital divide 55–56
digital economy 51
digital literacy 92, 108, 146
digital phenotyping 49–50, 53–54
digital psychiatry 49, 54, 57–58
dignity: harm in overriding autonomous 121; robotic care assistants 116–117, 119–121, 123, 126, 130; Treaty on European Union 119; Universal Declaration of Human Rights 119
disclosure: balancing harm with benefits of disclosure 23–24; duty of care 84; patient-oriented theory 85; physician-oriented theory 85; to at risk/genetic relatives 34; standard of care 85
discrimination 15, 67–68, 70, 73, 87
disparities: health/healthcare 6, 66–67, 76, 99, 107; racial 91
distributive justice 68
DIY diabetes management 28–41
DIY looping 5, 28–41; benefits 31–32; challenges of 32; duties of healthcare professionals 37–38; duties of parents 35–37; legal liability of healthcare

professionals 38–39; parental choice to use 32–34; regulation, role of 39–40; Zone of Parental Discretion 34–35, 41
DNA 11
DNA sequencing technologies 11–12
doctor–patient relationship: artificial intelligence 69–70; confidence 70, 90, 109; confidential information 109; fiduciary obligations 70; telehealth 99, 106–107, 111; therapeutic relationship 35, 37, 54, 89, 106
do not attempt resuscitation (DNAR) 135
Dresser, Rebecca 138
duty of care 13; AI in diagnosis 73–74; disclosure 84; DIY looping 37–39; sharing genetic information 21; standard 54, 74

e-consultation 100
electronic health record 52, 147
ELIZA (chatbot) 90
e-Mental health 48
empathy, clinical 92
epistemic humility 3
e-privacy 52
equity, telemedicine and 107–108
ethics: artificial intelligence 67; autonomy 120–122; beneficence 23, 104–105, 122–124; consequentialism 68; Four Principles approach 119–120, 130; justice 125–126; non-maleficence 23, 67, 105, 124–125; Nuffield Council on Bioethics 3, 6, 107, 137; principles of bioethics 119–126; robotic care assistants 118–126, 129–130; telemedicine 103–106
ethics by design principle 129
ethics committees 129–130
European Convention on Human Rights and Biomedicine 14
European Court of Human Rights 34
European General Data Protection Regulation 6, 68
European Group on Ethics 71
ex ante regulation 72
exome 11
eye disease, AI diagnosis of 64

Facebook 2
fairness, and AI ethics 67
fall sensors 48, 116
FASTQ files 16
feedback (return of secondary findings) 13–15, 58, 82, 123

fertility, apps used to monitor 47
fiduciary obligations 36, 70
Firlik, Andrew 138
FOCUS (app) 50
Food and Drug Administration, FDA (United States) 30, 39–40; Artificial Intelligence/Machine Learning Action Plan 73; medical device and software safety 30, 56, 73, 128

Gard, Charlie 28–29, 34
General Data Protection Regulation, GDPR 18–19, 51, 87, 110
General Medical Council 22, 37, 109
general practice/general practitioners 12, 17, 20, 63, 66, 81, 83, 116, 137, 141; portability and accessibility 146–147; Royal Australian College of General Practitioners Guidelines 102, 110–111; telehealth 98–104, 107, 110–111
genetic counsellors 19–21
genome 11
genomic data: return of raw 10, 16–20; return of secondary findings 12–14; right to access 16–20
genomic medicine 11, 24
genomic (genome) sequencing 4–5, 10–24; balancing harm with benefits of disclosure 23–24; DNA sequencing technologies 11–12; return of raw genomic data 10, 16–20; return of secondary findings, obligations of researchers and 12–14; sharing information with genetic relatives 20–24
genotyping 14
Gillam, Lynn 34
Gillick-competence 33
global positioning system (GPS) 50
Gold Standards Framework (UK) 139
Good Medical Practice: Australia 37; United Kingdom 37
Google: DeepMind 2, 64, 76; LaMDA 64–65; searches for health information 83–84
guidelines 38, 108; AI ethics 67; Australian NHMRC 22–23, European Commissions' Ethics Guidelines for Trustworthy AI 67; Royal Australian College of General Practice 102, 110

haiku 109
Hale, Lady 145
harm: artificial intelligence 71–76; balancing with benefits of disclosure

23–24; best interests standard 34; ex ante regulation 72; foreseeability of 75–76; non-maleficence 124–125; obligation to avoid 23; potential with use of smartphone health apps 56; protection from as justification for limiting autonomy 121–122; of sharenting 36; telehealth 105; tort 72–76; Zone of Parental Discretion 35
Harris, John 8
Hayden, J 145
head and neck cancer 64
healthcare: access to 1, 82, 98, 107, 111; decisions 21, 33, 76, 137, 147 (*see also* decision making); disparities 6, 66–67, 76, 99, 107; information 21, 82, 109 (*see also* health information); values in decision making 136–138
healthcare professionals: disclosure of risks and consequences 84; duties of 37–38; legal liability of 38–39; patient confidence 70, 90, 109; *see also* doctor–patient relationship
health data: privacy of 51–53; *see also* health information
health data poverty 2
health information: data breaches involving 53; readability level 84; sources of 83–84; symptom checker triage role 83; telehealth 99
Health Insurance Portability and Accountability Act (United States) 18, 110
Health Talks Online 142
Her (film) 82
high-throughput sequencing 11, 15, 20, 24
Ho, Anita 3
Hobbit (robotic care assistant) 118
human flourishing 69, 76
Human Genome Project 11
Huntington disease 20, 23–24
hybrid closed loop system 28–31, 39

incidental findings *see* secondary findings
informed choice, by parents 33
informed consent 81–93; defined 69; readability of terms 86; robotic care assistant 126–127; symptom checker chatbots 6–7; telemedicine 108–109
In My Own Words 142
insulin, automated delivery of 28–41
interaction, human 3
International Medical Device Regulators Forum 56

Internet of Things 5, 29, 39–41
Isabel (symptom checker) 88
isolation, robot use and 7, 116, 119, 124, 126

Jackson, Peter J 145
joint account model, of confidentiality 22–23
judgement, human 3, 130
justice: distributive 68; robotic care assistants 125–126; telemedicine and 105–106

labour theory 17
LaMDA (Language Model for Dialogue Applications) 64–65
legislation: advance care decision (ACD) 139–140, 141, 147; regulating AI 72; robotic care assistants 127–128
Leibrand, Scott 30
Lewis, Dana 30, 32
liability 73–76, 128; causation 75–76; of healthcare professionals and DIY looping 38–39
Lio (robotic care assistant) 119
literacy: digital 92, 108, 146; health 84, 141
living will 136
Loop 30
looping 31–32; *see also* DIY looping
Lowrance, William 5

machine learning 66–68; AI in diagnosis of health conditions 64–67, 71; algorithm 65–68, 71; Artificial Intelligence/Machine Learning Action Plan, FDA 73; bias 67–68; definition of 65; digital phenotyping 50; symptom checker chatbots 91–92; terminology 66
Magnusson, Roger 6
maleficence 33, 130
Margo's Logo 137–138
medical device: Food and Drug Administration, FDA (United States) regulation of 30, 56, 128; harm from 74; linked devices through a networked system 29; regulation 39, 56, 73, 128; robot as 128; Software as a Medical Device (SaMD) 30, 56
Medical Treatment Planning and Decisions Act (Victoria, Australia) 140, 143–144
Medicare: Australia 101; United States 101
Medicare Benefits Scheme (Australia) 101
medication reminder systems 54
melanoma 6, 63, 65–68, 73–74

Mental Capacity Act (England and Wales) 123, 138–140, 145
mental health: chatbots 82, 88, 91–92; digital psychiatry 49, 54, 57–58; prevalence of mental disorders 47; self-binding directives 135; smartphone apps for 5–6, 47–58; telehealth consultations 101, 106; telemedicine 105; therapeutic relationship, digital technology and 54–55
mHealth 48, 55
Mill, John Stuart 21, 121
Moleanalyzer-Pro 63, 73–74
morbidification 15
My Directives 142
My Health Record (Australia) 136, 147
My Health Record Act (Australia) 147
My Spoon (robotic care assistant) 118

narratives 137
National Aeronautics and Space Administration 100
National Digital Health Strategy (Australia) 146
National Health and Medical Research Council (NHMRC) 22–23
National Statement on Ethical Conduct in Human Research (Australia) 16
Near Me (video consulting services) 101, 103–105
negligence 73–76; causation 75–76; DIY systems 38–39; failure to inform patients of risks, benefits, and alternatives 84–85; standards of care for claims in 74–75; tele-negligence 110–111
next-generation sequencing (NGS) 11, 21, 24
non-maleficence 23, 67, 105, 124–125
Nuffield Council on Bioethics 3, 6, 107, 137

Obama, Barack 100
older adults: ageing demographic 117–118; robotic care assistants 7, 116–131; technology use by 145–146
O'Neill, Onora 87
On Liberty (Mill) 121
Open Artificial Pancreas System (OpenAPS) 28, 30
open-source software to manage type 1 diabetes 2, 5, 28–29, 31–32, 37–40
Organisation for Economic Co-operation and Development (OECD) 67
Ostler, William 3

ownership: collective 18; of genetic data 11, 17–18; moral rather than legal claim of research participants 18

parental choice to use DIY looping 32–34
parental responsibility 33–35, 37
parents: DIY diabetes management by 28–41; fiduciary obligations 36; sharenting 5, 31, 35–37
Paro (companion robot) 117, 118, 122, 124, 128
passive data 49, 53
passive monitoring 50, 53
patient-centred care 8, 54, 69, 123, 136–137, 139, 142, 145
Pearl (nursebot) 118–119
personal account model, of confidentiality 22
personal(ly) identifiable information 51, 72
personal information: confidentiality 109; divulged in chatbots 81, 85–88; mandatory notification schemes for compromised 53; privacy of health data 51–53
personalised medicine 28–41
phronesis 90–91
Physician Orders for Life-Sustaining Treatment (POLST) 135, 142
pop-up advertisements 81
Postman, Neil 7
power of attorney 135
prescriptive fiduciary obligation 70
PRIME (app) 50
The Principles and Practices of Medicine (Ostler) 3
privacy: access to personal data 18–19; advance care decision (ACD) 146–147; artificial intelligence 72; of children 36; constant tracking as infringement 50; contact tracing apps 48; e-privacy 52; as fundamental human right 52; haiku 109; health data 51–53; information 124; invasion of 36; legislation 72; physical 124; recording conferences 108–109; regulation 51; robotic care assistants and 116–117, 124–125; security 108; sharing genetic information 22–23; Universal Declaration of Human Rights 124; working definition of right to 52
Privacy Act (Australia) 2, 19, 22, 87
privacy policies: of apps 52; chatbots 86; as long and difficult to understand 6, 87; readability of terms 86; robotic care assistants 125
property rights: biosamples 17–18; data 18

proximity 13, 24
prudence 90–91
prudent practitioner 58
public good 3

randomized clinical trial (RCT) 57
reciprocity 13
regulation: of artificial intelligence 71–73; co-regulation 128; defined 127; DIY systems 39–40; ex ante 72; legislation 127–128; privacy 51; responsive 129; robotic care assistants 127–130; self-regulation 73, 128, 129; smartphone apps for mental health 56–57
regulatory agencies, artificial intelligence and 72–73
Replika (chatbot companion) 82
research: genomic sequencing 10–16; obligations to return secondary findings 12–14
residential aged care facilities, use of telehealth in 100
respect: AI ethics and 67; for patient autonomy 41, 53–54, 85, 103–104, 136–137; for self-determination 14
responsibility, and AI ethics 67
return of raw genomic data 10, 16–20; implications for 19–20
return of secondary findings 12–14
Riba (Robot for Interactive Body Assistance) 118
right not to know 5, 14–16
right to access genomic data 16–20
right to know 5, 14
right to privacy, working definition of 52
risk: of device failure 32; disclosure by healthcare professionals 84; failure to inform patients of 84–85; of genetic conditions 5, 10, 14–16, 21, 23, 34; of harm 3, 21, 23, 34, 105, 122; of skin cancer 63, 66; telehealth and 104–105, 107
RNA 11
RNA sequencing 10, 24
Robodebt program 89
robot(s): artificial intelligence use 123; companion 118–119; range of applications in personal use 116; use in care of older adults 118–119
robotic care assistant(s) 7, 116–131; autonomy 120–122; beneficence 122–124; clinical/robot ethics committees 129–130; consent 125, 126–127; cost 117, 127; ethical issues 118–126, 129–130; forms of 118–119; harms and benefits 119–122; information provision 127; justice 125–126; non-maleficence 124–125; privacy 116–117, 124–125; regulation 127–130; use by elderly with declining cognitive capacity 122–124; uses in care of older adults 118–119
Robot Strategy (Japan) 118
Rosetta Life 142
Royal Australian College of General Practitioners Guidelines 102, 110–111
Royal Free Hospital (London) 2, 76
RP-7 robot 119

safety, and AI ethics 67
SaMD (Software as a Medical Device) 30, 56
Sandel, Michael 3
schizophrenia 6, 47–58
Schönberger, Daniel 68, 74
secondary findings: return of 12–14; terminology defined 11
self-determination, respect for 14
self-regulation 73, 128, 129
sentience 65
sharenting 5, 31, 35–37
skin cancer 2, 6, 47, 63, 66–67; *see also* melanoma
smartphone: apps for mental health 5–6, 47–58; digital phenotyping 50; equality in access and digital skills 55–56; ownership, prevalence of 55; regulation of health apps 56–57; terminology 48–49
social isolation: AI use and 69; during COVID-19 pandemic 49, 82, 106
social media, sharing information about children on 35–37
social support, artificial agents as 82
Software as a Medical Device (SaMD) 30, 56
standard of care: AI use in diagnosis 63, 65, 73–75; digital psychiatry 54; for disclosure 85; DIY looping 38; failure to meet reasonable 38, 73, 75; smartphone monitoring apps 58; telehealth 110–111; tele-negligence 110–111
state-of-the-art defence 128
stigma/stigmatisation 47, 88, 116, 122
support groups, peer 32, 37
Symptom Checker (Australia) 83
symptom checker chatbots 6–7, 81–93; accuracy 88–89, 92; health literacy 84; triage 82–85, 89–92

targeted advertising 87
targeted therapies 2, 10–11, 15
telehealth 98–111; access and equity 107–108; COVID-19 and 7; doctor–patient relationship 99, 106–107, 111; ethical issues 103–106; legal issues 108–110; meaning and history 99–101; robots and 119; standard of care 110–111; telephone *versus* video consultation 102–103
telemedicine: access and equity 107–108; beneficence 104–105; during COVID-19 pandemic 101–102; ethical issues 103–106; justice 105–106; legal issues 108–110; meaning and history 99–101; non-maleficence 105; recording conferences 108–109; respect for autonomy 103–104; robots and 119
tele-negligence 110–111
telephone consultation 98, 101–103, 106, 111
telepsychiatry 106
Therapeutic Goods Act 73, 128
Therapeutic Goods Administration (Australia) 28, 30, 39–40, 56, 73, 128
therapeutic relationship: digital technology and 54–55; DIY looping and 37–38; telehealth 99, 106–107
third-party interpretive services (TPIs) 20
Tidepool 40
tort 72–76
translational medicine 10, 24
transparency, and AI ethics 67
Treaty on European Union 119
triage, chatbots 82–85, 89–92
trust: in artificial intelligence 70, 76; chatbots 89–91; patient–healthcare professional relationship 70

UK Biobank 12–15
UK Data Protection Act 2
United Nations Convention on the Rights of Persons with Disabilities (CRPD) 123, 144–145
United Nations Convention on the Rights of the Child 33

United Nations Universal Declaration of Human Rights 52, 119, 124
utilitarianism 68, 125

values video 8, 136, 142–145; authentication of identity 143; capacity 143; co-creation 147; format of 142–143; key information 144; legal status of 144–145; portability and accessibility 146–147
VCF (Variant Call Format) files 16
video conferencing platforms 109–110
video consultation 99–111
videotherapy 106
virtual assistant 82, 89
voice, patient 40
vulnerability 3, 54–55, 70, 85, 87, 90, 99, 104, 107, 129

Wachsmuth, Ipke 126
Wagner, Isabel 87
wearable devices/technology 1, 47; to assist older adults 116; cost 55; digital phenotyping 49; passive data 49; privacy of data 51–52; privacy policies 52; self-monitoring 29; smartphone apps for mental health 5, 47–48, 55; terminology 48–49
#WeAreNotWaiting movement 5, 28, 70
Weizenbaum, Joseph 90
WES (whole exome sequencing) 10–11, 15, 24
WGS (whole genome sequencing) 10–11, 15–16, 19, 24
whole exome sequencing (WES) 10–11, 15, 24
whole genome sequencing (WGS) 10–11, 15–16, 19, 24
Woebot (therapy chatbot) 82
World Health Organization (WHO) 49, 98–100, 111
World Medical Association Declaration of Taipai 14

Yip, J 24

Zone of Parental Discretion 34–35, 41

Taylor & Francis eBooks

www.taylorfrancis.com

A single destination for eBooks from Taylor & Francis with increased functionality and an improved user experience to meet the needs of our customers.

90,000+ eBooks of award-winning academic content in Humanities, Social Science, Science, Technology, Engineering, and Medical written by a global network of editors and authors.

TAYLOR & FRANCIS EBOOKS OFFERS:

- A streamlined experience for our library customers
- A single point of discovery for all of our eBook content
- Improved search and discovery of content at both book and chapter level

REQUEST A FREE TRIAL
support@taylorfrancis.com

Printed in the USA
CPSIA information can be obtained
at www.ICGtesting.com
LVHW020826170924
791293LV00003B/501